PHRASEBOOK
— HEBREW —

THE MOST IMPORTANT PHRASES

This phrasebook contains
the most important
phrases and questions
for basic communication
Everything you need
to survive overseas

T&P BOOKS

Phrasebook + 3000-word dictionary

English-Hebrew phrasebook & topical vocabulary

By Andrey Taranov

The collection of "Everything Will Be Okay" travel phrasebooks published by T&P Books is designed for people traveling abroad for tourism and business. The phrasebooks contain what matters most - the essentials for basic communication. This is an indispensable set of phrases to "survive" while abroad.

This book also includes a small topical vocabulary that contains roughly 3,000 of the most frequently used words. Another section of the phrasebook provides a gastronomical dictionary that may help you order food at a restaurant or buy groceries at the store.

T&P Books Publishing
www.tpbooks.com

ISBN: 978-1-78716-979-1

This book is also available in E-book formats.
Please visit www.tpbooks.com or the major online bookstores.

FOREWORD

The collection of "Everything Will Be Okay" travel phrasebooks published by T&P Books is designed for people traveling abroad for tourism and business. The phrasebooks contain what matters most - the essentials for basic communication. This is an indispensable set of phrases to "survive" while abroad.

This phrasebook will help you in most cases where you need to ask something, get directions, find out how much something costs, etc. It can also resolve difficult communication situations where gestures just won't help.

This book contains a lot of phrases that have been grouped according to the most relevant topics. The edition also includes a small vocabulary that contains roughly 3,000 of the most frequently used words. Another section of the phrasebook provides a gastronomical dictionary that may help you order food at a restaurant or buy groceries at the store.

Take "Everything Will Be Okay" phrasebook with you on the road and you'll have an irreplaceable traveling companion who will help you find your way out of any situation and teach you to not fear speaking with foreigners.

TABLE OF CONTENTS

T&P Books Publishing

PRONUNCIATION

Letter's name	Letter	Hebrew example	T&P phonetic alphabet	English example
Alef	א	אריה	[ɑ], [ɑː]	bath, to pass
	א	אחד	[ɛ], [ɛː]	habit, bad
	א	מָאָה	[ ] (hamza)	glottal stop
Bet	ב	בית	[b]	baby, book
Gimel	ג	גמל	[g]	game, gold
Gimel+geresh	ג׳	ג׳וּנְגַל	[dʒ]	joke, general
Dalet	ד	דג	[d]	day, doctor
Hei	ה	הר	[h]	home, have
Vav	ו	וסת	[v]	very, river
Zayin	ז	זאב	[z]	zebra, please
Zayin+geresh	ז׳	ז׳וּרְנָל	[ʒ]	forge, pleasure
Chet	ח	חוט	[x]	as in Scots 'loch'
Tet	ט	טוב	[t]	tourist, trip
Yud	י	יום	[j]	yes, New York
Kaph	ך כ	בריש	[k]	clock, kiss
Lamed	ל	לחם	[l]	lace, people
Mem	ם מ	מלך	[m]	magic, milk
Nun	ן נ	גר	[n]	name, normal
Samech	ס	סוס	[s]	city, boss
Ayin	ע	עין	[ɑ], [ɑː]	bath, to pass
	ע	תּשעִים	[ ] (ayn)	voiced pharyngeal fricative
Pei	ף פ	פיל	[p]	pencil, private
Tsadi	ץ צ	צעצוע	[ts]	cats, tsetse fly
Tsadi+geresh	צ׳/ץ׳	צ׳יק	[tʃ]	church, French
Qoph	ק	קוף	[k]	clock, kiss
Resh	ר	רכבת	[r]	French (guttural) R
Shin	ש	שלחן, עָשׂרִים	[s], [ʃ]	city, machine
Tav	ת	תפוז	[t]	tourist, trip

LIST OF ABBREVIATIONS

Explication

⇨ man	- addressing a man
⇨ woman	- addressing a woman
couple, men ⇨	- a couple or men are speaking
man ⇨	- man is speaking
man ⇨ man	- a man speaks to a man
man ⇨ woman	- a man speaks to a woman
woman ⇨	- woman is speaking
woman ⇨ man	- a woman speaks to a man
woman ⇨ woman	- a woman speaks to a woman
women ⇨	- women are speaking

English abbreviations

ab.	- about
adj	- adjective
adv	- adverb
anim.	- animate
as adj	- attributive noun used as adjective
e.g.	- for example
etc.	- et cetera
fam.	- familiar
fem.	- feminine
form.	- formal
inanim.	- inanimate
masc.	- masculine
math	- mathematics
mil.	- military
n	- noun
pl	- plural
pron.	- pronoun
sb	- somebody
sing.	- singular
sth	- something
v aux	- auxiliary verb

vi	-	intransitive verb
vi, vt	-	intransitive, transitive verb
vt	-	transitive verb

Hebrew abbreviations

ז	-	masculine
ז"ר	-	masculine plural
ז ,נ	-	masculine, feminine
נ	-	feminine
נ"ר	-	feminine plural

HEBREW
PHRASEBOOK

This section contains
important phrases that may
come in handy in various
real-life situations.
The phrasebook will help
you ask for directions, clarify
a price, buy tickets, and
order food at a restaurant

T&P Books Publishing

PHRASEBOOK
CONTENTS

T&P Books Publishing

The bare minimum

Excuse me, ... (→ man)	slaχ li, ... סלח לי, ...
Excuse me, ... (→ woman)	silχi li, ... סלחי לי, ...
Hello.	ʃalom. שלום.
Thank you.	toda. תודה.
Good bye.	lehitra'ot. להתראות.

Yes.	ken. כן.
No.	lo. לא.
I don't know. (man →)	ani lo yo'de'a. אני לא יודע.
I don't know. (woman →)	ani lo yo'da'at. אני לא יודעת.
Where? | Where to? | When?	eifo? | le'an? | matai? איפה? | לאן? | מתי?

I need ... (man →)	ani tsariχ ... אני צריך ...
I need ... (woman →)	ani tsriχa ... אני צריכה ...
I want ... (man →)	ani rotse ... אני רוצה ...
I want ... (woman →)	ani rotsa ... אני רוצה ...

Do you have ...? (→ man)	ha'im yeʃ leχa ...? האם יש לך ...?
Do you have ...? (→ woman)	ha'im yeʃ laχ ...? האם יש לך ...?
Is there a ... here?	ha'im yeʃ po ...? האם יש פה ...?

May I ...? (man →)	ha'im ani yaχol ...? האם אני יכול ...?
May I ...? (woman →)	ha'im ani yeχola ...? האם אני יכולה ...?
..., please (polite request)	..., bevakaʃa ..., בבקשה

I'm looking for ... (man)

ani meχapes ...
אני מחפש ...

I'm looking for ... (woman)

ani meχa'peset ...
אני מחפשת ...

the restroom

ʃerutim
שירותים

an ATM

kaspomat
כספומט

a pharmacy (drugstore)

beit mer'kaχat
בית מרקחת

a hospital

beit χolim
בית חולים

the police station

taχanat miʃtara
תחנת משטרה

the subway

ra'kevet taχtit
רכבת תחתית

a taxi

monit, 'teksi
מונית, טקסי

the train station

taχanat ra'kevet
תחנת רכבת

My name is ...

kor'im li ...
קוראים לי ...

What's your name? (man)

eiχ kor'im leχa?
איך קוראים לך?

What's your name? (woman)

eiχ kor'im laχ?
איך קוראים לך?

Could you please help me? (man)

ha'im ata yaχol la'azor li?
האם אתה יכול לעזור לי?

Could you please help me? (woman)

ha'im at yeχola la'azor li?
האם את יכולה לעזור לי?

I've got a problem.

yeʃ li be'aya.
יש לי בעייה.

I don't feel well. (man)

ani lo margiʃ tov.
אני לא מרגיש טוב.

I don't feel well. (woman)

ani lo margiʃa tov.
אני לא מרגישה טוב.

Call an ambulance! (man)

hazmen 'ambulans!
הזמן אמבולנס!

Call an ambulance! (woman)

haz'mini 'ambulans!
הזמיני אמבולנס!

May I make a call? (man)

ha'im ani yaχol lehitkaʃer?
האם אני יכול להתקשר?

May I make a call? (woman)

ha'im ani yeχola lehitkaʃer?
האם אני יכולה להתקשר?

I'm sorry. (man)

ani mitsta'er.
אני מצטער.

I'm sorry. (woman)

ani mitsta'eret.
אני מצטערת.

You're welcome.

ein be'ad ma, bevakaʃa.
אין בעד מה, בבקשה.

I, me	ani אני
you (inform.) (masc.)	ata אתה
you (inform.) (fem.)	at את
he	hu הוא
she	hi היא
they (masc.)	hem הם
they (fem.)	hen הן
we	a'naxnu אנחנו
you (pl) (masc.)	atem אתם
you (pl) (fem.)	aten אתן
you (sg, form.) (masc.)	ata אתה
you (sg, form.) (fem.)	at את

ENTRANCE	knisa כניסה
EXIT	yetsi'a יציאה
OUT OF ORDER	lo po'el לא פועל
CLOSED	sagur סגור
OPEN	pa'tuax פתוח
FOR WOMEN	lenaʃim לנשים
FOR MEN	ligvarim לגברים

Questions

Where?	eifo?
	?איפה
Where to?	le'an?
	?לאן
Where from?	me''eifo?
	?מאיפה
Why?	lama?
	?למה
For what reason?	me''eizo siba?
	?מאיזו סיבה
When?	matai?
	?מתי
How long?	kama zman?
	?כמה זמן
At what time?	be''eizo ʃa'a?
	?באיזו שעה
How much?	kama?
	?כמה
Do you have ...? (man)	ha'im yeʃ leχa ...?
	?... האם יש לך
Do you have ...? (woman)	ha'im yeʃ laχ ...?
	?... האם יש לך
Where is ...?	eifo ...?
	?... איפה
What time is it?	ma ʃaʃa'a?
	?מה השעה
May I make a call? (man)	ha'im ani yaχol lehitkaʃer?
	?האם אני יכול להתקשר
May I make a call? (woman)	ha'im ani yeχola lehitkaʃer?
	?האם אני יכולה להתקשר
Who's there?	mi ʃam?
	?מי שם
Can I smoke here?	ha'im mutar le'aʃen kan?
	?האם מותר לעשן כאן
May I ...? (man)	ha'im ani yaχol ...?
	?... האם אני יכול
May I ...? (woman)	ha'im ani yeχola ...?
	?... האם אני יכולה

Needs

I'd like ... (man ♂)	ha'yiti rotse ... הייתי רוצה ...
I'd like ... (woman ♀)	ha'yiti rotsa ... הייתי רוצה ...
I don't want ... (man ♂)	ani lo rotse ... אני לא רוצה ...
I don't want ... (woman ♀)	ani lo rotsa ... אני לא רוצה ...
I'm thirsty. (man ♂)	ani tsame. אני צמא.
I'm thirsty. (woman ♀)	ani tsme'a. אני צמאה.
I want to sleep.	ani rotse lishon. אני רוצה לישון.
I want ... (man ♂)	ani rotse ... אני רוצה ...
I want ... (woman ♀)	ani rotsa ... אני רוצה ...

to wash up	lishtof panim veya'dayim לשטוף פנים וידיים
to brush my teeth	letsaχ'tseaχ ʃi'nayim לצחצח שיניים
to rest a while	la'nuaχ ktsat לנוח קצת
to change my clothes	lehaχlif bgadim להחליף בגדים
to go back to the hotel	laχazor lamalon לחזור למלון
to buy ...	liknot ... לקנות ...
to go to ...	la'leχet le... ללכת ל ...
to visit ...	levaker be... לבקר ב ...
to meet with ...	lehipageʃ im... להיפגש עם...
to make a call	letalfen, lehitkaʃer לטלפן, להתקשר

I'm tired. (man ♂)	ani ayef. אני עייף.
I'm tired. (woman ♀)	ani ayefa. אני עייפה.

We are tired. (couple , men)
a'naχnu ayefim.
אנחנו עייפים.

We are tired. (women)
anaχnu ayefot.
אנחנו עייפות.

I'm cold.
kar li.
קר לי.

I'm hot.
χam li.
חם לי.

I'm OK.
ani be'seder.
אני בסדר.

I need to make a call. (man)
ani tsariχ lehitkaʃer.
אני צריך להתקשר.

I need to make a call. (woman)
ani tsriχa lehitkaʃer.
אני צריכה להתקשר.

I need to go to the restroom. (man)
ani tsariχ leʃerutim.
אני צריך ללכת לשירותים.

I need to go to the restroom. (woman)
ani tsriχa leʃerutim.
אני צריכה ללכת לשירותים.

I have to go. (man)
ani tsariχ la'leχet.
אני צריך ללכת.

I have to go. (woman)
ani tsriχa la'leχet.
אני צריכה ללכת.

I have to go now. (man)
ani χayav la'leχet aχʃav.
אני חייב ללכת עכשיו.

I have to go now. (woman)
ani χa'yevet la'leχet aχʃav.
אני חייבת ללכת עכשיו.

Asking for directions

Excuse me, ... (man ⏴)	slaχ li, ... ,סלח לי
Excuse me, ... (woman ⏴)	silχi li, ... ,סלחי לי
Where is ...?	eifo ...? ?... איפה
Which way is ...?	eiχ megi'im le ...? ?... איך מגיעים ל
Could you help me, please? (⏴ man)	ha'im ata yaχol la'azor li, bevakaʃa? ?האם אתה יכול לעזור לי, בבקשה
Could you help me, please? (⏴ woman)	ha'im at yeχola la'azor li, bevakaʃa? ?האם את יכולה לעזור לי, בבקשה

I'm looking for ... (man ⏴)	ani meχapes ... ... אני מחפש
I'm looking for ... (woman ⏴)	ani meχa'peset ... ... אני מחפשת
I'm looking for the exit. (man ⏴)	ani meχapes et hayetsi'a. .אני מחפש את היציאה
I'm looking for the exit. (woman ⏴)	ani meχa'peset et hayetsi'a. .אני מחפשת את היציאה
I'm going to ... (man ⏴)	ani holeχ le ... ... אני הולך ל
I'm going to ... (woman ⏴)	ani ho'leχet le ... ... אני הולכת ל
Am I going the right way to ...?	ha'im ani bakivun hanaχon le ...? ?... האם אני בכיוון הנכון ל

Is it far?	ha'im ze raχok? ?האם זה רחוק
Can I get there on foot?	ha'im efʃar leha'gi'a leʃam ba'regel? ?האם אפשר להגיע לשם ברגל
Can you show me on the map? (⏴ man)	ha'im ata yaχol lehar'ot li al hamapa? ?האם אתה יכול להראות לי על המפה
Can you show me on the map? (⏴ woman)	ha'im at yeχola lehar'ot li al hamapa? ?האם את יכולה להראות לי על המפה
Show me where we are right now. (⏴ man)	har'e li heiχan 'anu nimtsa'im aχʃav. .הראה לי היכן אנו נמצאים עכשיו
Show me where we are right now. (⏴ woman)	har'i li heiχan 'anu nimtsa'im aχʃav. .הראי לי היכן אנו נמצאים עכשיו
Here	kan, po כאן, פה
There	ʃam שם

This way	lekan
	לכאן
Turn right. (man)	pne ya'mina.
	פנה ימינה.
Turn right. (woman)	pni ya'mina.
	פני ימינה.
Turn left. (man)	pne 'smola.
	פנה שמאלה.
Turn left. (woman)	pni 'smola.
	פני שמאלה.
first (second, third) turn	pniya riʃona (ʃniya, ʃliʃit)
	פנייה ראשונה (שנייה, שלישית)
to the right	ya'mina
	ימינה
to the left	smola
	שמאלה
Go straight ahead. (man)	leχ yaʃar.
	לך ישר.
Go straight ahead. (woman)	leχi yaʃar.
	לכי ישר.

Signs

WELCOME!	bruχim haba'im! !ברוכים הבאים
ENTRANCE	knisa כניסה
EXIT	yetsi'a יציאה

PUSH	dχof דחוף
PULL	mʃoχ משוך
OPEN	pa'tuaχ פתוח
CLOSED	sagur סגור

FOR WOMEN	lenaʃim לנשים
FOR MEN	ligvarim לגברים
GENTLEMEN, GENTS	gvarim גברים
WOMEN	naʃim נשים

DISCOUNTS	hanaχot הנחות
SALE	mivtsa מבצע
FREE	χinam, beχinam חינם, בחינם
NEW!	χadaʃ! !חדש
ATTENTION!	sim lev! !שים לב

NO VACANCIES	ein mekomot pnuyim אין מקומות פנויים
RESERVED	ʃamur שמור
ADMINISTRATION	hanhala הנהלה
STAFF ONLY	le'ovdim bilvad לעובדים בלבד

BEWARE OF THE DOG!   zehirut, 'kelev!
זהירות כלב!

NO SMOKING!   asur le'aʃen!
אסור לעשן!

DO NOT TOUCH!   asur la'ga'at!
אסור לגעת!

DANGEROUS   mesukan
מסוכן

DANGER   sakana
סכנה

HIGH VOLTAGE   metaχ ga'voha
מתח גבוה

NO SWIMMING!   asur lisχot!
אסור לשחות!

OUT OF ORDER   lo po'el
לא פועל

FLAMMABLE   dalik
דליק

FORBIDDEN   asur
אסור

NO TRESPASSING!   ein ma'avar
אין מעבר

WET PAINT   tseva laχ, 'tseva tari
צבע לח, צבע טרי

CLOSED FOR RENOVATIONS   sagur leʃiputsim
סגור לשיפוצים

WORKS AHEAD   avodot bakviʃ
עבודות בכביש

DETOUR   ma'akaf
מעקף

Transportation. General phrases

plane	matos מטוס
train	ra'kevet רכבת
bus	'otobus אוטובוס
ferry	ma'a'boret מעבורת
taxi	monit מונית
car	meχonit מכונית
schedule	luaχ zmanim לוח זמנים
Where can I see the schedule?	heiχan efʃar lir'ot et 'luaχ hazmanim? היכן אפשר לראות את לוח הזמנים?
workdays (weekdays)	yemei avoda ימי עבודה
weekends	sofei ʃa'vu'a סופי שבוע
holidays	χagim חגים
DEPARTURE	hamra'a המראה
ARRIVAL	neχita נחיתה
DELAYED	ikuv עיכוב
CANCELLED	bitul ביטול
next (train, etc.)	haba /haba'a/ הבא /הבאה/
first	riʃon /riʃona/ ראשון /ראשונה/
last	aχaron /aχrona/ אחרון /אחרונה/
When is the next ...?	matai ha... haba /haba'a/? מתי ה ... הבא /הבאה/?
When is the first ...?	matai ha... hariʃon /hariʃona/? מתי ה ... הראשון /הראשונה/?

When is the last ...?

matai ha… ha'aχaron /ha'aχrona/?

מתי ה ... האחרון /האחרונה?

transfer (change of trains, etc.)

haχlafa, ko'nekʃen

החלפה, קונקשן

to make a transfer

la'asot haχlafa

לעשות החלפה

Do I need to make a transfer? (man ↗)

ha'im ani tsariχ la'asot haχlafa?

האם אני צריך לעשות החלפה?

Do I need to make a transfer? (woman ↗)

ha'im ani tsriχa la'asot haχlafa?

האם אני צריכה לעשות החלפה?

Buying tickets

Where can I buy tickets?	heiχan efʃar liknot kartisim? היכן אפשר לקנות כרטיסים?
ticket	kartis כרטיס
to buy a ticket	liknot kartis לקנות כרטיס
ticket price	meχir kartis מחיר כרטיס
Where to?	le'an? לאן?
To what station?	le''eizo taχana? לאיזו תחנה?
I need ... (man -)	ani tsariχ ... אני צריך ...
I need ... (woman -)	ani tsriχa ... אני צריכה ...
one ticket	kartis eχad כרטיס אחד
two tickets	ʃnei kartisim שני כרטיסים
three tickets	ʃloʃa kartisim שלושה כרטיסים
one-way	kivun eχad כיוון אחד
round-trip	haloχ vaʃov הלוך ושוב
first class	maχlaka riʃona מחלקה ראשונה
second class	maχlaka ʃniya מחלקה שנייה
today	hayom היום
tomorrow	maχar מחר
the day after tomorrow	maχara'tayim מחרתיים
in the morning	ba'boker בבוקר
in the afternoon	aχar hatsaha'rayim אחר הצהריים
in the evening	ba''erev בערב

aisle seat	moʃav bama'avar
	מושב במעבר
window seat	moʃav leyad haχalon
	מושב ליד החלון
How much?	kama?
	כמה?
Can I pay by credit card?	ha'im efʃar leʃalem bekatrtis aʃrai?
	האם אפשר לשלם בכרטיס אשראי?

Bus

bus	'otobus אוטובוס
intercity bus	'otobus bein ironi אוטובוס בין-עירוני
bus stop	taχanat 'otobus תחנת אוטובוס
Where's the nearest bus stop?	eifo taχanat ha''otobus hakrova beyoter? איפה תחנת האוטובוס הקרובה ביותר?
number (bus ~, etc.)	mispar מספר
Which bus do I take to get to …?	eize 'otobus tsariχ la'kaχat kedei leha'gi'a le …? איזה אוטובוס צריך לקחת כדי להגיע ל …?
Does this bus go to …?	ha'im ha''otobus haze ma'gi'a le …? האם האוטובוס הזה מגיע ל …?
How frequent are the buses?	ma hatadirut ʃel ha'oto'busim? מה התדירות של האוטובוסים?
every 15 minutes	kol χameʃ esre dakot כל חמש עשרה דקות
every half hour	kol χatsi ʃa'a כל חצי שעה
every hour	kol ʃa'a כל שעה
several times a day	mispar pe'amim beyom מספר פעמים ביום
… times a day	… pe'amim beyom … פעמים ביום
schedule	luaχ zmanim לוח זמנים
Where can I see the schedule?	heiχan efʃar lir'ot et 'luaχ hazmanim? היכן אפשר לראות את לוח הזמנים?
When is the next bus?	matai ha''otobus haba? מתי האוטובוס הבא?
When is the first bus?	matai ha''otobus hariʃon? מתי האוטובוס הראשון?
When is the last bus?	matai ha''otobus ha'aχaron? מתי האוטובוס האחרון?

stop	taχanat atsira
	תחנת עצירה
next stop	hataχana haba'a
	התחנה הבאה
last stop (terminus)	taχana aχrona
	תחנה אחרונה
Stop here, please. (man)	atsor kan, bevakaʃa.
	עצור כאן, בבקשה.
Stop here, please. (woman)	itsri kan, bevakaʃa.
	עצרי כאן, בבקשה.
Excuse me, this is my stop. (man)	slaχ li, zo hataχana ʃeli.
	סלח לי, זו התחנה שלי.
Excuse me, this is my stop. (woman)	silχi li, zo hataχana ʃeli.
	סלחי לי, זו התחנה שלי.

Train

train	ra'kevet רכבת
suburban train	ra'kevet parvarim רכבת פרברים
long-distance train	ra'kevet bein ironit רכבת בין-עירונית
train station	taχanat ra'kevet תחנת רכבת
Excuse me, where is the exit to the platform? (⇽ man)	slaχ li, 'eifo hayetsi'a laratsif? סלח לי, איפה היציאה לרציף?
Excuse me, where is the exit to the platform? (⇽ woman)	silχi li, 'eifo hayetsi'a laratsif? סלחי לי, איפה היציאה לרציף?
Does this train go to ...?	ha'im hara'kevet hazo megi'a le ...? האם הרכבת הזו מגיעה ל ...?
next train	hara'kevet haba'a הרכבת הבאה
When is the next train?	matai hara'kevet haba'a? מתי הרכבת הבאה?
Where can I see the schedule?	heiχan efʃar lir'ot et 'luaχ hazmanim? היכן אפשר לראות את לוח הזמנים?
From which platform?	me''eize ratsif? מאיזה רציף?
When does the train arrive in ...?	matai hara'kevet megi'a le ...? מתי הרכבת מגיעה ל ...?
Please help me. (⇽ man)	azor li bevakaʃa. עזור לי בבקשה.
Please help me. (⇽ woman)	izri li bevakaʃa. עזרי לי בבקשה.
I'm looking for my seat. (man ⇽)	ani meχapes et hamoʃav ʃeli. אני מחפש את המושב שלי.
I'm looking for my seat. (woman ⇽)	ani meχa'peset et hamoʃav ʃeli. אני מחפשת את המושב שלי.
We're looking for our seats. (couple , men ⇽)	anu meχapsim et hamoʃavim ʃe'lanu אנו מחפשים את המושבים שלנו.
We're looking for our seats. (women ⇽)	anu meχapsot et hamoʃavim ʃe'lanu אנו מחפשות את המושבים שלנו.
My seat is taken.	hamoʃav ʃeli tafus. המושב שלי תפוס.
Our seats are taken.	hamoʃavim ʃe'lanu tfusim. המושבים שלנו תפוסים.
I'm sorry but this is my seat. (man ⇽)	ani mitsta'er, aval ze hamoʃav ʃeli. אני מצטער, אבל זה המושב שלי.

I'm sorry but this is my seat. (woman ⌐)

ani mitsta'eret, aval ze hamoʃav ʃeli.
אני מצטערת, אבל זה המושב שלי.

Is this seat taken?

ha'im hamoʃav haze tafus?
האם המושב הזה תפוס?

May I sit here? (man ⌐)

ha'im ani yaχol la'ʃevet kan?
האם אני יכול לשבת כאן?

May I sit here? (woman ⌐)

ha'im ani yeχola laʃevet kan?
האם אני יכולה לשבת כאן?

On the train. Dialogue (No ticket)

Ticket, please.	kartis, bevakaʃa. כרטיס, בבקשה.
I don't have a ticket.	ein li kartis. אין לי כרטיס.
I lost my ticket.	i'badti et hakartis ʃeli. איבדתי את הכרטיס שלי.
I forgot my ticket at home.	ʃa'χaχti et hakartis ʃeli ba'bayit שכחתי את הכרטיס שלי בבית.
You can buy a ticket from me. (↝ man)	ata yaχol liknot kartis mi'meni. אתה יכול לקנות כרטיס ממני.
You can buy a ticket from me. (↝ woman)	at yeχola liknot kartis mi'meni. את יכולה לקנות כרטיס ממני.
You will also have to pay a fine. (↝ man)	titstareχ gam leʃalem knas. תצטרך גם לשלם קנס.
You will also have to pay a fine. (↝ woman)	titstarχi gam leʃalem knas. תצטרכי גם לשלם קנס.
Okay.	okei. אוקיי.
Where are you going? (↝ man)	le'an ata no'se'a? לאן אתה נוסע?
Where are you going? (↝ woman)	le'an at nos'a'at? לאן את נוסעת?
I'm going to … (man ↝)	ani no'se'a le… אני נוסע ל...
I'm going to … (woman ↝)	ani nos'a'at le… אני נוסעת ל...
How much? I don't understand. (man ↝)	kama? ani lo mevin. כמה? אני לא מבין.
How much? I don't understand. (woman ↝)	kama? ani lo mevina. כמה? אני לא מבינה.
Write it down, please. (↝ man)	ktov li et ze, bevakaʃa. כתוב לי את זה, בבקשה.
Write it down, please. (↝ woman)	kitvi li et ze, bevakaʃa. כתבי לי את זה, בבקשה.
Okay. Can I pay with a credit card?	okei. ha'im efʃar leʃalem bekartis aʃrai? אוקיי. האם אפשר לשלם בכרטיס אשראי?
Yes, you can.	ken, efʃar. כן, אפשר.
Here's your receipt. (↝ man)	hine hakabala ʃelχa. הנה הקבלה שלך.
Here's your receipt. (↝ woman)	hine hakabala ʃelaχ' הינה הקבלה שלך

Sorry about the fine. (man)

ani mitsta'er be'kefer laknas.
אני מצטער בקשר לקנס.

Sorry about the fine. (woman)

ani mitsta''eret be'kefer laknas.
אני מצטערת בקשר לקנס.

That's okay. It was my fault.

ze be'seder. zo afmati.
זה בסדר. זו אשמתי.

Enjoy your trip.

tiyul mehane.
טיול מהנה.

Taxi

taxi	monit מונית
taxi driver (masc.)	nahag monit נהג מונית
taxi driver (fem.)	na'heget monit נהגת מונית
to catch a taxi	litpos monit לתפוס מונית
taxi stand	taχanat moniyot תחנת מוניות
Where can I get a taxi?	eifo efʃar la'kaχat monit? איפה אפשר לקחת מונית?
to call a taxi	lehazmin monit להזמין מונית
I need a taxi. (man ⇨)	ani tsariχ monit אני צריך מונית
I need a taxi. (woman ⇨)	ani tsriχa monit אני צריכה מונית
Right now.	aχʃav. עכשיו.
What is your address (location)? (⇦ man)	ma ha'ktovet ʃelχa? מה הכתובת שלך?
What is your address (location)? (⇦ woman)	ma ha'ktovet ʃelaχ? מה הכתובת שלך?
My address is …	ha'ktovet ʃeli hi … הכתובת שלי היא …
Your destination? (⇦ man)	le'an ata no'se'a? לאן אתה נוסע?
Your destination? (⇦ woman)	le'an at nos'a'at? לאן את נוסעת?
Excuse me, … (⇦ man)	slaχ li, … סלח לי, …
Excuse me, … (⇦ woman)	silχi li, … סלחי לי, …
Are you available? (⇦ man)	ha'im ata panui? האם אתה פנוי?
Are you available? (⇦ woman)	ha'im at pnuya? האם את פנויה?
How much is it to get to …?	kama ze ole lin'so'a le …? כמה זה עולה לנסוע ל …?
Do you know where it is? (⇦ man)	ha'im ata yo'de'a 'eifo ze? האם אתה יודע איפה זה?

Do you know where it is? (woman)	ha'im at yod'a'at 'eifo ze? האם את יודעת איפה זה?
Airport, please.	lisde hate'ufa, bevakaʃa. לשדה התעופה, בבקשה.
Stop here, please. (man)	atsor kan, bevakaʃa. עצור כאן, בבקשה.
Stop here, please. (woman)	itsri kan, bevakaʃa. עצרי כאן, בבקשה.
It's not here.	ze lo kan. זה לא כאן.
This is the wrong address.	zo lo ha'ktovet haneχona. זו לא הכתובת הנכונה.
Turn left. (man)	pne 'smola. פנה שמאלה.
Turn left. (woman)	pni 'smola. פני שמאלה.
Turn right. (man)	pne ya'mina. פנה ימינה.
Turn right. (woman)	pni ya'mina. פני ימינה.

How much do I owe you? (man)	kama me'gi'a leχa? כמה מגיע לך?
How much do I owe you? (woman)	kama me'gi'a laχ? כמה מגיע לך?
I'd like a receipt, please.	efʃar lekabel kabala, bevakaʃa? אפשר לקבל קבלה, בבקשה?
Keep the change. (man)	ʃmor et ha''odef. שמור את העודף.
Keep the change. (woman)	ʃimri et ha''odef. שמרי את העודף.

Would you please wait for me? (man)	ha'im ata muχan leχakot li, bevakaʃa? האם אתה מוכן לחכות לי, בבקשה?
Would you please wait for me? (woman)	ha'im at muχana leχakot li, bevakaʃa? האם את מוכנה לחכות לי, בבקשה?
five minutes	χameʃ dakot חמש דקות
ten minutes	eser dakot עשר דקות
fifteen minutes	χameʃ esre dakot חמש עשרה דקות
twenty minutes	esrim dakot עשרים דקות
half an hour	χatsi ʃa'a חצי שעה

Hotel

Hello.	ʃalom. שלום.
My name is …	kor'im li … קוראים לי …
I have a reservation.	yeʃ li hazmana. יש לי הזמנה.
I need … (man ⌐)	ani tsariχ … אני צריך …
I need … (woman ⌐)	ani tsriχa … אני צריכה …
a single room	χeder leyaχid חדר ליחיד
a double room	χeder zugi חדר זוגי
How much is that?	kama ze ole? כמה זה עולה?
That's a bit expensive.	ze ktsat yakar. זה קצת יקר.
Do you have anything else? (⌐ man)	ha'im yeʃ leχa 'optsiyot aχerot? האם יש לך אופציות אחרות?
Do you have anything else? (⌐ woman)	ha'im yeʃ laχ 'optsiyot aχerot? האם יש לך אופציות אחרות?
I'll take it.	ani ekaχ et ze. אני אקח את זה.
I'll pay in cash.	ani eʃalem bimzuman. אני אשלם במזומן.
I've got a problem.	yeʃ li be'aya. יש לי בעיה.
My … is broken. (masc.)	ha… ʃeli mekulkal. ה… שלי מקולקל.
My … is broken. (fem.)	ha… ʃeli mekul'kelet. ה… שלי מקולקלת.
My … is out of order. (masc.)	ha… ʃeli lo oved. ה… שלי לא עובד.
My … is out of order. (fem.)	ha… ʃeli lo o'vedet. ה… שלי לא עובדת.
TV	tele'vizya טלוויזיה
air conditioner	mizug avir מיזוג אוויר

tap	berez
	ברז
shower	mik'laxat
	מקלחת
sink	kiyor
	כיור
safe	ka'sefet
	כספת
door lock	man'ul
	מנעול
electrical outlet	ʃeka
	שקע
hairdryer	meyabeʃ se'ar
	מייבש שיער

I don't have ...	ein li ...
	... אין לי
water	mayim
	מים
light	te'ura
	תאורה
electricity	xaʃmal
	חשמל

Can you give me ...?	ha'im at yexola latet li ...?
	?... האם את יכולה לתת לי
a towel	ma'gevet
	מגבת
a blanket	smixa
	שמיכה
slippers	na'alei 'bayit
	נעלי בית
a robe	xaluk
	חלוק
shampoo	ʃampo
	שמפו
soap	sabon
	סבון

I'd like to change rooms. (man)	ani rotse lehaxlif 'xeder.
	אני רוצה להחליף חדר.
I'd like to change rooms. (woman)	ani rotsa lehaxlif 'xeder.
	אני רוצה להחליף חדר.
I can't find my key. (man)	ani lo motse et hamaf'teax ʃeli.
	אני לא מוצא את המפתח שלי.
I can't find my key. (woman)	ani lo motset et hamaf'teax ʃeli.
	אני לא מוצאת את המפתח שלי.
Could you open my room, please?	ha'im ata yaxol lif'toax et xadri, bevakaʃa?
	,האם אתה יכול לפתוח את חדרי
	?בבקשה

Who's there?	mi ʃam?
	?מי שם
Come in!	hikanes!
	!היכנס
Just a minute!	rak 'rega!
	!רק רגע
Not right now, please.	lo aχʃav, bevakaʃa.
	.לא עכשיו, בבקשה

Come to my room, please.	bo'i leχadri, bevakaʃa.
	.בואי לחדרי, בבקשה
I'd like to order food service. (man ◁)	ani mevakeʃ lehazmin ʃerut χadarim.
	.אני מבקש להזמין שירות חדרים
I'd like to order food service. (woman ◁)	ani meva'keʃet lehazmin ʃerut χadarim.
	.אני מבקשת להזמין שירות חדרים
My room number is …	mispar ha'χeder ʃeli hu …
	… מספר החדר שלי הוא

I'm leaving … (man ◁)	ani ozev …
	… אני עוזב
I'm leaving … (woman ◁)	ani o'zevet …
	… אני עוזבת
We're leaving … (couple , men ◁)	a'naχnu ozvim …
	… אנחנו עוזבים
We're leaving … (women ◁)	a'naχnu ozvot …
	… אנחנו עוזבות

right now	aχʃav
	עכשיו
this afternoon	aχar hatsaha'rayim
	אחר הצהריים
tonight	ha'laila
	הלילה
tomorrow	maχar
	מחר
tomorrow morning	maχar ba'boker
	מחר בבוקר
tomorrow evening	maχar ba''erev
	מחר בערב
the day after tomorrow	maχara'tayim
	מחרתיים

I'd like to pay. (man ◁)	ani rotse leʃalem.
	.אני רוצה לשלם
I'd like to pay. (woman ◁)	ani rotsa leʃalem.
	.אני רוצה לשלם
Everything was wonderful.	hakol haya nehedar.
	.הכל היה נהדר
Where can I get a taxi?	eifo efʃar la'kaχat monit?
	?איפה אפשר לקחת מונית

Would you call a taxi for me, please?
(⸬ man)

ha'im ata yaχol lehazmin li monit,
bevakaʃa?

**האם אתה יכול להזמין לי מונית,
בבקשה?**

Would you call a taxi for me, please?
(⸬ woman)

ha'im at yeχola lehazmin li monit,
bevakaʃa?

**האם את יכולה להזמין לי מונית,
בבקשה?**

Restaurant

Can I look at the menu, please?	ha'im efʃar lekabel tafrit, bevakaʃa? האם אפשר לקבל תפריט, בבקשה?
Table for one.	ʃulχan leyaχid. שולחן ליחיד.
There are two (three, four) of us.	a'naχnu 'ʃnayim (ʃloʃa, arba'a). אנחנו שניים (שלושה, ארבעה).
Smoking	me'aʃnim מעשנים
No smoking	lo me'aʃnim לא מעשנים
Excuse me! (addressing a waiter) (⊙ man)	slaχ li! סלח לי!
Excuse me! (addressing a waiter) (⊙ woman)	silχi li! סלחי לי!
menu	tafrit תפריט
wine list	reʃimat yeinot רשימת יינות
The menu, please.	tafrit, bevakaʃa. תפריט, בבקשה.
Are you ready to order? (⊙ man)	ha'im ata muχan lehazmin? האם אתה מוכן להזמין?
Are you ready to order? (⊙ woman)	ha'im at muχana lehazmin? האם את מוכנה להזמין?
What will you have? (⊙ man)	ma tirtse? מה תרצה?
What will you have? (⊙ woman)	ma tirtsi? מה תרצי?
I'll have ... (man ⊙)	ani rotse ... אני רוצה ...
I'll have ... (woman ⊙)	ani rotsa ... אני רוצה ...
I'm a vegetarian. (man ⊙)	ani tsimχoni. אני צמחוני.
I'm a vegetarian. (woman ⊙)	ani tsimχonit. אני צמחונית.
meat	basar בשר
fish	dagim דגים
vegetables	yerakot ירקות

Do you have vegetarian dishes?

ha'im yeʃ laχem manot tsimχoniyot?
האם יש לכם מנות צמחוניות?

I don't eat pork. (man)

ani lo oχel χazir.
אני לא אוכל חזיר.

I don't eat pork. (woman)

ani lo o'χelet χazir.
אני לא אוכלת חזיר.

He doesn't eat meat.

hu lo oχel basar.
הוא לא אוכל בשר.

She doesn't eat meat.

hi lo o'χelet basar.
היא לא אוכלת בשר.

I am allergic to ... (man)

ani a'lergi le...
אני אלרגי ל...

I am allergic to ... (woman)

ani a'lergit le...
אני אלרגית ל...

Would you please bring me ... (man)

ha'im ata yaχol lehavi li, bevakaʃa, ...
האם אתה יכול להביא לי, בבקשה, ...

Would you please bring me ... (woman)

ha'im at yeχola lehavi li, bevakaʃa, ...
האם את יכולה להביא לי, בבקשה, ...

salt | pepper | sugar

melaχ | 'pilpel | sukar
מלח | פלפל | סוכר

coffee | tea | dessert

kafe | te | ki'nuaχ
קפה | תה | קינוח

water | sparkling | plain

mayim | mugazim | regilim
מים | מוגזים| רגילים

a spoon | fork | knife

kaf | mazleg | sakin
כף | מזלג | סכין

a plate | napkin

tsa'laχat | mapit
צלחת | מפית

Enjoy your meal!

bete'avon!
בתיאבון!

One more, please.

od eχad /aχat/, bevakaʃa.
עוד אחד /אחת/, בבקשה.

It was very delicious.

ze haya me'od ta'im.
זה היה מאוד טעים.

check | change | tip

χeʃbon | 'odef | tip
חשבון | עודף | טיפ

Check, please.
(Could I have the check, please?)

χeʃbon, bevakaʃa.
חשבון, בבקשה.

Can I pay by credit card?

ha'im efʃar leʃalem bekatrtis aʃrai?
האם אפשר לשלם בכרטיס אשראי?

I'm sorry, there's a mistake here.
(man)

ani mitsta'er, yeʃ kan ta'ut.
אני מצטער, יש כאן טעות.

I'm sorry, there's a mistake here.
(woman)

ani mitsta''eret, yeʃ kan ta'ut.
אני מצטערת, יש כאן טעות.

Shopping

Can I help you? (⌐ man)	ha'im efʃar la'azor leχa?
	האם אפשר לעזור לך?
Can I help you? (⌐ woman)	ha'im efʃar la'azor laχ?
	האם אפשר לעזור לך?
Do you have …?	ha'im yeʃ laχem …?
	?...האם יש לכם
I'm looking for … (man ⌐)	ani meχapes …
	... אני מחפש
I'm looking for … (woman ⌐)	ani meχa'peset …
	... אני מחפשת
I need … (man ⌐)	ani tsariχ …
	... אני צריך
I need … (woman ⌐)	ani tsriχa …
	... אני צריכה

I'm just looking. (man ⌐)	ani rak mistakel.
	אני רק מסתכל.
I'm just looking. (woman ⌐)	ani rak mista'kelet.
	אני רק מסתכלת.
We're just looking. (couple , men ⌐)	a'naχnu rak mistaklim.
	אנחנו רק מסתכלים.
We're just looking. (women ⌐)	a'naχnu rak mistaklot.
	אנחנו רק מסתכלות.
I'll come back later.	ani aχazor me'uχar yoter.
	אני אחזור מאוחר יותר.
We'll come back later.	a'naχnu naχazor me'uχar yoter.
	אנחנו נחזור מאוחר יותר.
discounts | sale	hanaχot | mivtsa
	הנחות | מבצע

Would you please show me … (⌐ man)	ha'im ata yaχol lehar'ot li …
	... האם אתה יכול להראות לי
Would you please show me … (⌐ woman)	ha'im at yeχola lehar'ot li …
	... האם את יכולה להראות לי
Would you please give me … (⌐ man)	ha'im ata yaχol latet li, bevakaʃa …
	... האם אתה יכול לתת לי, בבקשה
Would you please give me … (⌐ woman)	ha'im at yeχola latet li, bevakaʃa …
	... האם את יכולה לתת לי, בבקשה
Can I try it on? (man ⌐)	ha'im ani yaχol limdod et ze?
	?האם אני יכול למדוד את זה
Can I try it on? (woman ⌐)	ha'im ani yeχola limdod et ze?
	?האם אני יכולה למדוד את זה

Excuse me, where's the fitting room?
(₋ man)

slax li, 'eifo χadar hahalbaʃa?
סלח לי, איפה חדר ההלבשה?

Excuse me, where's the fitting room?
(₋ woman)

silχi li, 'eifo χadar hahalbaʃa?
סלחי לי, איפה חדר ההלבשה?

Which color would you like? (man)

eize 'tseva ha'yita rotse?
איזה צבע היית רוצה?

Which color would you like? (woman)

eize 'tseva hayit rotsa?
איזה צבע היית רוצה?

size | length

mida | 'oreχ
מידה | אורך

How does it fit? (man)

ha'im ze mat'im leχa?
האם זה מתאים לך?

How does it fit? (woman)

ha'im ze mat'im laχ?
האם זה מתאים לך?

How much is it?

kama ze ole?
כמה זה עולה?

That's too expensive.

ze yakar midai.
זה יקר מדי.

I'll take it.

ani ekaχ et ze.
אני אקח את זה.

Excuse me, where do I pay? (man ₋)

slax li, 'eifo meʃalmim?
סלח לי, איפה משלמים?

Excuse me, where do I pay? (woman ₋)

silχi li, 'eifo 'meʃalmim?
סלחי לי, איפה משלמים?

Will you pay in cash or credit card?
(₋ man)

ha'im ata meʃalem bimzuman
o bekartis aʃrai?
האם אתה משלם במזומן
או בכרטיס אשראי?

Will you pay in cash or credit card?
(₋ woman)

ha'im at meʃa'lemet bimzuman
o bekartis aʃrai?
האם את משלמת במזומן
או בכרטיס אשראי?

In cash | with credit card

bimzuman | bekartis aʃrai
במזומן | בכרטיס אשראי

Do you want the receipt? (man)

ha'im ata rotse et hakabala?
האם אתה רוצה את הקבלה?

Do you want the receipt? (woman)

ha'im at rotsa et hakabala?
האם את רוצה את הקבלה?

Yes, please.

ken, bevakaʃa.
כן, בבקשה.

No, it's OK.

lo, ze be'seder.
לא, זה בסדר.

Thank you. Have a nice day! (man)

toda. ʃeyihye leχa yom na'im!
תודה. שיהיה לך יום נעים!

Thank you. Have a nice day! (woman)

toda. ʃeyihye laχ yom na'im!
תודה. שיהיה לך יום נעים!

In town

Excuse me, please. (◌ man)	slaχ li, bevakaſa. סלח לי, בבקשה.
Excuse me, please. (◌ woman)	silχi li, bevakaſa. סלחי לי, בבקשה.
I'm looking for ... (man ◌)	ani meχapes ... אני מחפש ...
I'm looking for ... (woman ◌)	ani meχa'peset ... אני מחפשת ...
the subway	ra'kevet taχtit רכבת תחתית
my hotel	et hamalon ſeli את המלון שלי
the movie theater	et hakol'no'a את הקולנוע
a taxi stand	taχanat moniyot תחנת מוניות
an ATM	kaspomat כספומט
a foreign exchange office	misrad mat'be'a χuts משרד מטבע חוץ
an internet café	beit kafe 'internet בית קפה אינטרנט
... street	reχov ... רחוב ...
this place	hamakom haze המקום הזה
Do you know where ... is? (◌ man)	ha'im ata yo'de'a heiχan nimtsa ...? האם אתה יודע היכן נמצא ...?
Do you know where ... is? (◌ woman)	ha'im at yo'da'at heiχan nimtsa ...? האם את יודעת היכן נמצא ...?
Which street is this?	eize reχov ze? איזה רחוב זה?
Show me where we are right now. (◌ man)	har'e li heiχan 'anu nimtsa'im axſav. הראה לי היכן אנו נמצאים עכשיו.
Show me where we are right now. (◌ woman)	har'i li heiχan anu nimtsa'im axſav. הראי לי היכן אנו נמצאים עכשיו.
Can I get there on foot?	ha'im efſar leha'gi'a leſam ba'regel? האם אפשר להגיע לשם ברגל?
Do you have a map of the city? (◌ man)	ha'im yeſ leχa mapa ſel ha'ir? האם יש לך מפה של העיר?
Do you have a map of the city? (◌ woman)	ha'im yeſ laχ mapa ſel ha'ir? האם יש לך מפה של העיר?

How much is a ticket to get in?

kama ole kartis knisa?
כמה עולה כרטיס כניסה?

Can I take pictures here?

ha'im mutar letsalem kan?
האם מותר לצלם כאן?

Are you open?

ha'im atem ptuxim?
האם אתם פתוחים?

When do you open?

matai atem potxim?
מתי אתם פותחים?

When do you close?

matai atem sogrim?
מתי אתם סוגרים?

Money

money	kesef
	כסף
cash	mezuman
	מזומן
paper money	ʃtarot 'kesef
	שטרות כסף
loose change	kesef katan
	כסף קטן
check | change | tip	χeʃbon | 'odef | tip
	חשבון | עודף | טיפ

credit card	kartis aʃrai
	כרטיס אשראי
wallet	arnak
	ארנק
to buy	liknot
	לקנות
to pay	leʃalem
	לשלם
fine	knas
	קנס
free	χinam
	חינם

Where can I buy ...?	eifo efʃar liknot ...?
	איפה אפשר לקנות ...?
Is the bank open now?	ha'im ha'bank pa'tuaχ aχʃav?
	האם הבנק פתוח עכשיו?
When does it open?	matai ze nisgar?
	מתי זה נפתח?
When does it close?	matai ze niftaχ?
	מתי זה נסגר?

How much?	kama?
	כמה?
How much is this?	kama ze ole?
	כמה זה עולה?
That's too expensive.	ze yakar midai.
	זה יקר מידי.

Excuse me, where do I pay?	sliχa, 'eifo meʃalmim?
	סליחה, איפה משלמים?
Check, please.	χeʃbon, bevakaʃa.
	חשבון, בבקשה.

Can I pay by credit card?	ha'im efʃar leʃalem bekatrtis aʃrai?
	האם אפשר לשלם בכרטיס אשראי?
Is there an ATM here?	ha'im yeʃ kan kaspomat?
	האם יש כאן כספומט?
I'm looking for an ATM. (man)	ani meχapes kaspomat.
	אני מחפש כספומט.
I'm looking for an ATM. (woman)	ani meχa'peset kaspomat.
	אני מחפשת כספומט.

I'm looking for a foreign exchange office. (man)	ani meχapes misrad mat'be'a χuts.
	אני מחפש משרד מטבע חוץ.
I'm looking for a foreign exchange office. (woman)	ani meχa'peset misrad mat'be'a χuts.
	אני מחפשת משרד מטבע חוץ.
I'd like to change … (man)	ani rotse lehaχlif …
	… אני רוצה להחליף
I'd like to change … (woman)	ani rotsa lehaχlif …
	… אני רוצה להחליף
What is the exchange rate?	ma 'ʃa'ar haχalifin?
	מה שער החליפין?
Do you need my passport? (man)	ha'im ata tsariχ et hadarkon ʃeli?
	האם אתה צריך את הדרכון שלי?
Do you need my passport? (woman)	ha'im at tsriχa et hadarkon ʃeli?
	האם את צריכה את הדרכון שלי?

Time

What time is it?	ma haʃa'a? ?מה השעה
When?	matai? ?מתי
At what time?	be"eizo ʃa'a? ?באיזו שעה
now | later | after …	aχʃav | aχar kaχ | aχrei … עכשיו | אחר כך | אחרי ...

one o'clock	aχat אחת
one fifteen	aχat va'reva אחת ורבע
one thirty	aχat va'χetsi אחת וחצי
one forty-five	aχat arba'im veχameʃ אחת ארבעים וחמש

one | two | three	aχat | ʃtayim | ʃaloʃ אחת | שתיים | שלוש
four | five | six	arba | χameʃ | ʃeʃ ארבע | חמש | שש
seven | eight | nine	ʃeva | 'ʃmone | 'teʃa שבע | שמונה | תשע
ten | eleven | twelve	eser | aχat esre | ʃtem esre עשר | אחת עשרה | שתים עשרה

in …	toχ … תוך ...
five minutes	χameʃ dakot חמש דקות
ten minutes	eser dakot עשר דקות
fifteen minutes	χameʃ esre dakot חמש עשרה דקות
twenty minutes	esrim dakot עשרים דקות

half an hour	χatsi ʃa'a חצי שעה
an hour	ʃa'a שעה

in the morning	ba'boker בבוקר
early in the morning	mukdam ba'boker, haʃkem ba'boker מוקדם בבוקר, השכם בבוקר
this morning	ha'boker הבוקר
tomorrow morning	maxar ba'boker מחר בבוקר
in the middle of the day	batsaha'rayim בצהריים
in the afternoon	axar hatsaha'rayim אחר הצהריים
in the evening	ba''erev בערב
tonight	ha'laila הלילה
at night	ba'laila בלילה
yesterday	etmol אתמול
today	hayom היום
tomorrow	maxar מחר
the day after tomorrow	maxara'tayim מחרתיים
What day is it today?	eize yom hayom? איזה יום היום?
It's …	hayom … היום …
Monday	yom ʃeni יום שני
Tuesday	yom ʃliʃi יום שלישי
Wednesday	yom revi'i יום רביעי
Thursday	yom xamiʃi יום חמישי
Friday	yom ʃiʃi יום שישי
Saturday	ʃabat שבת
Sunday	yom riʃon יום ראשון

Greetings. Introductions

Pleased to meet you. (man → man)	ani sameaχ lehakir otχa. ‏אני שמח להכיר אותך.
Pleased to meet you. (man → woman)	ani sameaχ lehakir otaχ. ‏אני שמח להכיר אותך.
Pleased to meet you. (woman → man)	ani smeχa lifgoʃ otχa. ‏אני שמחה לפגוש אותך.
Pleased to meet you. (woman → woman)	ani smeχa lifgoʃ otaχ. ‏אני שמחה לפגוש אותך.
Hello.	ʃalom. ‏שלום.
Me too.	gam ani. ‏גם אני.

I'd like you to meet … (man → man)	ha'yiti rotse ʃetakir et … ‏הייתי רוצה שתכיר את ...
I'd like you to meet … (man → woman)	ha'yiti rotse ʃeta'kiri et … ‏הייתי רוצה שתכירי את ...
I'd like you to meet … (woman → man)	ha'yiti rotsa ʃetakir et … ‏הייתי רוצה שתכיר את ...
I'd like you to meet … (woman → woman)	ha'yiti rotsa ʃeta'kiri et … ‏הייתי רוצה שתכירי את ...
Nice to meet you. (→ man)	na'im lifgoʃ otχa. ‏נעים לפגוש אותך.
Nice to meet you. (→ woman)	na'im lifgoʃ otaχ. ‏נעים לפגוש אותך.

How are you? (→ man)	ma ʃlomχa? ‏מה שלומך?
How are you? (→ woman)	ma ʃlomeχ? ‏מה שלומך?
My name is …	kor'im li … ‏קוראים לי ...
His name is …	kor'im lo … ‏קוראים לו ...
Her name is …	kor'im la … ‏קוראים לה ...
What's your name? (→ man)	eiχ kor'im leχa? ‏איך קוראים לך?
What's your name? (→ woman)	eiχ kor'im laχ? ‏איך קוראים לך?
What's his name?	eiχ kor'im lo? ‏איך קוראים לו?
What's her name?	eiχ kor'im la? ‏איך קוראים לה?

What's your last name? (to man)	ma ʃem hamiʃpaχa ʃelχa?
	מה שם המשפחה שלך?
What's your last name? (to woman)	ma ʃem hamiʃpaχa ʃelaχ?
	מה שם המשפחה שלך?
You can call me ... (to man)	ata yaχol likro li ...
	אתה יכול לקרוא לי ...
You can call me ... (to woman)	at yeχola likro li ...
	את יכולה לקרוא לי ...
Where are you from? (to man)	me''eifo ata?
	מאיפה אתה?
Where are you from? (to woman)	me''eifo at?
	מאיפה את?

I'm from ...	ani mi...
	אני מ...
What do you do for a living? (to man)	bema ata oved?
	במה אתה עובד?
What do you do for a living? (to woman)	bema at o'vedet?
	במה את עובדת?

Who is this? (masc.)	mi ze?
	מי זה?
Who is this? (fem.)	mi zo?
	מי זו?
Who is he?	mi ze?
	מי זה?
Who is she?	mi zo?
	מי זו?
Who are they?	mi 'ele?
	מי אלה?

This is ...	ze ...
	זה ...
my friend (masc.)	χaver ʃeli
	חבר שלי
my husband	ba'ali
	בעלי
my father	avi
	אבי
my brother	aχi
	אחי
my son	bni
	בני

This is ...	zo ...
	זו ...
my friend (fem.)	χavera ʃeli
	חברה שלי
my wife	iʃti
	אשתי
my mother	immi
	אמי

my sister	aχoti
	אחותי
my daughter	biti
	בתי

This is our son.	ze haben ʃe'lanu.
	זה הבן שלנו.
This is our daughter.	zo habat ʃe'lanu.
	זו הבת שלנו.
These are my children.	ele hayeladim ʃeli.
	אלה הילדים שלי.
These are our children.	ele hayeladim ʃe'lanu.
	אלה הילדים שלנו.

Farewells

Good bye!	ʃalom! שלום!
Bye! (inform.)	bai! ביי!
See you tomorrow.	lehitra'ot maxar. להתראות מחר.
See you soon.	lehitra'ot bekarov. להתראות בקרוב.
See you at seven.	lehitra'ot be'ʃeva. להתראות בשבע.
Have fun!	asu xayim! עשו חיים!
Talk to you later.	lehiʃta'me'a. להשתמע.
Have a nice weekend.	sof ʃa'vu'a na'im. סוף שבוע נעים.
Good night.	laila tov. לילה טוב.
It's time for me to go.	hi'gi'a zmani la'lexet. הגיע זמני ללכת.
I have to go. (man)	ani xayav la'lexet. אני חייב ללכת.
I have to go. (woman)	ani xa'yevet la'lexet. אני חייבת ללכת.
I will be right back.	ani axazor miyad. אני אחזור מייד.
It's late.	kvar me'uxar. כבר מאוחר.
I have to get up early. (man)	ani tsariх lakum mukdam. אני צריך לקום מוקדם.
I have to get up early. (woman)	ani tsrixa lakum mukdam. אני צריכה לקום מוקדם.
I'm leaving tomorrow. (man)	ani ozev maxar. אני עוזב מחר.
I'm leaving tomorrow. (woman)	ani o'zevet maxar. אני עוזבת מחר.
We're leaving tomorrow. (couple , men)	a'naxnu ozvim maxar. אנחנו עוזבים מחר.
We're leaving tomorrow. (women)	a'naxnu ozvot maxar. אנחנו עוזבות מחר.

Have a nice trip!	nesi'a tova! !נסיעה טובה
It was nice meeting you. (☞ man)	haya neχmad lifgoʃ otχa. .היה נחמד לפגוש אותך
It was nice meeting you. (☞ woman)	haya neχmad lifgoʃ otaχ. .היה נחמד לפגוש אותך
It was nice talking to you. (☞ man)	haya na'im ledaber itχa. .היה נעים לדבר איתך
It was nice talking to you. (☞ woman)	haya na'im ledaber itaχ. .היה נעים לדבר איתך
Thanks for everything.	toda al hakol. .תודה על הכל

I had a very good time.	nehe'neti me'od. .נהניתי מאוד
We had a very good time.	nehe'nenu me'od. .נהנינו מאוד
It was really great.	ze haya mamaʃ nehedar. .זה היה ממש נהדר
I'm going to miss you. (☞ man)	ani etga'a'ge'a e'leχa. .אני אתגעגע אליך
I'm going to miss you. (☞ woman)	ani etga'a'ge'a e'layiχ. .אני אתגעגע אלייך
We're going to miss you. (☞ man)	a'naχnu nitga'a'ge'a e'leχa. .אנחנו נתגעגע אליך
We're going to miss you. (☞ woman)	a'naχnu nitga'a'ge'a e'layiχ. .אנחנו נתגעגע אלייך

Good luck!	behatslaχa! !בהצלחה
Say hi to ... (☞ man)	msor daʃ le... ...מסור ד"ש ל
Say hi to ... (☞ woman)	misri daʃ le... ...מסרי ד"ש ל

Foreign language

I don't understand. (man)	ani lo mevin.
	אני לא מבין.
I don't understand. (woman)	ani lo mevina.
	אני לא מבינה.
Write it down, please. (man)	ktov li et ze, bevakaʃa.
	כתוב לי את זה, בבקשה.
Write it down, please. (woman)	kitvi li et ze, bevakaʃa.
	כתבי לי את זה, בבקשה.
Do you speak ...? (man)	ha'im ata medaber ...?
	האם אתה מדבר ...?
Do you speak ...? (woman)	ha'im at meda'beret ...?
	האם את מדברת ...?

I speak a little bit of ... (man)	ani medaber ktsat ...
	אני מדבר קצת ...
I speak a little bit of ... (woman)	ani meda'beret ktsat ...
	אני מדברת קצת ...
English	anglit
	אנגלית
Turkish	turkit
	טורקית
Arabic	aravit
	ערבית
French	tsarfatit
	צרפתית

German	germanit
	גרמנית
Italian	italkit
	איטלקית
Spanish	sfaradit
	ספרדית
Portuguese	portu'gezit
	פורטוגזית
Chinese	sinit
	סינית
Japanese	ya'panit
	יפנית

Can you repeat that, please. (man)	ha'im ata yaχol laχazor al ze, bevakaʃa?
	האם אתה יכול לחזור על זה, בבקשה?
Can you repeat that, please. (woman)	ha'im at yeχola laχazor al ze, bevakaʃa?
	האם את יכולה לחזור על זה, בבקשה?

I understand. (man)

ani mevin.
אני מבין.

I understand. (woman)

ani mevina.
אני מבינה.

I don't understand. (man)

ani lo mevin.
אני לא מבין.

I don't understand. (woman)

ani lo mevina.
אני לא מבינה.

Please speak more slowly. (man)

ana daber yoter le'at.
אנא דבר יותר לאט.

Please speak more slowly. (woman)

ana dabri yoter le'at.
אנא דברי יותר לאט.

Is that correct? (Am I saying it right?)

ha'im ze naχon?
האם זה נכון?

What is this? (What does this mean?)

ma ze?
מה זה?

Apologies

Excuse me, please. (to man)	slax li, bevakaʃa.
	סלח לי, בבקשה.
Excuse me, please. (to woman)	silxi li, bevakaʃa.
	סלחי לי, בבקשה.
I'm sorry. (man)	ani mitsta'er.
	אני מצטער.
I'm sorry. (woman)	ani mitsta''eret.
	אני מצטערת.
I'm really sorry. (man)	ani mamaʃ mitsta'er.
	אני ממש מצטער.
I'm really sorry. (woman)	ani mamaʃ mitsta''eret.
	אני ממש מצטערת.
Sorry, it's my fault.	slixa, zo aʃmati.
	סליחה, זו אשמתי.
My mistake.	ta'ut ʃeli.
	טעות שלי.

May I ...? (man)	ha'im ani yaxol ...?
	האם אני יכול ...?
May I ...? (woman)	ha'im ani yexola ...?
	האם אני יכולה ...?
Do you mind if I ...? (to man)	ha'im ixpat lexa im ani ...?
	האם איכפת לך אם אני ...?
Do you mind if I ...? (to woman)	ha'im ixpat lax im ani ...?
	האם איכפת לך אם אני ...?
It's OK.	ze be'seder.
	זה בסדר.
It's all right.	ze be'seder.
	זה בסדר.
Don't worry about it. (to man)	al taxʃov al ze.
	אל תחשוב על זה.
Don't worry about it. (to woman)	al taxʃevi al ze.
	אל תחשבי על זה.

Agreement

Yes.	ken.
	כן.
Yes, sure.	ken, bevadai.
	כן, בוודאי.
OK (Good!)	tov!
	טוב!
Very well.	be'seder gamur.
	בסדר גמור.
Certainly!	bevadai!
	בוודאי!
I agree. (man ⌐)	ani maskim.
	אני מסכים.
I agree. (woman ⌐)	ani maskima.
	אני מסכימה.
That's correct.	ze naxon.
	זה נכון.
That's right.	ze naxon.
	זה נכון.
You're right. (⌐ man)	ata tsodek.
	אתה צודק.
You're right. (⌐ woman)	at tso'deket.
	את צודקת.
I don't mind.	lo mefane li.
	לא משנה לי.
Absolutely right.	naxon me'od.
	נכון מאוד.
It's possible.	yitaxen, ze efʃari.
	ייתכן, זה אפשרי.
That's a good idea.	ze ra'ayon tov.
	זה רעיון טוב.
I can't say no. (man ⌐)	ani lo yaxol lesarev.
	אני לא יכול לסרב.
I can't say no. (woman ⌐)	ani lo yexola lesarev.
	אני לא יכולה לסרב.
I'd be happy to.	esmax la'asot et ze.
	אשמח לעשות את זה.
With pleasure.	bekef.
	בכיף.

Refusal. Expressing doubt

No.	lo. לא.
Certainly not.	ba'tuaχ ʃelo. בטוח שלא.
I don't agree. (man)	ani lo maskim. אני לא מסכים.
I don't agree. (woman)	ani lo maskima. אני לא מסכימה.
I don't think so. (man)	ani lo χoʃev kaχ. אני לא חושב כך.
I don't think so. (woman)	ani lo χoʃevet kaχ. אני לא חושבת כך.
It's not true.	ze lo naχon. זה לא נכון.
You are wrong. (man)	ata to'e. אתה טועה.
You are wrong. (woman)	at to'a. את טועה.
I think you are wrong. (man man)	ani χoʃev ʃe'ata to'e. אני חושב שאתה טועה.
I think you are wrong. (man woman)	ani χoʃev ʃe'at to'a. אני חושב שאת טועה.
I think you are wrong. (woman man)	ani χo'ʃevet ʃe'ata to'e. אני חושבת שאתה טועה.
I think you are wrong. (woman woman)	ani χo'ʃevet ʃe'at to'a. אני חושבת שאת טועה.
I'm not sure. (man)	ani lo ba'tuaχ. אני לא בטוח.
I'm not sure. (woman)	ani lo betuχa. אני לא בטוחה.
It's impossible.	ze 'bilti efʃari. זה בלתי אפשרי.
Nothing of the kind (sort)!	beʃum panim va'ofen lo! בשום פנים ואופן לא!
The exact opposite.	bediyuk ha'hefeχ. בדיוק ההיפך.
I'm against it. (man)	ani mitnaged leze. אני מתנגד לזה.
I'm against it. (woman)	ani mitna'gedet leze. אני מתנגדת לזה.
I don't care.	lo iχpat li. לא איכפת לי.

I have no idea.

ein li musag.
אין לי מושג.

I doubt it. (man ◻)

ani lo ba'tuaχ.
אני לא בטוח.

I doubt it. (woman ◻)

ani lo betuχa.
אני לא בטוחה.

Sorry, I can't. (man ◻)

mitsta'er, ani lo yaχol.
מצטער, אני לא יכול.

Sorry, I can't. (woman ◻)

mitsta"eret, ani lo yeχola.
מצטערת, אני לא יכולה.

Sorry, I don't want to. (man ◻)

mitsta'er, ani lo me'unyan.
מצטער, אני לא מעוניין.

Sorry, I don't want to. (woman ◻)

mitsta"eret, ani lo me'un'yenet.
מצטערת, אני לא מעוניינת.

Thank you, but I don't need this. (man ◻)

toda, aval ani lo tsariχ et ze.
תודה, אבל אני לא צריך את זה.

Thank you, but I don't need this. (woman ◻)

toda, aval ani lo tsriχa et ze.
תודה, אבל אני לא צריכה את זה.

It's getting late.

matχil lihyot me'uχar.
מתחיל להיות מאוחר.

I have to get up early. (man ◻)

ani tsariχ lakum mukdam.
אני צריך לקום מוקדם.

I have to get up early. (woman ◻)

ani tsriχa lakum mukdam.
אני צריכה לקום מוקדם.

I don't feel well. (man ◻)

ani lo margiʃ tov.
אני לא מרגיש טוב.

I don't feel well. (woman ◻)

ani lo margiʃa tov.
אני לא מרגישה טוב.

Expressing gratitude

Thank you.	toda. ‏תודה.‏
Thank you very much.	toda raba. ‏תודה רבה.‏
I really appreciate it. (man)	ani be'emet ma'ariχ et ze. ‏אני באמת מעריך את זה.‏
I really appreciate it. (woman)	ani be'emet ma'riχa et ze. ‏אני באמת מעריכה את זה.‏
I'm really grateful to you. (man _ man)	ani mamaʃ asir toda leχa. ‏אני ממש אסיר תודה לך.‏
I'm really grateful to you. (man _ woman)	ani mamaʃ asir toda laχ. ‏אני ממש אסיר תודה לך.‏
I'm really grateful to you. (woman _ man)	ani mamaʃ asirat toda leχa. ‏אני ממש אסירת תודה לך.‏
I'm really grateful to you. (woman _ woman)	ani mamaʃ asirat toda laχ. ‏אני ממש אסירת תודה לך.‏
Thank you for your time. (_ man)	toda al hazman ʃehik'daʃta. ‏תודה על הזמן שהקדשת.‏
Thank you for your time. (_ woman)	toda al hazman ʃehikdaʃt. ‏תודה על הזמן שהקדשת.‏
Thanks for everything.	toda al hakol. ‏תודה על הכל.‏
Thank you for …	toda al … ‏תודה על …‏
your help (_ man)	ezratχa ‏עזרתך‏
your help (_ woman)	ezrateχ ‏עזרתך‏
a nice time	haχavaya hamehana ‏החוויה המהנה‏
a wonderful meal	aruχa nehe'deret ‏ארוחה נהדרת‏
a pleasant evening	erev na'im ‏ערב נעים‏
a wonderful day	yom nifla ‏יום נפלא‏
an amazing journey	tiyul madhim ‏טיול מדהים‏
Don't mention it.	ein be'ad ma. ‏אין בעד מה.‏
You are welcome.	bevakaʃa. ‏בבקשה.‏

Any time.

ein be'ad ma.
אין בעד מה.

My pleasure.

ha"oneg kulo ʃeli.
העונג כולו שלי.

Forget it.

lo meʃane.
לא משנה

Don't worry about it. (⌐ man)

al tid'ag.
אל תדאג.

Don't worry about it. (⌐ woman)

al tid'agi.
אל תדאגי.

Congratulations. Best wishes

Congratulations!

birχotai!
ברכותיי!

Happy birthday!

mazal tov leyom hahu'ledet!
מזל טוב ליום ההולדת!

Merry Christmas!

χag molad sa'meaχ!
חג מולד שמח!

Happy New Year!

ʃana tova!
שנה טובה!

Happy Easter!

χag pasχa sa'meaχ!
חג פסחא שמח!

Happy Hanukkah!

χag 'χanuka sa'meaχ!
חג חנוכה שמח!

I'd like to propose a toast. (man)

ani rotse leharim kosit.
אני רוצה להרים כוסית.

I'd like to propose a toast. (woman)

ani rotsa leharim kosit.
אני רוצה להרים כוסית.

Cheers!

le'χayim!
לחיים!

Let's drink to …!

bo'u niʃte le …!
בואו נשתה ל ...!

To our success!

lehatslaχa'tenu!
להצלחתנו!

To your success! (man)

lehatslaχatχa!
להצלחתך!

To your success! (woman)

lehatslaχateχ!
להצלחתך!

Good luck!

behatslaχa!
בהצלחה!

Have a nice day! (man)

ʃeyihye leχa yom na'im!
שיהיה לך יום נעים!

Have a nice day! (woman)

ʃeyihye laχ yom na'im!
שיהיה לך יום נעים!

Have a good holiday!

χufʃa ne'ima!
חופשה נעימה!

Have a safe journey!

nesi'a tova!
נסיעה טובה!

I hope you get better soon!
(man – man)

ani mekave ʃetaχlim maher!
אני מקווה שתחלים מהר!

I hope you get better soon!
(man – woman)

ani mekave ʃetaχ'limi maher!
אני מקווה שתחלימי מהר!

I hope you get better soon!
(woman — man)

ani mekava ʃetaχlim maher!
אני מקווה שתחלים מהר!

I hope you get better soon!
(woman — woman)

ani mekava ʃetaχ'limi maher!
אני מקווה שתחלימי מהר!

Socializing

Why are you sad? (man)	lama ata atsuv?
	?למה אתה עצוב
Why are you sad? (woman)	lama at atsuva?
	?למה את עצובה
Smile! Cheer up! (man)	xayex ktsat!
	!חייך קצת
Smile! Cheer up! (woman)	xaixi ktsat!
	!חייכי קצת
Are you free tonight? (man)	ha'im ata panui ha''erev?
	?האם אתה פנוי הערב
Are you free tonight? (woman)	ha'im at pnuya ha'erev?
	?האם את פנויה הערב

May I offer you a drink?	ha'im efʃar leha'tsi'a lax maʃke?
	?האם אפשר להציע לך משקה
Would you like to dance? (man)	ha'im ata rotse lirkod?
	?האם אתה רוצה לרקוד
Would you like to dance? (woman)	ha'im at rotsa lirkod?
	?האם את רוצה לרקוד
Let's go to the movies. (man)	bo nelex le'seret.
	.בוא נלך לסרט
Let's go to the movies. (woman)	bo'i nelex le'seret.
	.בואי נלך לסרט

May I invite you to ...?	ha'im efʃar lehazmin otax le ...?
	?...האם אפשר להזמין אותך ל
a restaurant	mis'ada
	מסעדה
the movies	seret
	סרט
the theater	te'atron
	תיאטרון
go for a walk	letiyul ba'regel
	לטיול ברגל

At what time?	be''eizo ʃa'a?
	?באיזו שעה
tonight	ha'laila
	הלילה
at six	beʃeʃ
	בשש
at seven	be'ʃeva
	בשבע

at eight	bi'ʃmone
	בשמונה
at nine	be'teʃa
	בתשע

Do you like it here? (← man)	ha'im hamakom motse χen be'ei'neχa?
	?האם המקום מוצא חן בעיניך
Do you like it here? (← woman)	ha'im hamakom motse χen be'ei'nayiχ?
	?האם המקום מוצא חן בעינייך
Are you here with someone? (← man)	ha'im ata nimtsa kan im 'miʃehu?
	?האם אתה נמצא כאן עם מישהו
Are you here with someone? (← woman)	ha'im at nimtset kan im 'miʃehu?
	?האם את נמצאת כאן עם מישהו
I'm with my friend.	ani kan im χaver /χavera/.
	.אני כאן עם חבר /חברה/
I'm with my friends.	ani kan im χaverim.
	.אני כאן עם חברים
No, I'm alone.	lo, ani levad.
	.לא, אני לבד
Do you have a boyfriend?	ha'im yeʃ laχ χaver?
	?האם יש לך חבר
I have a boyfriend.	yeʃ li χaver.
	.יש לי חבר
Do you have a girlfriend?	ha'im yeʃ leχa χavera?
	?האם יש לך חברה
I have a girlfriend.	yeʃ li χavera.
	.יש לי חברה

Can I see you again? (← man)	ha'im tirtse lehipageʃ ʃuv?
	?האם תרצה להיפגש שוב
Can I see you again? (← woman)	ha'im tirtsi lehipageʃ ʃuv?
	?האם תרצי להיפגש שוב
Can I call you? (man ← man)	ha'im ani yaχol lehitkaʃer e'leχa?
	?האם אני יכול להתקשר אליך
Can I call you? (man ← woman)	ha'im ani yaχol lehitkaʃer e'layiχ?
	?האם אני יכול להתקשר אלייך
Can I call you? (woman ← man)	ha'im ani yeχola lehitkaʃer e'leχa?
	?האם אני יכולה להתקשר אליך
Can I call you? (woman ← woman)	ha'im ani yeχola lehitkaʃer e'layiχ?
	?האם אני יכולה להתקשר אלייך
Call me. (Give me a call.) (← man)	hitkaʃer elai.
	.התקשר אליי
Call me. (Give me a call.) (← woman)	hitkaʃri elai.
	.התקשרי אליי
What's your number? (← man)	ma hamispar ʃelχa?
	?מה המספר שלך
What's your number? (← woman)	ma hamispar ʃelaχ?
	?מה המספר שלך
I miss you. (man ← man)	ani mitga'a''ge'a e'leχa.
	.אני מתגעגע אליך
I miss you. (man ← woman)	ani mitga'a''ge'a e'layiχ.
	.אני מתגעגע אלייך

I miss you. (woman → man)
ani mitga'a"ga'at e'leχa.
אני מתגעגעת אליך.

I miss you. (woman → woman)
ani mitga'a"ga'at e'layiχ.
אני מתגעגעת אלייך.

You have a beautiful name.
(man → man)
yeʃ leχa ʃem maksim.
יש לך שם מקסים.

You have a beautiful name.
(man → woman)
yeʃ laχ ʃem maksim.
יש לך שם מקסים.

I love you.
ani ohev otaχ.
אני אוהב אותך.

Will you marry me?
ha'im titχatni iti?
האם תתחתני איתי?

You're kidding!
at tso'χeket alai!
את צוחקת עליי!

I'm just kidding. (man →)
ani stam mitba'deaχ.
אני סתם מתבדח.

I'm just kidding. (woman →)
ani stam mitba'daχat.
אני סתם מתבדחת.

Are you serious? (→ man)
ha'im ata retsini?
האם אתה רציני?

Are you serious? (→ woman)
ha'im at retsinit?
האם את רצינית?

I'm serious. (man →)
ani retsini.
אני רציני.

I'm serious. (woman →)
ani retsinit.
אני רצינית.

Really?!
be'emet?!
באמת?!

It's unbelievable!
ze lo ye'uman!
זה לא יאומן!

I don't believe you. (man → man)
ani lo ma'amin leχa.
אני לא מאמין לך.

I don't believe you. (man → woman)
ani lo ma'amin laχ.
אני לא מאמין לך.

I don't believe you. (woman → man)
ani lo ma'amina leχa.
אני לא מאמינה לך.

I don't believe you. (woman → woman)
ani lo ma'amina laχ.
אני לא מאמינה לך.

I can't. (man →)
ani lo yaχol.
אני לא יכול.

I can't. (woman →)
ani lo yeχola.
אני לא יכולה.

I don't know. (man →)
ani lo yo'de'a.
אני לא יודע.

I don't know. (woman →)
ani lo yo'da'at.
אני לא יודעת.

I don't understand you. (man → man)
ani lo mevin otχa.
אני לא מבין אותך.

I don't understand you. (man → woman)

ani lo mevin otax
אני לא מבין אותך.

I don't understand you. (woman → man)

ani lo mevina otxa.
אני לא מבינה אותך.

I don't understand you. (woman → woman)

ani lo mevina otax.
אני לא מבינה אותך.

Please go away. (→ man)

lex mipo bevakaʃa.
לך מפה בבקשה.

Please go away. (→ woman)

lexi mipo bevakaʃa.
לכי מפה בבקשה.

Leave me alone! (→ man)

azov oti!
עזוב אותי!

Leave me alone! (→ woman)

izvi oti!
עזבי אותי!

I can't stand him. (man →)

ani lo sovel oto.
אני לא סובל אותו.

I can't stand him. (woman →)

ani lo so'velet oto.
אני לא סובלת אותו.

You are disgusting! (→ man)

ata mag'il!
אתה מגעיל!

You are disgusting! (→ woman)

at mag'ila!
את מגעילה!

I'll call the police!

ani azmin miʃtara!
אני אזמין משטרה!

Sharing impressions. Emotions

I like it.	ze motse χen be'einai. זה מוצא חן בעיניי.
Very nice.	neχmad me'od. נחמד מאוד.
That's great!	ze nehedar! זה נהדר!
It's not bad.	ze lo ra. זה לא רע.
I don't like it.	ze lo motse χen be'einai. זה לא מוצא חן בעיניי.
It's not good.	ze lo yafe. זה לא יפה.
It's bad.	ze ra. זה רע.
It's very bad.	ze ra me'od. זה רע מאוד.
It's disgusting.	ze mag'il. זה מגעיל.
I'm happy. (man)	ani me'uʃar. אני מאושר.
I'm happy. (woman)	ani me'u'ʃeret. אני מאושרת.
I'm content. (man)	ani merutse. אני מרוצה.
I'm content. (woman)	ani merutsa. אני מרוצה.
I'm in love. (man)	ani me'ohav. אני מאוהב.
I'm in love. (woman)	ani me'o'hevet. אני מאוהבת.
I'm calm. (man)	ani ra'gu'a. אני רגוע.
I'm calm. (woman)	ani regu'a. אני רגועה.
I'm bored. (man)	ani meʃu'amam. אני משועמם.
I'm bored. (woman)	ani meʃu'a'memet. אני משועממת.
I'm tired. (man)	ani ayef. אני עייף.
I'm tired. (woman)	ani ayefa. אני עייפה.

I'm sad. (man ⏴) — ani atsuv.
אני עצוב.

I'm sad. (woman ⏴) — ani atsuva.
אני עצובה.

I'm frightened. (man ⏴) — ani poχed.
אני פוחד.

I'm frightened. (woman ⏴) — ani po'χedet.
אני פוחדת.

I'm angry. (man ⏴) — ani ko'es.
אני כועס.

I'm angry. (woman ⏴) — ani ko''eset.
אני כועסת.

I'm worried. (man ⏴) — ani mud'ag.
אני מודאג.

I'm worried. (woman ⏴) — ani mud''eget.
אני מודאגת.

I'm nervous. (man ⏴) — ani atsbani.
אני עצבני.

I'm nervous. (woman ⏴) — ani atsbanit.
אני עצבנית.

I'm jealous. (envious) (man ⏴) — ani mekane.
אני מקנא.

I'm jealous. (envious) (woman ⏴) — ani mekanet.
אני מקנאת.

I'm surprised. (man ⏴) — ani mufta.
אני מופתע.

I'm surprised. (woman ⏴) — ani muf'ta'at.
אני מופתעת.

I'm perplexed. (man ⏴) — ani mevulbal.
אני מבולבל.

I'm perplexed. (woman ⏴) — ani mevul'belet.
אני מבולבלת.

Problems. Accidents

I've got a problem.
yeʃ li be'aya.
יש לי בעייה.

We've got a problem.
yeʃ 'lanu be'aya.
יש לנו בעייה.

I'm lost.
ha'laxti le'ibud.
הלכתי לאיבוד.

I missed the last bus.
fis'fasti et ha''otobus ha'axaron.
פספסתי את האוטובוס האחרון.

I missed the last train.
fis'fasti et hara'kevet ha'axrona.
פספסתי את הרכבת האחרונה.

I don't have any money left.
niʃ'arti bli 'kesef.
נשארתי בלי כסף.

I've lost my …
i'badti et ha… ʃeli
איבדתי את ה... שלי

Someone stole my …
miʃehu ganav et ha… ʃeli
מישהו גנב את ה... שלי

passport
darkon
דרכון

wallet
arnak
ארנק

papers
te'udot
תעודות

ticket
kartis
כרטיס

money
kesef
כסף

handbag
tik yad
תיק יד

camera
matslema
מצלמה

laptop
maxʃev nayad
מחשב נייד

tablet computer
maxʃev ʃulxani
מחשב שולחני

mobile phone
telefon nayad
טלפון נייד

Help me!
izru li!
עזרו לי!

What's happened?
ma kara?
מה קרה?

fire	srefa שריפה
shooting	yeriyot יריות
murder	retsaχ רצח
explosion	pitsuts פיצוץ
fight	ktata קטטה

Call the police!	haz'minu miʃtara !הזמינו משטרה
Please hurry up!	ana maharu! !אנא מהרו
I'm looking for the police station. (man ⇨)	ani meχapes et taχanat hamiʃtara. .אני מחפש את תחנת המשטרה
I'm looking for the police station. (woman ⇨)	ani meχa'peset et taχanat hamiʃtara. .אני מחפשת את תחנת המשטרה
I need to make a call. (man ⇨)	ani tsariχ lehitkaʃer. .אני צריך להתקשר
I need to make a call. (woman ⇨)	ani tsriχa lehitkaʃer. .אני צריכה להתקשר
May I use your phone? (⇨ man)	ha'im eʃʃar lehiʃtameʃ be'telefon ʃelχa? ?האם אפשר להשתמש בטלפון שלך
May I use your phone? (⇨ woman)	ha'im eʃʃar lehiʃtameʃ be'telefon ʃelaχ? ?האם אפשר להשתמש בטלפון שלך

I've been …	ani … … אני
mugged	hut'kafti הותקפתי
robbed	niʃ'dadti נשדדתי
raped	ne'e'nasti נאנסתי
attacked (beaten up)	hu'keti הוכיתי

Are you all right? (⇨ man)	ha'im ata be'seder? ?האם אתה בסדר
Are you all right? (⇨ woman)	ha'im at be'seder? ?האם את בסדר
Did you see who it was? (⇨ man)	ha'im ra''ita mi asa et ze? ?האם ראית מי עשה את זה
Did you see who it was? (⇨ woman)	ha'im ra'it mi asa et ze? ?האם ראית מי עשה את זה
Would you be able to recognize the person? (⇨ man)	ha'im tuχal lezahot et oto adam? ?האם תוכל לזהות את אותו אדם
Would you be able to recognize the person? (⇨ woman)	ha'im tuχli lezahot et oto adam? ?האם תוכלי לזהות את אותו אדם

Are you sure? (man) ha'im ata ba'tuaχ?
האם אתה בטוח?

Are you sure? (woman) ha'im at betuχa?
האם את בטוחה?

Please calm down. (man) heraga, bevakaſa.
הירגע בבקשה.

Please calm down. (woman) herag'i, bevakaſa.
הירגעי בבקשה.

Take it easy! (man) teraga!
תירגע!

Take it easy! (woman) terag'i!
תירגעי!

Don't worry! (man) al tid'ag!
אל תדאג!

Don't worry! (woman) al tid'agi!
אל תדאגי!

Everything will be fine. hakol yihye be'seder.
הכל יהיה בסדר.

Everything's all right. hakol be'seder.
הכל בסדר.

Come here, please. (man) bo 'hena, bevakaſa.
בוא הנה, בבקשה.

Come here, please. (woman) bo'i 'hena, bevakaſa.
בואי הנה, בבקשה.

I have some questions for you. (man) yeſ li 'kama ſe'elot e'leχa.
יש לי כמה שאלות אליך.

I have some questions for you. (woman) yeſ li 'kama ſe'elot e'layiχ.
יש לי כמה שאלות אלייך.

Wait a moment, please. (man) χake 'rega, bevakaſa.
חכה רגע, בבקשה.

Wait a moment, please. (woman) χaki 'rega, bevakaſa.
חכי רגע, בבקשה.

Do you have any I.D.? (man) ha'im yeſ leχa te'uda mezaha?
האם יש לך תעודה מזהה?

Do you have any I.D.? (woman) ha'im yeſ laχ te'uda mezaha?
האם יש לך תעודה מזהה?

Thanks. You can leave now. (man) toda. ata yaχol la'leχet aχſav.
תודה. אתה יכול ללכת עכשיו.

Thanks. You can leave now. (woman) toda. at yeχola la'leχet aχſav.
תודה. את יכולה ללכת עכשיו.

Hands behind your head! ya'dayim aχarei haroſ!
ידיים אחרי הראש!

You're under arrest! (man) ata atsur!
אתה עצור!

You're under arrest! (woman) at atsura!
את עצורה!

Health problems

Please help me. (– man)	azor li bevakaʃa. עזור לי בבקשה.
Please help me. (– woman)	izri li bevakaʃa. עזרי לי בבקשה.
I don't feel well. (man –)	ani lo margiʃ tov. אני לא מרגיש טוב.
I don't feel well. (woman –)	ani lo margiʃa tov. אני לא מרגישה טוב.
My husband doesn't feel well.	ba'ali lo margiʃ tov. בעלי לא מרגיש טוב.
My son …	haben ʃeli … הבן שלי ...
My father …	avi … אבי ...
My wife doesn't feel well.	iʃti lo margiʃa tov. אשתי לא מרגישה טוב.
My daughter …	habat ʃeli … הבת שלי ...
My mother …	immi … אמי ...
I've got a …	yeʃ li … יש לי ...
headache	ke'ev roʃ כאב ראש
sore throat	ke'ev garon כאב גרון
stomach ache	ke'ev 'beten כאב בטן
toothache	ke'ev ʃi'nayim כאב שיניים
I feel dizzy.	yeʃ li sχar'χoret. יש לי סחרחורת.
He has a fever.	yeʃ lo χom. יש לו חום.
She has a fever.	yeʃ la χom. יש לה חום.
I can't breathe. (man –)	ani lo yaχol linʃom. אני לא יכול לנשום.
I can't breathe. (woman –)	ani lo yeχola linʃom. אני לא יכולה לנשום.

I'm short of breath.

yeʃ li 'kotser neʃima.
יש לי קוצר נשימה.

I am asthmatic. (man)

ani ast'mati.
אני אסתמתי.

I am asthmatic. (woman)

ani ast'matit.
אני אסתמתית.

I am diabetic.

yeʃ li su'keret.
יש לי סוכרת.

I can't sleep. (man)

ani lo yaxol liʃon.
אני לא יכול לישון.

I can't sleep. (woman)

ani lo yexola liʃon.
אני לא יכולה לישון.

food poisoning

har'alat mazon
הרעלת מזון

It hurts here.

ko'ev li kan.
כואב לי כאן.

Help me!

izru li!
עזרו לי!

I am here!

ani po!
אני פה!

We are here!

a'naxnu kan!
אנחנו כאן!

Get me out of here!

hots'i'u oti mikan!
הוציאו אותי מכאן!

I need a doctor. (man)

ani tsarix rofe.
אני צריך רופא.

I need a doctor. (woman)

ani tsrixa rofe.
אני צריכה רופא.

I can't move. (man)

ani lo yaxol lazuz.
אני לא יכול לזוז.

I can't move. (woman)

ani lo yexola lazuz.
אני לא יכולה לזוז.

I can't move my legs. (man)

ani lo yaxol lehaziz et harag'layim.
אני לא יכול להזיז את הרגליים.

I can't move my legs. (woman)

ani lo yexola lehaziz et harag'layim.
אני לא יכולה להזיז את הרגליים.

I have a wound.

yeʃ li 'petsa.
יש לי פצע.

Is it serious?

ha'im ze retsini?
האם זה רציני?

My documents are in my pocket.

hate'udot ʃeli bakis.
התעודות שלי בכיס.

Calm down! (man)

heraga!
הירגע!

Calm down! (woman)

herag'i!
הירגעי!

May I use your phone? (man man)

ha'im ani yaxol lehiʃtameʃ
ba'telefon ʃelxa?
האם אני יכול להשתמש
בטלפון שלך?

May I use your phone? (man → woman)	ha'im ani yaχol lehiſtameſ ba'telefon ſelaχ?
	?האם אני יכול להשתמש בטלפון שלך
May I use your phone? (woman → woman)	ha'im ani yeχola lehiſtameſ ba'telefon ſelaχ?
	?האם אני יכולה להשתמש בטלפון שלך
May I use your phone? (woman → man)	ha'im ani yeχola lehiſtameſ ba'telefon ſelχa?
	?האם אני יכולה להשתמש בטלפון שלך

Call an ambulance!	haz'minu 'ambulans!
	!הזמינו אמבולנס
It's urgent!	ze daχuf!
	!זה דחוף
It's an emergency!	ze matsav χerum!
	!זה מצב חירום
Please hurry up!	ana maharu!
	!אנא מהרו
Would you please call a doctor? (→ man)	ha'im ata yaχol lehazmin rofe, bevakaſa?
	?האם אתה יכול להזמין רופא בבקשה
Would you please call a doctor? (→ woman)	ha'im at yeχola lehazmin rofe, bevakaſa?
	?האם את יכולה להזמין רופא בבקשה
Where is the hospital?	eifo beit haχolim?
	?איפה בית החולים

How are you feeling? (→ man)	eiχ ata margiſ?
	?איך אתה מרגיש
How are you feeling? (→ woman)	eiχ at margiſa?
	?איך את מרגישה
Are you all right? (→ man)	ha'im ata be'seder?
	?האם אתה בסדר
Are you all right? (→ woman)	ha'im at be'seder?
	?האם את בסדר
What's happened?	ma kara?
	?מה קרה
I feel better now. (man →)	ani margiſ yoter tov aχſav.
	.אני מרגיש טוב יותר עכשיו
I feel better now. (woman →)	ani margiſa yoter tov aχſav.
	.אני מרגישה טוב יותר עכשיו
It's OK.	ze be'seder.
	.זה בסדר
It's all right.	ze be'seder.
	.זה בסדר

At the pharmacy

pharmacy (drugstore)	beit mer'kaxat
	בית מרקחת
24-hour pharmacy	beit mer'kaxat pa'tuax esrim ve'arba ʃa'ot biymama
	בית מרקחת פתוח עשרים וארבע שעות ביממה
Where is the closest pharmacy?	eifo beit hamer'kaxat hakarov beyoter?
	איפה בית המרקחת הקרוב ביותר?
Is it open now?	ha'im ze pa'tuax axʃav?
	האם זה פתוח עכשיו?
At what time does it open?	be''eizo ʃa'a ze niftax?
	באיזו שעה זה נפתח?
At what time does it close?	be''eizo ʃa'a ze nisgar?
	באיזו שעה זה נסגר?
Is it far?	ha'im ze raxok?
	האם זה רחוק?
Can I get there on foot? (man ⌐)	ha'im ani yaxol la'lexet leʃam ba'regel?
	האם אני יכול ללכת לשם ברגל?
Can I get there on foot? (woman ⌐)	ha'im ani yexola la'lexet leʃam ba'regel?
	האם אני יכולה ללכת לשם ברגל?
Can you show me on the map? (⌐ man)	ha'im ata yaxol lehar'ot li al hamapa?
	האם אתה יכול להראות לי על המפה?
Can you show me on the map? (⌐ woman)	ha'im at yexola lehar'ot li al hamapa?
	האם את יכולה להראות לי על המפה?
Please give me something for … (⌐ man)	ten li bevakaʃa 'maʃehu 'neged …
	תן לי בבקשה משהו נגד ...
Please give me something for … (⌐ woman)	tni li bevakaʃa 'maʃehu 'neged …
	תני לי בבקשה משהו נגד ...
a headache	ke'ev roʃ
	כאב ראש
a cough	ʃi'ul
	שיעול
a cold	hitkarerut
	התקררות
the flu	ʃa'pa'at
	שפעת
a fever	xom
	חום
a stomach ache	ke'ev 'beten
	כאב בטן

nausea	bχila	בחילה
diarrhea	ʃilʃul	שלשול
constipation	atsirut	עצירות

pain in the back	ke'ev bagav	כאב בגב
chest pain	ke'ev baχaze	כאב בחזה
side stitch	dkirot batsad	דקירות בצד
abdominal pain	ke'ev ba'beten	כאב בבטן

pill	glula	גלולה
ointment, cream	miʃχa, krem	משחה, קרם
syrup	sirop	סירופ
spray	tarsis	תרסיס
drops	tipot	טיפות

You need to go to the hospital. (← man)	ata tsariχ la'leχet leveit χolim.	אתה צריך ללכת לבית חולים.
You need to go to the hospital. (← woman)	at tsriχa la'leχet leveit χolim.	את צריכה ללכת לבית חולים.
health insurance	bi'tuaχ bri'ut	ביטוח בריאות
prescription	mirʃam	מרשם
insect repellant	doχe χarakim	דוחה חרקים
Band Aid	plaster	פלסטר

The bare minimum

Excuse me, ... (man)	slaχ li, ... סלח לי, ...
Excuse me, ... (woman)	silχi li, ... סלחי לי, ...
Hello.	ʃalom. שלום.
Thank you.	toda. תודה.
Good bye.	lehitra'ot. להתראות.
Yes.	ken. כן.
No.	lo. לא.
I don't know. (man)	ani lo yo'de'a. אני לא יודע.
I don't know. (woman)	ani lo yo'da'at. אני לא יודעת.
Where? | Where to? | When?	eifo? | le'an? | matai? איפה? | לאן? | מתי?
I need ... (man)	ani tsariχ ... אני צריך ...
I need ... (woman)	ani tsriχa ... אני צריכה ...
I want ... (man)	ani rotse ... אני רוצה ...
I want ... (woman)	ani rotsa ... אני רוצה ...
Do you have ...? (man)	ha'im yeʃ leχa ...? האם יש לך ...?
Do you have ...? (woman)	ha'im yeʃ laχ ...? האם יש לך ...?
Is there a ... here?	ha'im yeʃ po ...? האם יש פה ...?
May I ...? (man)	ha'im ani yaχol ...? האם אני יכול ...?
May I ...? (woman)	ha'im ani yeχola ...? האם אני יכולה ...?
..., please (polite request)	..., bevakaʃa ..., בבקשה

I'm looking for … (man ⬄)	ani meχapes … אני מחפש ...
I'm looking for … (woman ⬄)	ani meχa'peset … אני מחפשת ...
the restroom	ʃerutim שירותים
an ATM	kaspomat כספומט
a pharmacy (drugstore)	beit mer'kaχat בית מרקחת
a hospital	beit χolim בית חולים
the police station	taχanat miʃtara תחנת משטרה
the subway	ra'kevet taχtit רכבת תחתית
a taxi	monit, 'teksi מונית, טקסי
the train station	taχanat ra'kevet תחנת רכבת

My name is …	kor'im li … קוראים לי ...
What's your name? (⬄ man)	eiχ kor'im leχa? איך קוראים לך?
What's your name? (⬄ woman)	eiχ kor'im laχ? איך קוראים לך?
Could you please help me? (⬄ man)	ha'im ata yaχol la'azor li? האם אתה יכול לעזור לי?
Could you please help me? (⬄ woman)	ha'im at yeχola la'azor li? האם את יכולה לעזור לי?
I've got a problem.	yeʃ li be'aya. יש לי בעייה.
I don't feel well. (man ⬄)	ani lo margiʃ tov. אני לא מרגיש טוב.
I don't feel well. (woman ⬄)	ani lo margiʃa tov. אני לא מרגישה טוב.
Call an ambulance! (⬄ man)	hazmen 'ambulans! הזמן אמבולנס!
Call an ambulance! (⬄ woman)	haz'mini 'ambulans! הזמיני אמבולנס!
May I make a call? (man ⬄)	ha'im ani yaχol lehitkaʃer? האם אני יכול להתקשר?
May I make a call? (woman)	ha'im ani yeχola lehitkaʃer? האם אני יכולה להתקשר?

I'm sorry. (man ⬄)	ani mitsta'er. אני מצטער.
I'm sorry. (woman ⬄)	ani mitsta''eret. אני מצטערת.
You're welcome.	ein be'ad ma, bevakaʃa. אין בעד מה, בבקשה.

I, me	ani
	אני
you (inform.) (masc.)	ata
	אתה
you (inform.) (fem.)	at
	את
he	hu
	הוא
she	hi
	היא
they (masc.)	hem
	הם
they (fem.)	hen
	הן
we	a'naχnu
	אנחנו
you (pl) (masc.)	atem
	אתם
you (pl) (fem.)	aten
	אתן
you (sg, form.) (masc.)	ata
	אתה
you (sg, form.) (fem.)	at
	את

ENTRANCE	knisa
	כניסה
EXIT	yetsi'a
	יציאה
OUT OF ORDER	lo po'el
	לא פועל
CLOSED	sagur
	סגור
OPEN	pa'tuaχ
	פתוח
FOR WOMEN	lenaʃim
	לנשים
FOR MEN	ligvarim
	לגברים

TOPICAL VOCABULARY

This section contains more than 3,000 of the most important words.
The dictionary will provide invaluable assistance while traveling abroad, because frequently individual words are enough for you to be understood.
The dictionary includes a convenient transcription of each foreign word

T&P Books Publishing

VOCABULARY
CONTENTS

T&P Books Publishing

BASIC CONCEPTS

T&P Books Publishing

BASIC CONCEPTS

T&P Books Publishing

1. Pronouns

I, me	ani	אֲנִי (נ, ז)
you (masc.)	ata	אַתָּה (ז)
you (fem.)	at	אַתְּ (נ)
he	hu	הוּא (ז)
she	hi	הִיא (נ)
we	a'naχnu	אֲנַחְנוּ (נ, ז)
you (masc.)	atem	אַתֶּם (ז-ר)
you (fem.)	aten	אַתֶּן (נ-ר)
you (polite, sing.)	ata, at	אַתָּה (ז), אַתְּ (נ)
you (polite, pl)	atem, aten	אַתֶּם (ז-ר), אַתֶּן (נ-ר)
they (masc.)	hem	הֵם (ז-ר)
they (fem.)	hen	הֵן (נ-ר)

2. Greetings. Salutations

Hello! (fam.)	ʃalom!	שָׁלוֹם!
Hello! (form.)	ʃalom!	שָׁלוֹם!
Good morning!	'boker tov!	בּוֹקֶר טוֹב!
Good afternoon!	tsaha'rayim tovim!	צָהֳרַיִם טוֹבִים!
Good evening!	'erev tov!	עֶרֶב טוֹב!
to say hello	lomar ʃalom	לוֹמַר שָׁלוֹם
Hi! (hello)	hai!	הַיי!
greeting (n)	ahlan	אַהְלָן
to greet (vt)	lomar ʃalom	לוֹמַר שָׁלוֹם
How are you? (form.)	ma ʃlomeχ?, ma ʃlomχa?	מַה שְׁלוֹמֵךְ? (נ), מַה שְׁלוֹמְךָ? (ז)
How are you? (fam.)	ma niʃma?	מַה נִשְׁמַע?
What's new?	ma χadaʃ?	מַה חָדָשׁ?
Bye-Bye! Goodbye!	lehitra'ot!	לְהִתְרָאוֹת!
Bye!	bai!	בַּיי!
See you soon!	lehitra'ot bekarov!	לְהִתְרָאוֹת בְּקָרוֹב!
Farewell!	heye ʃalom!	הֱיֵה שָׁלוֹם!
Farewell! (form.)	lehitra'ot!	לְהִתְרָאוֹת!
to say goodbye	lomar lehitra'ot	לוֹמַר לְהִתְרָאוֹת
So long!	bai!	בַּיי!
Thank you!	toda!	תּוֹדָה!
Thank you very much!	toda raba!	תּוֹדָה רַבָּה!
You're welcome	bevakaʃa	בְּבַקָּשָׁה

Don't mention it!	al lo davar	עַל לֹא דָּבָר
It was nothing	ein be'ad ma	אֵין בְּעַד מָה
Excuse me!	sliχa!	סְלִיחָה!
to excuse (forgive)	lis'loaχ	לִסְלוֹחַ
to apologize (vi)	lehitnatsel	לְהִתְנַצֵּל
My apologies	ani mitnatsel,	אֲנִי מִתְנַצֵּל (ז),
	ani mitna'tselet	אֲנִי מִתְנַצֶּלֶת (נ)
I'm sorry!	ani mitsta'er,	אֲנִי מִצְטַעֵר (ז),
	ani mitsta''eret	אֲנִי מִצְטַעֶרֶת (נ)
to forgive (vt)	lis'loaχ	לִסְלוֹחַ
It's okay! (that's all right)	lo nora	לֹא נוֹרָא
please (adv)	bevakaʃa	בְּבַקָּשָׁה
Don't forget!	al tiʃkaχ!	אַל תִּשְׁכַּח! (ז)
Certainly!	'betaχ!	בֶּטַח!
Of course not!	'betaχ ʃelo!	בֶּטַח שֶׁלֹּא!
Okay! (I agree)	okei!	אוֹקֵיי!
That's enough!	maspik!	מַסְפִּיק!

3. Questions

Who?	mi?	מִי?
What?	ma?	מָה?
Where? (at, in)	'eifo?	אֵיפֹה?
Where (to)?	le'an?	לְאָן?
From where?	me''eifo?	מֵאֵיפֹה?
When?	matai?	מָתַי?
Why? (What for?)	'lama?	לָמָּה?
Why? (~ are you crying?)	ma'du'a?	מַדּוּעַ?
What for?	biʃvil ma?	בִּשְׁבִיל מָה?
How? (in what way)	eiχ, keitsad?	כֵּיצַד? אֵיךְ?
What? (What kind of ...?)	'eize?	אֵיזֶה?
Which?	'eize?	אֵיזֶה?
To whom?	lemi?	לְמִי?
About whom?	al mi?	עַל מִי?
About what?	al ma?	עַל מָה?
With whom?	im mi?	עִם מִי?
How many? How much?	'kama?	כַּמָּה?
Whose?	ʃel mi?	שֶׁל מִי?

4. Prepositions

with (accompanied by)	im	עִם
without	bli, lelo	בְּלִי, לְלֹא

to (indicating direction)	le…	...ְל
about (talking ~ …)	al	עַל
before (in time)	lifnei	לִפְנֵי
in front of …	lifnei	לִפְנֵי
under (beneath, below)	mi'taxat le…	...ְל מִתַּחַת
above (over)	me'al	מֵעַל
on (atop)	al	עַל
from (off, out of)	mi, me	מ, מֶ
of (made from)	mi, me	מ, מֶ
in (e.g., ~ ten minutes)	tox	תּוֹך
over (across the top of)	'derex	דֶּרֶך

5. Function words. Adverbs. Part 1

Where? (at, in)	'eifo?	אֵיפֹה?
here (adv)	po, kan	פֹּה, כָּאן
there (adv)	ʃam	שָׁם
somewhere (to be)	'eifo ʃehu	אֵיפֹה שֶׁהוּא
nowhere (not anywhere)	beʃum makom	בְּשׁוּם מָקוֹם
by (near, beside)	leyad …	...ְ לְיַד
by the window	leyad haxalon	לְיַד הַחַלוֹן
Where (to)?	le'an?	לְאָן?
here (e.g., come ~!)	'hena, lekan	הֵנָּה; לְכָאן
there (e.g., to go ~)	leʃam	לְשָׁם
from here (adv)	mikan	מִכָּאן
from there (adv)	miʃam	מִשָּׁם
close (adv)	karov	קָרוֹב
far (adv)	raxok	רָחוֹק
near (e.g., ~ Paris)	leyad	לְיַד
nearby (adv)	karov	קָרוֹב
not far (adv)	lo raxok	לֹא רָחוֹק
left (adj)	smali	שְׂמָאלִי
on the left	mismol	מִשְׂמֹאל
to the left	'smola	שְׂמֹאלָה
right (adj)	yemani	יְמָנִי
on the right	miyamin	מִיָמִין
to the right	ya'mina	יָמִינָה
in front (adv)	mika'dima	מִקְּדִימָה
front (as adj)	kidmi	קַדְמִי
ahead (the kids ran ~)	ka'dima	קָדִימָה

behind (adv)	me'aχor	מֵאָחוֹר
from behind	me'aχor	מֵאָחוֹר
back (towards the rear)	a'χora	אָחוֹרָה
middle	'emtsa	אֶמְצַע (ז)
in the middle	ba''emtsa	בָּאֶמְצַע
at the side	mehatsad	מֵהַצַּד
everywhere (adv)	beχol makom	בְּכָל מָקוֹם
around (in all directions)	misaviv	מִסָּבִיב
from inside	mibifnim	מִבִּפְנִים
somewhere (to go)	le'an ʃehu	לְאָן שֶׁהוּא
straight (directly)	yaʃar	יָשָׁר
back (e.g., come ~)	baχazara	בַּחֲזָרָה
from anywhere	me'ei ʃam	מֵאֵי שָׁם
from somewhere	me'ei ʃam	מֵאֵי שָׁם
firstly (adv)	reʃit	רֵאשִׁית
secondly (adv)	ʃenit	שֵׁנִית
thirdly (adv)	ʃliʃit	שְׁלִישִׁית
suddenly (adv)	pit'om	פִּתְאוֹם
at first (in the beginning)	behatslaχa	בַּהַתְחָלָה
for the first time	lariʃona	לָרִאשׁוֹנָה
long before …	zman rav lifnei …	זְמַן רַב לִפְנֵי …
anew (over again)	meχadaʃ	מֵחָדָשׁ
for good (adv)	letamid	לְתָמִיד
never (adv)	af 'pa'am, me'olam	מֵעוֹלָם, אַף פַּעַם
again (adv)	ʃuv	שׁוּב
now (adv)	aχʃav, ka'et	עַכְשָׁיו, כָּעֵת
often (adv)	le'itim krovot	לְעִיתִים קְרוֹבוֹת
then (adv)	az	אָז
urgently (quickly)	bidχifut	בִּדְחִיפוּת
usually (adv)	be'dereχ klal	בְּדֶרֶךְ כְּלָל
by the way, …	'dereχ 'agav	דֶּרֶךְ אַגַּב
possible (that is ~)	efʃari	אֶפְשָׁרִי
probably (adv)	kanir'e	כַּנִּרְאֶה
maybe (adv)	ulai	אוּלַי
besides …	χuts mize …	חוּץ מִזֶּה …
that's why …	laχen	לָכֵן
in spite of …	lamrot …	לַמְרוֹת …
thanks to …	hodot le…	הוֹדוֹת לְ…
what (pron.)	ma	מַה
that (conj.)	ʃe	שֶׁ
something	'maʃehu	מַשֶּׁהוּ
anything (something)	'maʃehu	מַשֶּׁהוּ
nothing	klum	כְּלוּם

who (pron.)	mi	מִי
someone	'miʃehu, 'miʃehi	מִישֶׁהוּ (ז), מִישֶׁהִי (נ)
somebody	'miʃehu, 'miʃehi	מִישֶׁהוּ (ז), מִישֶׁהִי (נ)
nobody	af eχad, af aχat	אַף אֶחָד (ז), אַף אַחַת (נ)
nowhere (a voyage to ~)	leʃum makom	לְשׁוּם מָקוֹם
nobody's	lo ʃayaχ le'af eχad	לֹא שַׁיָּךְ לְאַף אֶחָד
somebody's	ʃel 'miʃehu	שֶׁל מִישֶׁהוּ
so (I'm ~ glad)	kol kaχ	כָּל־כָּךְ
also (as well)	gam	גַּם
too (as well)	gam	גַּם

6. Function words. Adverbs. Part 2

Why?	ma'du'a?	מַדּוּעַ?
for some reason	miʃum ma	מִשּׁוּם־מָה
because …	miʃum ʃe	מִשּׁוּם שֶׁ
for some purpose	lematara 'kolʃehi	לְמַטָּרָה כָּלְשֶׁהִי
and	ve …	וְ ...
or	o	אוֹ
but	aval, ulam	אֲבָל, אוּלָם
for (e.g., ~ me)	biʃvil	בִּשְׁבִיל
too (~ many people)	yoter midai	יוֹתֵר מִדַּי
only (exclusively)	rak	רַק
exactly (adv)	bediyuk	בְּדִיּוּק
about (more or less)	be''ereχ	בְּעֵרֶךְ
approximately (adv)	be''ereχ	בְּעֵרֶךְ
approximate (adj)	meʃo'ar	מְשׁוֹעָר
almost (adv)	kim'at	כִּמְעַט
the rest	ʃe'ar	שְׁאָר (ז)
the other (second)	aχer	אַחֵר
other (different)	aχer	אַחֵר
each (adj)	kol	כֹּל
any (no matter which)	kolʃehu	כָּלְשֶׁהוּ
many, much (a lot of)	harbe	הַרְבֵּה
many people	harbe	הַרְבֵּה
all (everyone)	kulam	כּוּלָם
in return for …	tmurat …	תְּמוּרַת ...
in exchange (adv)	bitmura	בִּתְמוּרָה
by hand (made)	bayad	בַּיָּד
hardly (negative opinion)	safek im	סָפֵק אִם
probably (adv)	karov levadai	קָרוֹב לְוַודַאי
on purpose (intentionally)	'davka	דַּוְוקָא

by accident (adv)	bemikre	בְּמִקְרֶה
very (adv)	me'od	מְאוֹד
for example (adv)	lemaʃal	לְמָשָׁל
between	bein	בֵּין
among	be'kerev	בְּקֶרֶב
so much (such a lot)	kol kaχ harbe	כָּל־כָּךְ הַרבֵּה
especially (adv)	bimyuχad	בִּמיוּחָד

NUMBERS.
MISCELLANEOUS

T&P Books Publishing

0 zero	'efes	אֶפֶס (ז)
1 one	eχad	אֶחָד (ז)
1 one (fem.)	aχat	אַחַת (נ)
2 two	'ʃtayim	שְׁתַּיִם (נ)
3 three	ʃaloʃ	שָׁלוֹשׁ (נ)
4 four	arba	אַרְבַּע (נ)
5 five	χameʃ	חָמֵשׁ (נ)
6 six	ʃeʃ	שֵׁשׁ (נ)
7 seven	'ʃeva	שֶׁבַע (נ)
8 eight	'ʃmone	שְׁמוֹנֶה (נ)
9 nine	'teʃa	תֵּשַׁע (נ)
10 ten	'eser	עֶשֶׂר (נ)
11 eleven	aχat esre	אַחַת־עֶשְׂרֵה (נ)
12 twelve	ʃteim esre	שְׁתֵּים־עֶשְׂרֵה (נ)
13 thirteen	ʃloʃ esre	שְׁלוֹשׁ־עֶשְׂרֵה (נ)
14 fourteen	arba esre	אַרְבַּע־עֶשְׂרֵה (נ)
15 fifteen	χameʃ esre	חֲמֵשׁ־עֶשְׂרֵה (נ)
16 sixteen	ʃeʃ esre	שֵׁשׁ־עֶשְׂרֵה (נ)
17 seventeen	ʃva esre	שְׁבַע־עֶשְׂרֵה (נ)
18 eighteen	ʃmone esre	שְׁמוֹנֶה־עֶשְׂרֵה (נ)
19 nineteen	tʃa esre	תְּשַׁע־עֶשְׂרֵה (נ)
20 twenty	esrim	עֶשְׂרִים
21 twenty-one	esrim ve'eχad	עֶשְׂרִים וְאֶחָד
22 twenty-two	esrim u'ʃnayim	עֶשְׂרִים וּשְׁנַיִים
23 twenty-three	esrim uʃloʃa	עֶשְׂרִים וּשְׁלוֹשָׁה
30 thirty	ʃloʃim	שְׁלוֹשִׁים
31 thirty-one	ʃloʃim ve'eχad	שְׁלוֹשִׁים וְאֶחָד
32 thirty-two	ʃloʃim u'ʃnayim	שְׁלוֹשִׁים וּשְׁנַיִים
33 thirty-three	ʃloʃim uʃloʃa	שְׁלוֹשִׁים וּשְׁלוֹשָׁה
40 forty	arba'im	אַרְבָּעִים
41 forty-one	arba'im ve'eχad	אַרְבָּעִים וְאֶחָד
42 forty-two	arba'im u'ʃnayim	אַרְבָּעִים וּשְׁנַיִים
43 forty-three	arba'im uʃloʃa	אַרְבָּעִים וּשְׁלוֹשָׁה
50 fifty	χamiʃim	חֲמִישִׁים
51 fifty-one	χamiʃim ve'eχad	חֲמִישִׁים וְאֶחָד
52 fifty-two	χamiʃim u'ʃnayim	חֲמִישִׁים וּשְׁנַיִים
53 fifty-three	χamiʃim uʃloʃa	חֲמִישִׁים וּשְׁלוֹשָׁה

60 sixty	ʃiʃim	שִׁשִּׁים
61 sixty-one	ʃiʃim ve'exad	שִׁשִּׁים וְאֶחָד
62 sixty-two	ʃiʃim u'ʃnayim	שִׁשִּׁים וּשְׁנַיִם
63 sixty-three	ʃiʃim uʃloʃa	שִׁשִּׁים וּשְׁלוֹשָׁה

70 seventy	ʃiv'im	שִׁבְעִים
71 seventy-one	ʃiv'im ve'exad	שִׁבְעִים וְאֶחָד
72 seventy-two	ʃiv'im u'ʃnayim	שִׁבְעִים וּשְׁנַיִם
73 seventy-three	ʃiv'im uʃloʃa	שִׁבְעִים וּשְׁלוֹשָׁה

80 eighty	ʃmonim	שְׁמוֹנִים
81 eighty-one	ʃmonim ve'exad	שְׁמוֹנִים וְאֶחָד
82 eighty-two	ʃmonim u'ʃnayim	שְׁמוֹנִים וּשְׁנַיִם
83 eighty-three	ʃmonim uʃloʃa	שְׁמוֹנִים וּשְׁלוֹשָׁה

90 ninety	tiʃim	תִּשְׁעִים
91 ninety-one	tiʃim ve'exad	תִּשְׁעִים וְאֶחָד
92 ninety-two	tiʃim u'ʃayim	תִּשְׁעִים וּשְׁנַיִם
93 ninety-three	tiʃim uʃloʃa	תִּשְׁעִים וּשְׁלוֹשָׁה

8. Cardinal numbers. Part 2

100 one hundred	'me'a	מֵאָה (נ)
200 two hundred	ma'tayim	מָאתַיִם
300 three hundred	ʃloʃ me'ot	שְׁלוֹשׁ מֵאוֹת (נ)
400 four hundred	arba me'ot	אַרְבַּע מֵאוֹת (נ)
500 five hundred	xameʃ me'ot	חֲמֵשׁ מֵאוֹת (נ)

600 six hundred	ʃeʃ me'ot	שֵׁשׁ מֵאוֹת (נ)
700 seven hundred	ʃva me'ot	שְׁבַע מֵאוֹת (נ)
800 eight hundred	ʃmone me'ot	שְׁמוֹנֶה מֵאוֹת (נ)
900 nine hundred	tʃa me'ot	תְּשַׁע מֵאוֹת (נ)

1000 one thousand	'elef	אֶלֶף (ז)
2000 two thousand	al'payim	אַלְפַּיִם (ז)
3000 three thousand	'ʃloʃet alafim	שְׁלוֹשֶׁת אֲלָפִים (ז)
10000 ten thousand	a'seret alafim	עֲשֶׂרֶת אֲלָפִים (ז)
one hundred thousand	'me'a 'elef	מֵאָה אֶלֶף (ז)
million	milyon	מִילְיוֹן (ז)
billion	milyard	מִילְיַארְד (ז)

9. Ordinal numbers

first (adj)	riʃon	רִאשׁוֹן
second (adj)	ʃeni	שֵׁנִי
third (adj)	ʃliʃi	שְׁלִישִׁי
fourth (adj)	revi'i	רְבִיעִי
fifth (adj)	xamiʃi	חֲמִישִׁי

sixth (adj)	ʃiʃi	שִׁישִׁי
seventh (adj)	ʃvi'i	שְׁבִיעִי
eighth (adj)	ʃmini	שְׁמִינִי
ninth (adj)	tʃi'i	תְּשִׁיעִי
tenth (adj)	asiri	עֲשִׁירִי

COLOURS. UNITS OF MEASUREMENT

T&P Books Publishing

10. Colors

color	'tseva	צֶבַע (ז)
shade (tint)	gavan	גָּוֶון (ז)
hue	gavan	גָּוֶון (ז)
rainbow	'keʃet	קֶשֶׁת (נ)
white (adj)	lavan	לָבָן
black (adj)	ʃaχor	שָׁחוֹר
gray (adj)	afor	אָפוֹר
green (adj)	yarok	יָרוֹק
yellow (adj)	tsahov	צָהֹב
red (adj)	adom	אָדֹם
blue (adj)	kaχol	כָּחֹל
light blue (adj)	taχol	תְּכֹל
pink (adj)	varod	וָרוֹד
orange (adj)	katom	כָּתֹם
violet (adj)	segol	סָגֹל
brown (adj)	χum	חוּם
golden (adj)	zahov	זָהֹב
silvery (adj)	kasuf	כָּסוּף
beige (adj)	beʒ	בֶּז'
cream (adj)	be'tseva krem	בְּצֶבַע קְרֶם
turquoise (adj)	turkiz	טוּרְקִיז
cherry red (adj)	bordo	בּוֹרְדוֹ
lilac (adj)	segol	סָגֹל
crimson (adj)	patol	פָּטֹל
light (adj)	bahir	בָּהִיר
dark (adj)	kehe	כֵּהֶה
bright, vivid (adj)	bohek	בּוֹהֵק
colored (pencils)	tsiv'oni	צִבְעוֹנִי
color (e.g., ~ film)	tsiv'oni	צִבְעוֹנִי
black-and-white (adj)	ʃaχor lavan	שָׁחוֹר-לָבָן
plain (one-colored)	χad tsiv'i	חַד-צִבְעִי
multicolored (adj)	sasgoni	סַסְגוֹנִי

11. Units of measurement

weight	miʃkal	מִשְׁקָל (ז)
length	'oreχ	אֹרֶךְ (ז)

width	'roχav	רוֹחַב (ז)
height	'gova	גּוֹבַה (ז)
depth	'omek	עוֹמֶק (ז)
volume	'nefaχ	נֶפַח (ז)
area	'ʃetaχ	שֶׁטַח (ז)
gram	gram	גְרַם (ז)
milligram	miligram	מִילִיגְרַם (ז)
kilogram	kilogram	קִילוֹגְרַם (ז)
ton	ton	טוֹן (ז)
pound	'pa'und	פָּאונד (ז)
ounce	'unkiya	אונקְיָה (נ)
meter	'meter	מֶטֶר (ז)
millimeter	mili'meter	מִילִימֶטֶר (ז)
centimeter	senti'meter	סֶנטִימֶטֶר (ז)
kilometer	kilo'meter	קִילוֹמֶטֶר (ז)
mile	mail	מַייל (ז)
inch	intʃ	אִינצ' (ז)
foot	'regel	רֶגֶל (נ)
yard	yard	יַרד (ז)
square meter	'meter ra'vu'a	מֶטֶר רָבוּע (ז)
hectare	hektar	הֶקטָר (ז)
liter	litr	לִיטר (ז)
degree	ma'ala	מַעֲלָה (נ)
volt	volt	ווֹלט (ז)
ampere	amper	אַמפֶּר (ז)
horsepower	'koaχ sus	כּוֹחַ סוּס (ז)
quantity	kamut	כָּמוּת (נ)
a little bit of …	ktsat …	קְצָת …
half	'χetsi	חֲצִי (ז)
dozen	tresar	תרֵיסָר (ז)
piece (item)	yeχida	יְחִידָה (נ)
size	'godel	גוֹדֶל (ז)
scale (map ~)	kne mida	קנֵה מִידָה (ז)
minimal (adj)	mini'mali	מִינִימָאלִי
the smallest (adj)	hakatan beyoter	הַקָטָן בְּיוֹתֵר
medium (adj)	memutsa	מְמוּצָע
maximal (adj)	maksi'mali	מַקסִימָלִי
the largest (adj)	hagadol beyoter	הַגָדוֹל בְּיוֹתֵר

12. Containers

canning jar (glass ~)	tsin'tsenet	צְנצֶנֶת (נ)
can	paχit	פַּחִית (נ)

bucket	dli	דְּלִי (ז)
barrel	χavit	חָבִית (נ)
wash basin (e.g., plastic ~)	gigit	גִּיגִית (נ)
tank (100L water ~)	meiχal	מֵיכָל (ז)
hip flask	meimiya	מֵימִיָּה (נ)
jerrycan	'dʒerikan	גֶ'רִיקָן (ז)
tank (e.g., tank car)	meχalit	מֵיכָלִית (נ)
mug	'sefel	סֵפֶל (ז)
cup (of coffee, etc.)	'sefel	סֵפֶל (ז)
saucer	taχtit	תַּחְתִּית (נ)
glass (tumbler)	kos	כּוֹס (נ)
wine glass	ga'vi'a	גָּבִיעַ (ז)
stock pot (soup pot)	sir	סִיר (ז)
bottle (~ of wine)	bakbuk	בַּקְבּוּק (ז)
neck (of the bottle, etc.)	tsavar habakbuk	צַוַּאר הַבַּקְבּוּק (ז)
carafe (decanter)	kad	כַּד (ז)
pitcher	kankan	קַנְקַן (ז)
vessel (container)	kli	כְּלִי (ז)
pot (crock, stoneware ~)	sir 'χeres	סִיר חֶרֶס (ז)
vase	agartal	אֲגַרְטָל (ז)
bottle (perfume ~)	tsloχit	צְלוֹחִית (נ)
vial, small bottle	bakbukon	בַּקְבּוּקוֹן (ז)
tube (of toothpaste)	ʃfo'feret	שְׁפוֹפֶרֶת (נ)
sack (bag)	sak	שַׂק (ז)
bag (paper ~, plastic ~)	sakit	שַׂקִּית (נ)
pack (of cigarettes, etc.)	χafisa	חֲפִיסָה (נ)
box (e.g., shoebox)	kufsa	קוּפְסָה (נ)
crate	argaz	אַרְגָּז (ז)
basket	sal	סַל (ז)

MAIN VERBS

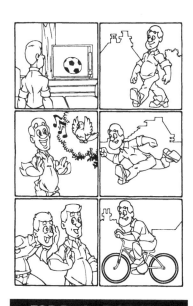

T&P Books Publishing

to advise (vt)	leya'ets	לְיָיעֵץ
to agree (say yes)	lehaskim	לְהַסְכִּים
to answer (vi, vt)	la'anot	לַעֲנוֹת
to apologize (vi)	lehitnatsel	לְהִתְנַצֵּל
to arrive (vi)	leha'gi'a	לְהַגִּיעַ
to ask (~ oneself)	liʃol	לִשְׁאוֹל
to ask (~ sb to do sth)	levakeʃ	לְבַקֵּשׁ
to be (vi)	lihyot	לִהְיוֹת
to be afraid	lefaxed	לְפַחֵד
to be hungry	lihyot ra'ev	לִהְיוֹת רָעֵב
to be interested in …	lehit'anyen be…	לְהִתְעַנְיֵין בְּ…
to be needed	lehidareʃ	לְהִידָרֵשׁ
to be surprised	lehitpale	לְהִתְפַּלֵּא
to be thirsty	lihyot tsame	לִהְיוֹת צָמֵא
to begin (vt)	lehatxil	לְהַתְחִיל
to belong to …	lehiʃtayex	לְהִשְׁתַּיֵּיךְ
to boast (vi)	lehitravrev	לְהִתְרַבְרֵב
to break (split into pieces)	liʃbor	לִשְׁבּוֹר
to call (~ for help)	likro	לִקְרוֹא
can (v aux)	yaxol	יָכוֹל
to catch (vt)	litfos	לִתְפּוֹס
to change (vt)	leʃanot	לְשַׁנּוֹת
to choose (select)	livxor	לִבְחוֹר
to come down (the stairs)	la'redet	לָרֶדֶת
to compare (vt)	lehaʃvot	לְהַשְׁווֹת
to complain (vi, vt)	lehitlonen	לְהִתְלוֹנֵן
to confuse (mix up)	lehitbalbel	לְהִתְבַּלְבֵּל
to continue (vt)	lehamʃix	לְהַמְשִׁיךְ
to control (vt)	liʃlot	לִשְׁלוֹט
to cook (dinner)	levaʃel	לְבַשֵּׁל
to cost (vt)	la'alot	לַעֲלוֹת
to count (add up)	lispor	לִסְפּוֹר
to count on …	lismox al	לִסְמוֹךְ עַל
to create (vt)	litsor	לִיצוֹר
to cry (weep)	livkot	לִבְכּוֹת

14. The most important verbs. Part 2

to deceive (vi, vt)	leramot	לְרַמוֹת
to decorate (tree, street)	lekaʃet	לְקַשֵׁט
to defend (a country, etc.)	lehagen	לְהָגֵן
to demand (request firmly)	lidroʃ	לִדרוֹשׁ
to dig (vt)	laxpor	לַחפוֹר
to discuss (vt)	ladun	לָדוּן
to do (vt)	la'asot	לַעֲשׂוֹת
to doubt (have doubts)	lefakpek	לְפַקפֵּק
to drop (let fall)	lehapil	לְהַפִּיל
to enter	lehikanes	לְהִיכָּנֵס
(room, house, etc.)		
to excuse (forgive)	lis'loax	לִסלוֹחַ
to exist (vi)	lehitkayem	לְהִתקַייֵם
to expect (foresee)	laxazot	לַחֲזוֹת
to explain (vt)	lehasbir	לְהַסבִּיר
to fall (vi)	lipol	לִיפּוֹל
to find (vt)	limtso	לִמצוֹא
to finish (vt)	lesayem	לְסַייֵם
to fly (vi)	la'uf	לָעוּף
to follow ... (come after)	la'akov axarei	לַעֲקוֹב אַחֲרֵי
to forget (vi, vt)	liʃ'koax	לִשכּוֹחַ
to forgive (vt)	lis'loax	לִסלוֹחַ
to give (vt)	latet	לָתֵת
to give a hint	lirmoz	לִרמוֹז
to go (on foot)	la'lexet	לָלֶכֶת
to go for a swim	lehitraxets	לְהִתרַחֵץ
to go out (for dinner, etc.)	latset	לָצֵאת
to guess (the answer)	lenaxeʃ	לְנַחֵשׁ
to have (vt)	lehaxzik	לְהַחזִיק
to have breakfast	le'exol aruxat 'boker	לֶאֱכוֹל אֲרוּחַת בּוֹקֶר
to have dinner	le'exol aruxat 'erev	לֶאֱכוֹל אֲרוּחַת עֶרֶב
to have lunch	le'exol aruxat tsaha'rayim	לֶאֱכוֹל אֲרוּחַת צָהֳרַיים
to hear (vt)	liʃ'mo'a	לִשמוֹעַ
to help (vt)	la'azor	לַעֲזוֹר
to hide (vt)	lehastir	לְהַסתִּיר
to hope (vi, vt)	lekavot	לְקַווֹת
to hunt (vi, vt)	latsud	לָצוּד
to hurry (vi)	lemaher	לְמַהֵר

15. The most important verbs. Part 3

to inform (vt)	leho'dia	לְהוֹדִיעַ
to insist (vi, vt)	lehit'akef	לְהִתְעַקֵּשׁ
to insult (vt)	leha'aliv	לְהַעֲלִיב
to invite (vt)	lehazmin	לְהַזְמִין
to joke (vi)	lehitba'deax	לְהִתְבַּדֵּחַ
to keep (vt)	lifmor	לִשְׁמוֹר
to keep silent	liftok	לִשְׁתוֹק
to kill (vt)	laharog	לַהֲרוֹג
to know (sb)	lehakir et	לְהַכִּיר אֶת
to know (sth)	la'da'at	לָדַעַת
to laugh (vi)	litsxok	לִצְחוֹק
to liberate (city, etc.)	lefaxrer	לְשַׁחְרֵר
to like (I like …)	limtso xen be'ei'nayim	לִמְצוֹא חֵן בְּעֵינַיִים
to look for … (search)	lexapes	לְחַפֵּשׂ
to love (sb)	le'ehov	לֶאֱהוֹב
to make a mistake	lit'ot	לִטְעוֹת
to manage, to run	lenahel	לְנַהֵל
to mean (signify)	lomar	לוֹמַר
to mention (talk about)	lehazkir	לְהַזְכִּיר
to miss (school, etc.)	lehaxsir	לְהַחְסִיר
to notice (see)	lasim lev	לָשִׂים לֵב
to object (vi, vt)	lehitnaged	לְהִתְנַגֵּד
to observe (see)	litspot, lehafkif	לִצְפּוֹת, לְהַשְׁקִיף
to open (vt)	liftoax	לִפְתוֹחַ
to order (meal, etc.)	lehazmin	לְהַזְמִין
to order (mil.)	lifkod	לִפְקוֹד
to own (possess)	lihyot 'ba'al fel	לִהְיוֹת בַּעַל שֶׁל
to participate (vi)	lehiftatef	לְהִשְׁתַתֵּף
to pay (vi, vt)	lefalem	לְשַׁלֵּם
to permit (vt)	leharfot	לְהַרְשׁוֹת
to plan (vt)	letaxnen	לְתַכְנֵן
to play (children)	lesaxek	לְשַׂחֵק
to pray (vi, vt)	lehitpalel	לְהִתְפַּלֵּל
to prefer (vt)	leha'adif	לְהַעֲדִיף
to promise (vt)	lehav'tiax	לְהַבְטִיחַ
to pronounce (vt)	levate	לְבַטֵּא
to propose (vt)	leha'tsi'a	לְהַצִּיעַ
to punish (vt)	leha'anif	לְהַעֲנִישׁ

16. The most important verbs. Part 4

to read (vi, vt)	likro	לִקְרוֹא
to recommend (vt)	lehamlits	לְהַמְלִיץ

to refuse (vi, vt)	lesarev	לְסָרֵב
to regret (be sorry)	lehitsta'er	לְהִצְטַעֵר
to rent (sth from sb)	liskor	לִשְׂכּוֹר

to repeat (say again)	laxazor al	לַחֲזוֹר עַל
to reserve, to book	lehazmin meroʃ	לְהַזְמִין מֵרֹאש
to run (vi)	laruts	לָרוּץ
to save (rescue)	lehatsil	לְהַצִּיל
to say (~ thank you)	lomar	לוֹמַר

to scold (vt)	linzof	לִנְזוֹף
to see (vt)	lir'ot	לִרְאוֹת
to sell (vt)	limkor	לִמְכּוֹר
to send (vt)	liʃ'loax	לִשְׁלוֹחַ
to shoot (vi)	lirot	לִירוֹת

to shout (vi)	lits'ok	לִצְעוֹק
to show (vt)	lehar'ot	לְהַרְאוֹת
to sign (document)	laxtom	לַחְתוֹם
to sit down (vi)	lehityaʃev	לְהִתְיַישֵׁב

to smile (vi)	lexayex	לְחַיֵּךְ
to speak (vi, vt)	ledaber	לְדַבֵּר
to steal (money, etc.)	lignov	לִגְנוֹב
to stop (for pause, etc.)	la'atsor	לַעֲצוֹר
to stop (please ~ calling me)	lehafsik	לְהַפְסִיק

to study (vt)	lilmod	לִלְמוֹד
to swim (vi)	lisxot	לִשְׂחוֹת
to take (vt)	la'kaxat	לָקַחַת
to think (vi, vt)	laxʃov	לַחֲשוֹב
to threaten (vt)	le'ayem	לְאַיֵּם

to touch (with hands)	la'ga'at	לָגַעַת
to translate (vt)	letargem	לְתַרְגֵּם
to trust (vt)	liv'toax	לִבְטוֹחַ
to try (attempt)	lenasot	לְנַסּוֹת
to turn (e.g., ~ left)	lifnot	לִפְנוֹת

to underestimate (vt)	leham'it be''erex	לְהַמְעִיט בְּעֵרֶךְ
to understand (vt)	lehavin	לְהָבִין
to unite (vt)	le'axed	לְאַחֵד
to wait (vt)	lehamtin	לְהַמְתִּין

to want (wish, desire)	lirtsot	לִרְצוֹת
to warn (vt)	lehazhir	לְהַזְהִיר
to work (vi)	la'avod	לַעֲבוֹד
to write (vt)	lixtov	לִכְתוֹב
to write down	lirʃom	לִרְשוֹם

TIME. CALENDAR

T&P Books Publishing

Monday	yom ʃeni	יוֹם שֵׁנִי (ז)
Tuesday	yom ʃliʃi	יוֹם שְׁלִישִׁי (ז)
Wednesday	yom revi'i	יוֹם רְבִיעִי (ז)
Thursday	yom χamiʃi	יוֹם חֲמִישִׁי (ז)
Friday	yom ʃiʃi	יוֹם שִׁישִׁי (ז)
Saturday	ʃabat	שַׁבָּת (נ)
Sunday	yom riʃon	יוֹם רִאשׁוֹן (ז)

today (adv)	hayom	הַיּוֹם
tomorrow (adv)	maχar	מָחָר
the day after tomorrow	maχara'tayim	מָחֳרָתַיִם
yesterday (adv)	etmol	אֶתמוֹל
the day before yesterday	ʃilʃom	שִׁלשׁוֹם

day	yom	יוֹם (ז)
working day	yom avoda	יוֹם עֲבוֹדָה (ז)
public holiday	yom χag	יוֹם חַג (ז)
day off	yom menuχa	יוֹם מְנוּחָה (ז)
weekend	sof ʃa'vu'a	סוֹף שָׁבוּעַ

all day long	kol hayom	כָּל הַיּוֹם
the next day (adv)	lamaχarat	לַמָּחֳרָת
two days ago	lifnei yo'mayim	לִפנֵי יוֹמַיִים
the day before	'erev	עֶרֶב
daily (adj)	yomyomi	יוֹמיוֹמִי
every day (adv)	midei yom	מִדֵי יוֹם

week	ʃa'vua	שָׁבוּעַ (ז)
last week (adv)	baʃa'vu'a ʃe'avar	בַּשָׁבוּעַ שֶׁעָבַר
next week (adv)	baʃa'vu'a haba	בַּשָׁבוּעַ הַבָּא
weekly (adj)	ʃvu'i	שבוּעִי
every week (adv)	kol ʃa'vu'a	כָּל שָׁבוּעַ
twice a week	pa'a'mayim beʃa'vu'a	פַּעֲמַיִים בְּשָׁבוּעַ
every Tuesday	kol yom ʃliʃi	כָּל יוֹם שְׁלִישִׁי

morning	'boker	בּוֹקֶר (ז)
in the morning	ba'boker	בַּבּוֹקֶר
noon, midday	tsaha'rayim	צָהֳרַיִים (ז״ר)
in the afternoon	aχar hatsaha'rayim	אַחַר הַצָּהֳרַיִים
evening	'erev	עֶרֶב (ז)

in the evening	ba''erev	בָּעֶרֶב
night	'laila	לַיְלָה (ז)
at night	ba'laila	בַּלַּיְלָה
midnight	χatsot	חֲצוֹת (נ)
second	ʃniya	שְׁנִיָּה (נ)
minute	daka	דַּקָּה (נ)
hour	ʃa'a	שָׁעָה (נ)
half an hour	χatsi ʃa'a	חֲצִי שָׁעָה (נ)
a quarter-hour	'reva ʃa'a	רֶבַע שָׁעָה (ז)
fifteen minutes	χameʃ esre dakot	חֲמֵשׁ עֶשְׂרֵה דַּקּוֹת
24 hours	yemama	יְמָמָה (נ)
sunrise	zriχa	זְרִיחָה (נ)
dawn	'ʃaχar	שַׁחַר (ז)
early morning	'ʃaχar	שַׁחַר (ז)
sunset	ʃki'a	שְׁקִיעָה (נ)
early in the morning	mukdam ba'boker	מוּקְדָּם בַּבּוֹקֶר
this morning	ha'boker	הַבּוֹקֶר
tomorrow morning	maχar ba'boker	מָחָר בַּבּוֹקֶר
this afternoon	hayom aχarei hatzaha'rayim	הַיּוֹם אַחֲרֵי הַצָּהֳרַיִים
in the afternoon	aχar hatsaha'rayim	אַחַר הַצָּהֳרַיִים
tomorrow afternoon	maχar aχarei hatsaha'rayim	מָחָר אַחֲרֵי הַצָּהֳרַיִים
tonight (this evening)	ha''erev	הָעֶרֶב
tomorrow night	maχar ba''erev	מָחָר בַּעֶרֶב
at 3 o'clock sharp	beʃa'a ʃaloʃ bediyuk	בָּשָׁעָה שָׁלוֹשׁ בְּדִיּוּק
about 4 o'clock	bisvivot arba	בַּסְּבִיבוֹת אַרְבַּע
by 12 o'clock	ad ʃteim esre	עַד שְׁתֵּים-עֶשְׂרֵה
in 20 minutes	be'od esrim dakot	בְּעוֹד עֶשְׂרִים דַּקּוֹת
in an hour	be'od ʃa'a	בְּעוֹד שָׁעָה
on time (adv)	bazman	בַּזְּמַן
a quarter of ...	'reva le...	רֶבַע לְ...
within an hour	toχ ʃa'a	תּוֹךְ שָׁעָה
every 15 minutes	kol 'reva ʃa'a	כָּל רֶבַע שָׁעָה
round the clock	misaviv laʃa'on	מִסָּבִיב לַשָּׁעוֹן

19. Months. Seasons

January	'yanu'ar	יָנוּאָר (ז)
February	'febru'ar	פֶבְּרוּאָר (ז)
March	merts	מֵרְץ (ז)
April	april	אַפְּרִיל (ז)

May	mai	מַאי (ז)
June	'yuni	יוּנִי (ז)
July	'yuli	יוּלִי (ז)
August	'ogust	אוֹגוּסְט (ז)
September	sep'tember	סֶפְּטֶמְבֶּר (ז)
October	ok'tober	אוֹקְטוֹבֶּר (ז)
November	no'vember	נוֹבֶמְבֶּר (ז)
December	de'tsember	דֶצֶמְבֶּר (ז)
spring	aviv	אָבִיב (ז)
in spring	ba'aviv	בָּאָבִיב
spring (as adj)	avivi	אֲבִיבִי
summer	'kayits	קַיִץ (ז)
in summer	ba'kayits	בַּקַיִץ
summer (as adj)	ketsi	קֵיצִי
fall	stav	סְתָיו (ז)
in fall	bestav	בְּסְתָיו
fall (as adj)	stavi	סְתָווִי
winter	'χoref	חוֹרֶף (ז)
in winter	ba'χoref	בַּחוֹרֶף
winter (as adj)	χorpi	חוֹרְפִּי
month	'χodeʃ	חוֹדֶשׁ (ז)
this month	ha'χodeʃ	הַחוֹדֶשׁ
next month	ba'χodeʃ haba	בַּחוֹדֶשׁ הַבָּא
last month	ba'χodeʃ ʃe'avar	בַּחוֹדֶשׁ שֶׁעָבַר
a month ago	lifnei 'χodeʃ	לִפְנֵי חוֹדֶשׁ
in a month (a month later)	be'od 'χodeʃ	בְּעוֹד חוֹדֶשׁ
in 2 months (2 months later)	be'od χod'ʃayim	בְּעוֹד חוֹדְשַׁיִים
the whole month	kol ha'χodeʃ	כָּל הַחוֹדֶשׁ
all month long	kol ha'χodeʃ	כָּל הַחוֹדֶשׁ
monthly (~ magazine)	χodʃi	חוֹדְשִׁי
monthly (adv)	χodʃit	חוֹדְשִׁית
every month	kol 'χodeʃ	כָּל חוֹדֶשׁ
twice a month	pa'a'mayim be'χodeʃ	פַּעֲמַיִים בְּחוֹדֶשׁ
year	ʃana	שָׁנָה (נ)
this year	haʃana	הַשָׁנָה
next year	baʃana haba'a	בְּשָׁנָה הַבָּאָה
last year	baʃana ʃe'avra	בְּשָׁנָה שֶׁעָבְרָה
a year ago	lifnei ʃana	לִפְנֵי שָׁנָה
in a year	be'od ʃana	בְּעוֹד שָׁנָה
in two years	be'od ʃna'tayim	בְּעוֹד שְׁנָתַיִים
the whole year	kol haʃana	כָּל הַשָׁנָה

all year long	kol haʃana	כָּל הַשָּׁנָה
every year	kol ʃana	כָּל שָׁנָה
annual (adj)	ʃnati	שְׁנָתִי
annually (adv)	midei ʃana	מִדֵי שָׁנָה
4 times a year	arba pa'amim be'χodeʃ	אַרבַּע פְּעָמִים בְּחוֹדֶשׁ
date (e.g., today's ~)	ta'ariχ	תַאֲרִיךְ (ז)
date (e.g., ~ of birth)	ta'ariχ	תַאֲרִיךְ (ז)
calendar	'luaχ ʃana	לוּחַ שָׁנָה (ז)
half a year	χatsi ʃana	חֲצִי שָׁנָה (ז)
six months	ʃiʃa χodaʃim, χatsi ʃana	חֲצִי שָׁנָה, שִׁישָׁה חוֹדָשִׁים
season (summer, etc.)	ona	עוֹנָה (נ)
century	'me'a	מֵאָה (נ)

TRAVEL. HOTEL

T&P Books Publishing

20. Trip. Travel

tourism, travel	tayarut	תַּיָּירוּת (נ)
tourist	tayar	תַּיָּיר (ז)
trip, voyage	tiyul	טִיּוּל (ז)
adventure	harpatka	הַרְפַּתְקָה (נ)
trip, journey	nesi'a	נְסִיעָה (נ)
vacation	χuffa	חוּפְשָׁה (נ)
to be on vacation	lihyot beχuffa	לִהְיוֹת בְּחוּפְשָׁה
rest	menuχa	מְנוּחָה (נ)
train	ra'kevet	רַכֶּבֶת (נ)
by train	bera'kevet	בְּרַכֶּבֶת
airplane	matos	מָטוֹס (ז)
by airplane	bematos	בְּמָטוֹס
by car	bemeχonit	בְּמְכוֹנִית
by ship	be'oniya	בָּאוֹנִיָּה
luggage	mit'an	מִטְעָן (ז)
suitcase	mizvada	מִזְוָדָה (נ)
luggage cart	eglat mit'an	עֶגְלַת מִטְעָן (נ)
passport	darkon	דַּרְכּוֹן (ז)
visa	'viza, aſra	וִיזָה, אַשְׁרָה (נ)
ticket	kartis	כַּרְטִיס (ז)
air ticket	kartis tisa	כַּרְטִיס טִיסָה (ז)
guidebook	madriχ	מַדְרִיךְ (ז)
map (tourist ~)	mapa	מַפָּה (נ)
area (rural ~)	ezor	אֵזוֹר (ז)
place, site	makom	מָקוֹם (ז)
exotica (n)	ek'zotika	אֶקְזוֹטִיקָה (נ)
exotic (adj)	ek'zoti	אֶקְזוֹטִי
amazing (adj)	nifla	נִפְלָא
group	kvuſsa	קְבוּצָה (נ)
excursion, sightseeing tour	tiyul	טִיּוּל (ז)
guide (person)	madriχ tiyulim	מַדְרִיךְ טִיּוּלִים (ז)

21. Hotel

hotel	malon	מָלוֹן (ז)
motel	motel	מוֹטֶל (ז)

three-star (~ hotel)	ʃloʃa koxavim	שְׁלוֹשָׁה כּוֹכָבִים
five-star	xamiʃa koxavim	חֲמִישָׁה כּוֹכָבִים
to stay (in a hotel, etc.)	lehit'axsen	לְהִתְאַכְסֵן
room	'xeder	חֶדֶר (ז)
single room	'xeder yaxid	חֶדֶר יָחִיד (ז)
double room	'xeder zugi	חֶדֶר זוּגִי (ז)
to book a room	lehazmin 'xeder	לְהַזְמִין חֶדֶר
half board	xatsi pensiyon	חֲצִי פֶּנְסִיוֹן (ז)
full board	pensyon male	פֶּנְסִיוֹן מָלֵא (ז)
with bath	im am'batya	עִם אַמְבַּטְיָה
with shower	im mik'laxat	עִם מִקְלַחַת
satellite television	tele'vizya bekvalim	טֶלֶוִויזְיָה בְּכְבָלִים (נ)
air-conditioner	mazgan	מַזְגָן (ז)
towel	ma'gevet	מַגֶּבֶת (נ)
key	maf'teax	מַפְתֵּחַ (ז)
administrator	amarkal	אֲמַרְכָּל (ז)
chambermaid	xadranit	חַדְרָנִית (נ)
porter, bellboy	sabal	סַבָּל (ז)
doorman	pakid kabala	פְקִיד קַבָּלָה (ז)
restaurant	mis'ada	מִסְעָדָה (נ)
pub, bar	bar	בָּר (ז)
breakfast	aruxat 'boker	אֲרוּחַת בּוֹקֶר (נ)
dinner	aruxat 'erev	אֲרוּחַת עֶרֶב (נ)
buffet	miznon	מִזְנוֹן (ז)
lobby	'lobi	לוֹבִּי (ז)
elevator	ma'alit	מַעֲלִית (נ)
DO NOT DISTURB	lo lehaf'ri'a	לֹא לְהַפְרִיעַ
NO SMOKING	asur le'aʃen!	אָסוּר לְעַשֵׁן!

22. Sightseeing

monument	an'darta	אַנְדַּרְטָה (נ)
fortress	mivtsar	מִבְצָר (ז)
palace	armon	אַרְמוֹן (ז)
castle	tira	טִירָה (נ)
tower	migdal	מִגְדָּל (ז)
mausoleum	ma'uzo'le'um	מָאוֹזוֹלֵיאוֹם (ז)
architecture	adrixalut	אַדְרִיכָלוּת (נ)
medieval (adj)	benaimi	בֵּינַיימִי
ancient (adj)	atik	עַתִּיק
national (adj)	le'umi	לְאוּמִי
famous (monument, etc.)	mefursam	מְפוֹרְסָם

tourist	tayar	תַּיָּיר (ז)
guide (person)	madriχ tiyulim	מַדְרִיךְ טִיּוּלִים (ז)
excursion, sightseeing tour	tiyul	טִיּוּל (ז)
to show (vt)	lehar'ot	לְהַרְאוֹת
to tell (vt)	lesaper	לְסַפֵּר
to find (vt)	limtso	לִמְצוֹא
to get lost (lose one's way)	la'leχet le'ibud	לָלֶכֶת לְאִיבּוּד
map (e.g., subway ~)	mapa	מַפָּה (נ)
map (e.g., city ~)	tarʃim	תַּרְשִׁים (ז)
souvenir, gift	maz'keret	מַזְכֶּרֶת (נ)
gift shop	χanut matanot	חֲנוּת מַתָּנוֹת (נ)
to take pictures	letsalem	לְצַלֵּם
to have one's picture taken	lehitstalem	לְהִצְטַלֵּם

TRANSPORTATION

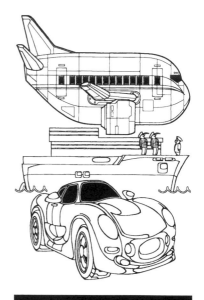

T&P Books Publishing

airport	nemal te'ufa	נְמַל תְּעוּפָה (ז)
airplane	matos	מָטוֹס (ז)
airline	xevrat te'ufa	חֶבְרַת תְּעוּפָה (נ)
air traffic controller	bakar tisa	בַּקָּר טִיסָה (ז)
departure	hamra'a	הַמְרָאָה (נ)
arrival	nexita	נְחִיתָה (נ)
to arrive (by plane)	leha'gi'a betisa	לְהַגִּיעַ בְּטִיסָה
departure time	zman hamra'a	זְמַן הַמְרָאָה (ז)
arrival time	zman nexita	זְמַן נְחִיתָה (ז)
to be delayed	lehit'akev	לְהִתְעַכֵּב
flight delay	ikuv hatisa	עִיכּוּב הַטִּיסָה (ז)
information board	'luax meida	לוּחַ מֵידָע (ז)
information	meida	מֵידָע (ז)
to announce (vt)	leho'dia	לְהוֹדִיעַ
flight (e.g., next ~)	tisa	טִיסָה (נ)
customs	'mexes	מֶכֶס (ז)
customs officer	pakid 'mexes	פָּקִיד מֶכֶס (ז)
customs declaration	hatsharat mexes	הַצְהָרַת מֶכֶס (נ)
to fill out (vt)	lemale	לְמַלֵּא
to fill out the declaration	lemale 'tofes hatshara	לְמַלֵּא טוֹפֶס הַצְהָרָה
passport control	bdikat darkonim	בְּדִיקַת דַּרְכּוֹנִים (נ)
luggage	kvuda	כְּבוּדָה (נ)
hand luggage	kvudat yad	כְּבוּדַת יָד (נ)
luggage cart	eglat kvuda	עֶגְלַת כְּבוּדָה (נ)
landing	nexita	נְחִיתָה (נ)
landing strip	maslul nexita	מַסְלוּל נְחִיתָה (ז)
to land (vi)	linxot	לַנְחוֹת
airstairs	'keveʃ	כֶּבֶשׁ (ז)
check-in	tʃek in	צֶ'ק אִין (ז)
check-in counter	dalpak tʃek in	דַּלְפָּק צֶ'ק אִין (ז)
to check-in (vi)	leva'tse'a tʃek in	לְבַצֵּעַ צֶ'ק אִין
boarding pass	kartis aliya lematos	כַּרְטִיס עֲלִיָּה לְמָטוֹס (ז)
departure gate	'ʃa'ar yetsi'a	שַׁעַר יְצִיאָה (ז)
transit	ma'avar	מַעֲבָר (ז)
to wait (vt)	lehamtin	לְהַמְתִּין

departure lounge	traklin tisa	טְרַקְלִין טִיסָה (ז)
to see off	lelavot	לְלַוּוֹת
to say goodbye	lomar lehitra'ot	לוֹמַר לְהִתְרָאוֹת

24. Airplane

airplane	matos	מָטוֹס (ז)
air ticket	kartis tisa	כַּרְטִיס טִיסָה (ז)
airline	xevrat te'ufa	חֶבְרַת תְעוּפָה (נ)
airport	nemal te'ufa	נְמַל תְעוּפָה (ז)
supersonic (adj)	al koli	עַל קוֹלִי

captain	kabarnit	קַבַּרְנִיט (ז)
crew	'tsevet	צֶוֶת (ז)
pilot	tayas	טַיָיס (ז)
flight attendant (fem.)	da'yelet	דַיֶילֶת (נ)
navigator	navat	נַוָוט (ז)

wings	kna'fayim	כְּנָפַיִים (נ"ר)
tail	zanav	זָנָב (ז)
cockpit	'kokpit	קוֹקְפִּיט (ז)
engine	ma'no'a	מָנוֹעַ (ז)
undercarriage (landing gear)	kan nesi'a	כַּן נְסִיעָה (ז)
turbine	tur'bina	טוּרבִּינָה (נ)

propeller	madxef	מַדחֵף (ז)
black box	kufsa ʃxora	קוּפְסָה שְחוֹרָה (נ)
yoke (control column)	'hege	הֶגֶה (ז)
fuel	'delek	דֶלֶק (ז)
safety card	hora'ot betixut	הוֹרָאוֹת בְּטִיחוּת (נ"ר)
oxygen mask	masexat xamtsan	מַסֵיכַת חַמצָן (נ)
uniform	madim	מַדִים (ז"ר)
life vest	xagorat hatsala	חֲגוֹרַת הַצָלָה (נ)
parachute	mitsnax	מִצנָח (ז)

takeoff	hamra'a	הַמרָאָה (נ)
to take off (vi)	lehamri	לְהַמרִיא
runway	maslul hamra'a	מַסלוּל הַמרָאָה (ז)

visibility	re'ut	רְאוּת (נ)
flight (act of flying)	tisa	טִיסָה (נ)
altitude	'gova	גוֹבַה (ז)
air pocket	kis avir	כִּיס אֲוִויר (ז)

seat	moʃav	מוֹשָב (ז)
headphones	ozniyot	אוֹזנִיוֹת (נ"ר)
folding tray (tray table)	magaʃ mitkapel	מַגָש מִתקַפֵּל (ז)
airplane window	tsohar	צוֹהַר (ז)
aisle	ma'avar	מַעֲבָר (ז)

25. Train

train	ra'kevet	רַכֶּבֶת (נ)
commuter train	ra'kevet parvarim	רַכֶּבֶת פַּרְבָרִים (נ)
express train	ra'kevet mehira	רַכֶּבֶת מְהִירָה (נ)
diesel locomotive	katar 'dizel	קַטָּר דִיזֶל (ז)
steam locomotive	katar	קַטָּר (ז)
passenger car	karon	קָרוֹן (ז)
dining car	kron mis'ada	קְרוֹן מִסְעָדָה (ז)
rails	mesilot	מְסִילוֹת (נ־ר)
railroad	mesilat barzel	מְסִילַת בַּרְזֶל (נ)
railway tie	'eden	אֶדֶן (ז)
platform (railway ~)	ratsif	רָצִיף (ז)
track (~ 1, 2, etc.)	mesila	מְסִילָה (נ)
semaphore	ramzor	רַמְזוֹר (ז)
station	taχana	תַחֲנָה (נ)
engineer (train driver)	nahag ra'kevet	נֶהָג רַכֶּבֶת (ז)
porter (of luggage)	sabal	סַבָּל (ז)
car attendant	sadran ra'kevet	סַדְרָן רַכֶּבֶת (ז)
passenger	no'se'a	נוֹסֵעַ (ז)
conductor (ticket inspector)	bodek	בּוֹדֵק (ז)
corridor (in train)	prozdor	פְּרוֹזְדוֹר (ז)
emergency brake	ma'atsar χirum	מַעֲצָר חִירוּם (ז)
compartment	ta	תָא (ז)
berth	dargaʃ	דַרְגָש (ז)
upper berth	dargaʃ elyon	דַרְגָש עֶלְיוֹן (ז)
lower berth	dargaʃ taχton	דַרְגָש תַחְתוֹן (ז)
bed linen, bedding	matsa'im	מַצָעִים (ז־ר)
ticket	kartis	כַּרְטִיס (ז)
schedule	'luaχ zmanim	לוּחַ זְמַנִים (ז)
information display	'ʃelet meida	שֶׁלֶט מֵידָע (ז)
to leave, to depart	latset	לָצֵאת
departure (of train)	yetsi'a	יְצִיאָה (נ)
to arrive (ab. train)	leha'gi'a	לְהַגִּיעַ
arrival	haga'a	הַגָעָה (נ)
to arrive by train	leha'gi'a bera'kevet	לְהַגִּיעַ בְּרַכֶּבֶת
to get on the train	la'alot lera'kevet	לַעֲלוֹת לְרַכֶּבֶת
to get off the train	la'redet mehara'kevet	לָרֶדֶת מֵהָרַכֶּבֶת
train wreck	hitraskut	הִתְרַסְקוּת (נ)
to derail (vi)	la'redet mipasei ra'kevet	לָרֶדֶת מִפַּסֵי רַכֶּבֶת

steam locomotive	katar	קַטָר (ז)
stoker, fireman	masik	מַסִיק (ז)
firebox	kivʃan	כִּבשָן (ז)
coal	peχam	פֶּחָם (ז)

26. Ship

ship	sfina	סְפִינָה (נ)
vessel	sfina	סְפִינָה (נ)
steamship	oniyat kitor	אוֹנִייַת קִיטוֹר (נ)
riverboat	sfinat nahar	סְפִינַת נָהָר (נ)
cruise ship	oniyat ta'anugot	אוֹנִייַת תַעֲנוּגוֹת (נ)
cruiser	sa'yeret	סַייֶרֶת (נ)
yacht	'yaχta	יַכטָה (נ)
tugboat	go'reret	גוֹרֶרֶת (נ)
barge	arba	אַרבָּה (נ)
ferry	ma'a'boret	מַעֲבּוֹרֶת (נ)
sailing ship	sfinat mifras	סְפִינַת מִפרָשׂ (נ)
brigantine	briganit	בּרִיגָנִית (נ)
ice breaker	ʃo'veret 'keraχ	שוֹבֶרֶת קֶרַח (נ)
submarine	tso'lelet	צוֹלֶלֶת (נ)
boat (flat-bottomed ~)	sira	סִירָה (נ)
dinghy	sira	סִירָה (נ)
lifeboat	sirat hatsala	סִירַת הַצָלָה (נ)
motorboat	sirat ma'no'a	סִירַת מָנוֹעַ (נ)
captain	rav χovel	רַב-חוֹבֵל (ז)
seaman	malaχ	מַלָח (ז)
sailor	yamai	יַמַאי (ז)
crew	'tsevet	צֶווֶת (ז)
boatswain	rav malaχim	רַב-מַלָחִים (ז)
ship's boy	'na'ar sipun	נַעַר סִיפּוּן (ז)
cook	tabaχ	טַבָּח (ז)
ship's doctor	rofe ha'oniya	רוֹפֵא הָאוֹנִייָה (ז)
deck	sipun	סִיפּוּן (ז)
mast	'toren	תוֹרֶן (ז)
sail	mifras	מִפרָשׂ (ז)
hold	'beten oniya	בֶּטֶן אוֹנִייָה (נ)
bow (prow)	χartom	חַרטוֹם (ז)
stern	yarketei hasfina	יַרכְּתֵי הַסְפִינָה (ז"ר)
oar	maʃot	מָשוֹט (ז)
screw propeller	madχef	מַדחֵף (ז)

cabin	ta	תָּא (ז)
wardroom	mo'adon ktsinim	מוֹעֲדוֹן קְצִינִים (ז)
engine room	χadar meχonot	חֲדַר מְכוֹנוֹת (ז)
bridge	'geʃer hapikud	גֶּשֶׁר הַפִּיקוּד (ז)
radio room	ta alχutan	תָּא אַלְחוּטָן (ז)
wave (radio)	'teder	תֶּדֶר (ז)
logbook	yoman ha'oniya	יוֹמַן הָאוֹנִיָּה (ז)

spyglass	miʃ'kefet	מִשְׁקֶפֶת (נ)
bell	pa'amon	פַּעֲמוֹן (ז)
flag	'degel	דֶּגֶל (ז)

| hawser (mooring ~) | avot ha'oniya | עֲבוֹת הָאוֹנִיָּה (נ) |
| knot (bowline, etc.) | 'keʃer | קֶשֶׁר (ז) |

| deckrails | ma'ake hasipun | מַעֲקֵה הַסִּיפּוּן (ז) |
| gangway | 'keveʃ | כֶּבֶשׁ (ז) |

anchor	'ogen	עוֹגֶן (ז)
to weigh anchor	leharim 'ogen	לְהָרִים עוֹגֶן
to drop anchor	la'agon	לַעֲגוֹן
anchor chain	ʃar'ʃeret ha'ogen	שַׁרְשֶׁרֶת הָעוֹגֶן (נ)

port (harbor)	namal	נָמֵל (ז)
quay, wharf	'mezaχ	מֶזַח (ז)
to berth (moor)	la'agon	לַעֲגוֹן
to cast off	lehaflig	לְהַפְלִיג

trip, voyage	masa, tiyul	מַסָּע (ז), טִיּוּל (ז)
cruise (sea trip)	'ʃayit	שַׁיִט (ז)
course (route)	kivun	כִּיוּוּן (ז)
route (itinerary)	nativ	נָתִיב (ז)

| fairway
(safe water channel) | nativ 'ʃayit | נָתִיב שַׁיִט (ז) |

| shallows | sirton | שִׂרְטוֹן (ז) |
| to run aground | la'alot al hasirton | לַעֲלוֹת עַל הַשִּׂרְטוֹן |

storm	sufa	סוּפָה (נ)
signal	ot	אוֹת (ז)
to sink (vi)	lit'bo'a	לִטְבּוֹעַ
Man overboard!	adam ba'mayim!	אָדָם בַּמַּיִם!
SOS (distress signal)	kri'at hatsala	קְרִיאַת הַצָּלָה
ring buoy	galgal hatsala	גַּלְגַּל הַצָּלָה (ז)

CITY

T&P Books Publishing

bus	'otobus	אוֹטוֹבּוּס (ז)
streetcar	ra'kevet kala	רַכֶּבֶת קַלָּה (נ)
trolley bus	tro'leibus	טְרוֹלֵיבּוּס (ז)
route (of bus, etc.)	maslul	מַסְלוּל (ז)
number (e.g., bus ~)	mispar	מִסְפָּר (ז)
to go by …	lin'so'a be…	לִנְסוֹעַ בְּ...
to get on (~ the bus)	la'alot	לַעֲלוֹת
to get off …	la'redet mi…	לָרֶדֶת מ...
stop (e.g., bus ~)	taxana	תַּחֲנָה (נ)
next stop	hataxana haba'a	הַתַּחֲנָה הַבָּאָה (נ)
terminus	hataxana ha'axrona	הַתַּחֲנָה הָאַחֲרוֹנָה (נ)
schedule	'luax zmanim	לוּחַ זְמַנִּים (ז)
to wait (vt)	lehamtin	לְהַמְתִּין
ticket	kartis	כַּרְטִיס (ז)
fare	mexir hanesiya	מְחִיר הַנְּסִיעָה (ז)
cashier (ticket seller)	kupai	קוּפַּאי (ז)
ticket inspection	bi'koret kartisim	בִּיקוֹרֶת כַּרְטִיסִים (נ)
ticket inspector	mevaker	מְבַקֵּר (ז)
to be late (for …)	le'axer	לְאַחֵר
to miss (~ the train, etc.)	lefasfes	לְפַסְפֵּס
to be in a hurry	lemaher	לְמַהֵר
taxi, cab	monit	מוֹנִית (נ)
taxi driver	nahag monit	נֶהַג מוֹנִית (ז)
by taxi	bemonit	בְּמוֹנִית
taxi stand	taxanat moniyot	תַּחֲנַת מוֹנִיוֹת (נ)
to call a taxi	lehazmin monit	לְהַזְמִין מוֹנִית
to take a taxi	la'kaxat monit	לָקַחַת מוֹנִית
traffic	tnu'a	תְּנוּעָה (נ)
traffic jam	pkak	פְּקָק (ז)
rush hour	ʃa'ot 'omes	שְׁעוֹת עוֹמֶס (נ"ר)
to park (vi)	laxanot	לַחֲנוֹת
to park (vt)	lehaxnot	לְהַחְנוֹת
parking lot	xanaya	חֲנָיָה (נ)
subway	ra'kevet taxtit	רַכֶּבֶת תַּחְתִּית (נ)
station	taxana	תַּחֲנָה (נ)
to take the subway	lin'so'a betaxtit	לִנְסוֹעַ בְּתַחְתִּית

| train | ra'kevet | רַכֶּבֶת (נ) |
| train station | taχanat ra'kevet | תַחֲנַת רַכֶּבֶת (נ) |

28. City. Life in the city

city, town	ir	עִיר (נ)
capital city	ir bira	עִיר בִּירָה (נ)
village	kfar	כְּפָר (ז)

city map	mapat ha'ir	מַפַּת הָעִיר (נ)
downtown	merkaz ha'ir	מֶרְכַּז הָעִיר (ז)
suburb	parvar	פַּרְוָור (ז)
suburban (adj)	parvari	פַּרְוָורִי

outskirts	parvar	פַּרְוָור (ז)
environs (suburbs)	svivot	סְבִיבוֹת (נ־ר)
city block	ʃχuna	שְׁכוּנָה (נ)
residential block (area)	ʃχunat megurim	שְׁכוּנַת מְגוּרִים (נ)

traffic	tnu'a	תְּנוּעָה (נ)
traffic lights	ramzor	רַמְזוֹר (ז)
public transportation	taχbura tsiburit	תַחְבּוּרָה צִיבּוּרִית (נ)
intersection	'tsomet	צוֹמֶת (ז)

crosswalk	ma'avar χatsaya	מַעֲבַר חֲצָיָה (ז)
pedestrian underpass	ma'avar tat karka'i	מַעֲבָר תַת־קַרְקָעִי (ז)
to cross (~ the street)	laχatsot	לַחֲצוֹת
pedestrian	holeχ 'regel	הוֹלֵך רֶגֶל (ז)
sidewalk	midraχa	מִדְרָכָה (נ)

bridge	'geʃer	גֶשֶׁר (ז)
embankment (river walk)	ta'yelet	טַיֶּילֶת (נ)
fountain	mizraka	מִזְרָקָה (נ)

allée (garden walkway)	sdera	שְׂדֵרָה (נ)
park	park	פַּארְק (ז)
boulevard	sdera	שְׂדֵרָה (נ)
square	kikar	כִּיכָּר (נ)
avenue (wide street)	reχov raʃi	רְחוֹב רָאשִׁי (ז)
street	reχov	רְחוֹב (ז)
side street	simta	סִמְטָה (נ)
dead end	mavoi satum	מָבוֹי סָתוּם (ז)

house	'bayit	בַּיִת (ז)
building	binyan	בְּנִיָין (ז)
skyscraper	gored ʃχakim	גּוֹרֵד שְׁחָקִים (ז)

facade	χazit	חֲזִית (נ)
roof	gag	גַּג (ז)
window	χalon	חַלוֹן (ז)

arch	'keʃet	קֶשֶׁת (ז)
column	amud	עַמּוּד (ז)
corner	pina	פִּינָה (נ)
store window	χalon ra'ava	חַלּוֹן רַאֲוָה (ז)
signboard (store sign, etc.)	'ʃelet	שֶׁלֶט (ז)
poster	kraza	כְּרָזָה (נ)
advertising poster	'poster	פּוֹסְטֵר (ז)
billboard	'luaχ pirsum	לוּחַ פִּרְסוּם (ז)
garbage, trash	'zevel	זֶבֶל (ז)
trashcan (public ~)	paχ aʃpa	פַּח אַשְׁפָּה (ז)
to litter (vi)	lelaχleχ	לְלַכְלֵךְ
garbage dump	mizbala	מִזְבָּלָה (נ)
phone booth	ta 'telefon	תָּא טֶלֶפוֹן (ז)
lamppost	amud panas	עַמּוּד פָּנָס (ז)
bench (park ~)	safsal	סַפְסָל (ז)
police officer	ʃoter	שׁוֹטֵר (ז)
police	miʃtara	מִשְׁטָרָה (נ)
beggar	kabtsan	קַבְּצָן (ז)
homeless (n)	χasar 'bayit	חֲסַר בַּיִת (ז)

29. Urban institutions

store	χanut	חֲנוּת (נ)
drugstore, pharmacy	beit mir'kaχat	בֵּית מִרְקַחַת (ז)
eyeglass store	χanut miʃka'fayim	חֲנוּת מִשְׁקָפַיִים (נ)
shopping mall	kanyon	קַנְיוֹן (ז)
supermarket	super'market	סוּפֵּרְמַרְקֶט (ז)
bakery	ma'afiya	מַאֲפִייָה (נ)
baker	ofe	אוֹפֶה (ז)
pastry shop	χanut mamtakim	חֲנוּת מַמְתָּקִים (נ)
grocery store	ma'kolet	מַכּוֹלֶת (נ)
butcher shop	itliz	אִטְלִיז (ז)
produce store	χanut perot viyerakot	חֲנוּת פֵּירוֹת וִירָקוֹת (נ)
market	ʃuk	שׁוּק (ז)
coffee house	beit kafe	בֵּית קָפֶה (ז)
restaurant	mis'ada	מִסְעָדָה (נ)
pub, bar	pab	פָּאבּ (ז)
pizzeria	pi'tseriya	פִּיצֵרִייָה (נ)
hair salon	mispara	מִסְפָּרָה (נ)
post office	'do'ar	דּוֹאַר (ז)
dry cleaners	nikui yaveʃ	נִיקּוּי יָבֵשׁ (ז)
photo studio	'studyo letsilum	סְטוּדְיוֹ לְצִילוּם (ז)

shoe store	χanut na'a'layim	(ז) חֲנוּת נַעֲלַיִם
bookstore	χanut sfarim	(ז) חֲנוּת סְפָרִים
sporting goods store	χanut sport	(ז) חֲנוּת סְפּוֹרט

clothes repair shop	χanut tikun bgadim	(ז) חֲנוּת תִּיקוּן בְּגָדִים
formal wear rental	χanut haskarat bgadim	(ז) חֲנוּת הַשְׂכָּרַת בְּגָדִים
video rental store	χanut haʃalat sratim	(ז) חֲנוּת הַשְׁאָלַת סְרָטִים

circus	kirkas	(ז) קִרקָס
zoo	gan hayot	(ז) גַּן חַיּוֹת
movie theater	kol'no'a	(ז) קוֹלנוֹעַ
museum	muze'on	(ז) מוּזֵיאוֹן
library	sifriya	(נ) סִפְרִיָּה

theater	te'atron	(ז) תֵּיאַטרוֹן
opera (opera house)	beit 'opera	(ז) בֵּית אוֹפֵּרָה
nightclub	mo'adon 'laila	(ז) מוֹעֲדוֹן לַיְלָה
casino	ka'zino	(ז) קָזִינוֹ

mosque	misgad	(ז) מִסגָּד
synagogue	beit 'kneset	(ז) בֵּית כְּנֶסֶת
cathedral	kated'rala	(נ) קָתֶדְרָלָה
temple	mikdaʃ	(ז) מִקדָּשׁ
church	knesiya	(נ) כְּנֵסִיָּה

college	miχlala	(נ) מִכְלָלָה
university	uni'versita	(נ) אוּנִיבֶרְסִיטָה
school	beit 'sefer	(ז) בֵּית סֵפֶר

prefecture	maχoz	(ז) מָחוֹז
city hall	iriya	(נ) עִירִיָּה
hotel	beit malon	(ז) בֵּית מָלוֹן
bank	bank	(ז) בַּנק

embassy	ʃagrirut	(נ) שַׁגרִירוּת
travel agency	soχnut nesi'ot	(נ) סוֹכְנוּת נְסִיעוֹת
information office	modi'in	(ז) מוֹדִיעִין
currency exchange	misrad hamarat mat'be'a	(ז) מִשְׂרַד הֲמָרַת מַטבֵּעַ

| subway | ra'kevet taχtit | (נ) רַכֶּבֶת תַּחְתִּית |
| hospital | beit χolim | (ז) בֵּית חוֹלִים |

| gas station | taχanat 'delek | (נ) תַחֲנַת דֶּלֶק |
| parking lot | migraʃ χanaya | (ז) מִגרָשׁ חֲנָיָה |

30. Signs

signboard (store sign, etc.)	'ʃelet	(ז) שֶׁלֶט
notice (door sign, etc.)	moda'a	(נ) מוֹדָעָה
poster	'poster	(ז) פּוֹסטֵר

direction sign	tamrur	תַּמְרוּר (ז)
arrow (sign)	χets	חֵץ (ז)
caution	azhara	אַזְהָרָה (נ)
warning sign	ʃelet azhara	שֶׁלֶט אַזְהָרָה (ז)
to warn (vt)	lehazhir	לְהַזְהִיר
rest day (weekly ~)	yom χofeʃ	יוֹם חוֹפֶשׁ (ז)
timetable (schedule)	luaχ zmanim	לוּחַ זְמַנִּים (ז)
opening hours	ʃa'ot avoda	שְׁעוֹת עֲבוֹדָה (נ"ר)
WELCOME!	bruχim haba'im!	ברוכים הַבָּאִים!
ENTRANCE	knisa	כְּנִיסָה
EXIT	yetsi'a	יְצִיאָה
PUSH	dχof	דחוֹף
PULL	mʃoχ	משוֹךְ
OPEN	pa'tuaχ	פָּתוּחַ
CLOSED	sagur	סָגוּר
WOMEN	lenaʃim	לְנָשִׁים
MEN	legvarim	לְגבָרִים
DISCOUNTS	hanaχot	הֲנָחוֹת
SALE	mivtsa	מבצע
NEW!	χadaʃ!	חָדָשׁ!
FREE	χinam	חִינָּם
ATTENTION!	sim lev!	שִׂים לֵב!
NO VACANCIES	ein makom panui	אֵין מָקוֹם פָּנוּי
RESERVED	ʃamur	שָׁמוּר
ADMINISTRATION	hanhala	הַנהָלָה
STAFF ONLY	le'ovdim bilvad	לְעוֹבדִים בִּלבָד
BEWARE OF THE DOG!	zehirut 'kelev noʃeχ!	זְהִירוּת, כֶּלֶב נוֹשֵׁךְ!
NO SMOKING	asur le'aʃen!	אָסוּר לְעַשֵׁן!
DO NOT TOUCH!	lo lagaat!	לֹא לָגַעַת!
DANGEROUS	mesukan	מְסוּכָּן
DANGER	sakana	סַכָּנָה
HIGH VOLTAGE	'metaχ ga'voha	מֶתַח גָּבוֹהַ
NO SWIMMING!	haraχatsa asura!	הָרַחֲצָה אֲסוּרָה!
OUT OF ORDER	lo oved	לֹא עוֹבֵד
FLAMMABLE	dalik	דָלִיק
FORBIDDEN	asur	אָסוּר
NO TRESPASSING!	asur la'avor	אָסוּר לַעֲבוֹר
WET PAINT	'tseva laχ	צֶבַע לַח

31. Shopping

to buy (purchase)	liknot	לִקְנוֹת
purchase	kniya	קְנִיָּה (נ)
to go shopping	la'leχet lekniyot	לָלֶכֶת לִקְנִיּוֹת
shopping	ariχat kniyot	עֲרִיכַת קְנִיּוֹת (נ)
to be open (ab. store)	pa'tuaχ	פָּתוּחַ
to be closed	sagur	סָגוּר
footwear, shoes	na'a'layim	נַעֲלַיִים (נ־ר)
clothes, clothing	bgadim	בְּגָדִים (ז־ר)
cosmetics	tamrukim	תַּמְרוּקִים (ז־ר)
food products	mutsrei mazon	מוּצְרֵי מָזוֹן (ז־ר)
gift, present	matana	מַתָּנָה (נ)
salesman	moχer	מוֹכֵר (ז)
saleswoman	mo'χeret	מוֹכֶרֶת (נ)
check out, cash desk	kupa	קוּפָּה (נ)
mirror	mar'a	מַרְאָה (נ)
counter (store ~)	duχan	דּוּכָן (ז)
fitting room	'χeder halbaʃa	חֶדֶר הַלְבָּשָׁה (ז)
to try on	limdod	לִמְדּוֹד
to fit (ab. dress, etc.)	lehat'im	לְהַתְאִים
to like (I like …)	limtso χen be'ei'nayim	לִמְצוֹא חֵן בְּעֵינַיִים
price	meχir	מְחִיר (ז)
price tag	tag meχir	תַּג מְחִיר (ז)
to cost (vt)	la'alot	לַעֲלוֹת
How much?	'kama?	כַּמָּה?
discount	hanaχa	הֲנָחָה (נ)
inexpensive (adj)	lo yakar	לֹא יָקָר
cheap (adj)	zol	זוֹל
expensive (adj)	yakar	יָקָר
It's expensive	ze yakar	זֶה יָקָר
rental (n)	haskara	הַשְׂכָּרָה (נ)
to rent (~ a tuxedo)	liskor	לִשְׂכּוֹר
credit (trade credit)	aʃrai	אַשְׁרַאי (ז)
on credit (adv)	be'aʃrai	בְּאַשְׁרַאי

CLOTHING &
ACCESSORIES

T&P Books Publishing

clothes	bgadim	בְּגָדִים (ז״ר)
outerwear	levuʃ elyon	לְבוּשׁ עֶלְיוֹן (ז)
winter clothing	bigdei 'xoref	בִּגְדֵי חוֹרֶף (ז״ר)
coat (overcoat)	me'il	מְעִיל (ז)
fur coat	me'il parva	מְעִיל פַּרְוָה (ז)
fur jacket	me'il parva katsar	מְעִיל פַּרְוָה קָצָר (ז)
down coat	me'il pux	מְעִיל פּוּךְ (ז)
jacket (e.g., leather ~)	me'il katsar	מְעִיל קָצָר (ז)
raincoat (trenchcoat, etc.)	me'il 'geʃem	מְעִיל גֶּשֶׁם (ז)
waterproof (adj)	amid be'mayim	עָמִיד בְּמַיִם

shirt (button shirt)	xultsa	חוּלְצָה (נ)
pants	mixna'sayim	מִכְנָסַיִם (ז״ר)
jeans	mixnesei 'dʒins	מִכְנְסֵי גִ׳ינְס (ז״ר)
suit jacket	ʒaket	זַ׳קֵט (ז)
suit	xalifa	חֲלִיפָה (נ)
dress (frock)	simla	שִׂמְלָה (נ)
skirt	xatsa'it	חֲצָאִית (נ)
blouse	xultsa	חוּלְצָה (נ)
knitted jacket (cardigan, etc.)	ʒaket 'tsemer	זַ׳קֵט צֶמֶר (ז)
jacket (of woman's suit)	ʒaket	זַ׳קֵט (ז)
T-shirt	ti ʃert	טִי שֶׁרְט (ז)
shorts (short trousers)	mixna'sayim ktsarim	מִכְנָסַיִם קְצָרִים (ז״ר)
tracksuit	'trening	טְרֶנִינְג (ז)
bathrobe	xaluk raxatsa	חָלוּק רַחְצָה (ז)
pajamas	pi'dʒama	פִּיגָ׳מָה (נ)
sweater	'sveder	סְוֶוֶדֶר (ז)
pullover	afuda	אֲפוּדָה (נ)
vest	vest	וֶסְט (ז)
tailcoat	frak	פְרָאק (ז)
tuxedo	tuk'sido	טוּקְסִידוֹ (ז)
uniform	madim	מַדִים (ז״ר)
workwear	bigdei avoda	בִּגְדֵי עֲבוֹדָה (ז״ר)

| overalls | sarbal | סַרְבָּל (ז) |
| coat (e.g., doctor's smock) | χaluk | חָלוּק (ז) |

34. Clothing. Underwear

underwear	levanim	לְבָנִים (ז"ר)
boxers, briefs	taχtonim	תַחְתּוֹנִים (ז"ר)
panties	taχtonim	תַחְתּוֹנִים (ז"ר)
undershirt (A-shirt)	gufiya	גוּפִייָה (נ)
socks	gar'bayim	גַרְבַּיִם (ז"ר)

nightgown	'ktonet 'laila	כּתוֹנֶת לַיְלָה (נ)
bra	χaziya	חֲזִייָה (נ)
knee highs	birkon	בִּרְכּוֹן (ז)
(knee-high socks)		

pantyhose	garbonim	גַרְבּוֹנִים (ז"ר)
stockings (thigh highs)	garbei 'nailon	גַרְבֵּי נַיְלוֹן (ז"ר)
bathing suit	'beged yam	בֶּגֶד יָם (ז)

35. Headwear

hat	'kova	כּוֹבַע (ז)
fedora	'kova 'leved	כּוֹבַע לֶבֶד (ז)
baseball cap	'kova 'beisbol	כּוֹבַע בֵּייסְבּוֹל (ז)
flatcap	'kova mitsχiya	כּוֹבַע מִצְחִייָה (ז)

beret	baret	בָּרֶט (ז)
hood	bardas	בַּרְדָס (ז)
panama hat	'kova 'tembel	כּוֹבַע טֶמְבֶּל (ז)
knit cap (knitted hat)	'kova 'gerev	כּוֹבַע גֶרֶב (ז)

| headscarf | mit'paχat | מִטְפַּחַת (נ) |
| women's hat | 'kova | כּוֹבַע (ז) |

hard hat	kasda	קַסְדָה (נ)
garrison cap	kumta	כּוּמְתָה (נ)
helmet	kasda	קַסְדָה (נ)

| derby | mig'ba'at me'u'gelet | מִגְבַּעַת מְעוּגֶלֶת (נ) |
| top hat | tsi'linder | צִילִינְדֶר (ז) |

36. Footwear

footwear	han'ala	הַנְעָלָה (נ)
shoes (men's shoes)	na'a'layim	נַעֲלַיִם (נ"ר)
shoes (women's shoes)	na'a'layim	נַעֲלַיִם (נ"ר)

| boots (e.g., cowboy ~) | maga'fayim | מַגָּפַיִם (ז״ר) |
| slippers | na'alei 'bayit | נַעֲלֵי בַּיִת (נ״ר) |

tennis shoes (e.g., Nike ~)	na'alei sport	נַעֲלֵי ספּוֹרט (נ״ר)
sneakers (e.g., Converse ~)	na'alei sport	נַעֲלֵי ספּוֹרט (נ״ר)
sandals	sandalim	סַנדָלִים (ז״ר)

cobbler (shoe repairer)	sandlar	סַנדלָר (ז)
heel	akev	עָקֵב (ז)
pair (of shoes)	zug	זוּג (ז)

| shoestring | sroχ | שׂרוֹך (ז) |
| to lace (vt) | lisroχ | לִשׂרוֹך |

| shoehorn | kaf na'a'layim | כַּף נַעֲלַיִם (נ) |
| shoe polish | miʃχat na'a'layim | מִשחַת נַעֲלַיִם (נ) |

37. Personal accessories

gloves	kfafot	כּפָפוֹת (נ״ר)
mittens	kfafot	כּפָפוֹת (נ״ר)
scarf (muffler)	tsa'if	צָעִיף (ז)

glasses (eyeglasses)	miʃka'fayim	מִשקָפַיִם (ז״ר)
frame (eyeglass ~)	mis'geret	מִסגֶרֶת (נ)
umbrella	mitriya	מַטרִייָה (נ)
walking stick	makel haliχa	מַקֵל הָלִיכָה (ז)

| hairbrush | miv'reʃet se'ar | מִברֶשֶת שֵׂיעָר (נ) |
| fan | menifa | מְנִיפָה (נ) |

| tie (necktie) | aniva | עֲנִיבָה (נ) |
| bow tie | anivat parpar | עֲנִיבַת פַּרפַּר (נ) |

| suspenders | ktefiyot | כּתֵפִיוֹת (נ״ר) |
| handkerchief | mimχata | מִמחָטָה (נ) |

| comb | masrek | מַסרֵק (ז) |
| barrette | sikat roʃ | סִיכַּת רֹאש (נ) |

| hairpin | sikat se'ar | סִיכַּת שֵׂעָר (נ) |
| buckle | avzam | אַבזָם (ז) |

| belt | χagora | חֲגוֹרָה (נ) |
| shoulder strap | reʦu'at katef | רְצוּעַת כָּתֵף (נ) |

bag (handbag)	tik	תִיק (ז)
purse	tik	תִיק (ז)
backpack	tarmil	תַרמִיל (ז)

38. Clothing. Miscellaneous

fashion	ofna	אוֹפְנָה (נ)
in vogue (adj)	ofnati	אוֹפְנָתִי
fashion designer	me'atsev ofna	מְעַצֵּב אוֹפְנָה (ז)
collar	tsavaron	צַוָּארוֹן (ז)
pocket	kis	כִּיס (ז)
pocket (as adj)	ʃel kis	שֶׁל כִּיס
sleeve	ʃarvul	שַׁרווּל (ז)
hanging loop	mitle	מִתְלֶה (ז)
fly (on trousers)	χanut	חֲנוּת (נ)
zipper (fastener)	roχsan	רוֹכְסָן (ז)
fastener	'keres	קֶרֶס (ז)
button	kaftor	כַּפְתּוֹר (ז)
buttonhole	lula'a	לוּלָאָה (נ)
to come off (ab. button)	lehitaleʃ	לְהִיתָלֵשׁ
to sew (vi, vt)	litpor	לִתְפּוֹר
to embroider (vi, vt)	lirkom	לִרְקוֹם
embroidery	rikma	רִקְמָה (נ)
sewing needle	'maχat tfira	מַחַט תְּפִירָה (נ)
thread	χut	חוּט (ז)
seam	'tefer	תֶּפֶר (ז)
to get dirty (vi)	lehitlaχleχ	לְהִתְלַכְלֵךְ
stain (mark, spot)	'ketem	כֶּתֶם (ז)
to crease, crumple (vi)	lehitkamet	לְהִתְקַמֵּט
to tear, to rip (vt)	lik'ro'a	לִקְרוֹעַ
clothes moth	aʃ	עָשׁ (ז)

39. Personal care. Cosmetics

toothpaste	miʃχat ʃi'nayim	מִשְׁחַת שִׁינַיִים (נ)
toothbrush	miv'reʃet ʃi'nayim	מִבְרֶשֶׁת שִׁינַיִים (נ)
to brush one's teeth	letsaχ'tseaχ ʃi'nayim	לְצַחְצֵחַ שִׁינַיִים
razor	'ta'ar	תַּעַר (ז)
shaving cream	'ketsef gi'luaχ	קֶצֶף גִּילּוּחַ (ז)
to shave (vi)	lehitga'leaχ	לְהִתְגַּלֵּחַ
soap	sabon	סַבּוֹן (ז)
shampoo	ʃampu	שַׁמְפּוּ (ז)
scissors	mispa'rayim	מִסְפָּרַיִים (ז-ר)
nail file	ptsira	פְּצִירָה (נ)
nail clippers	gozez tsipor'nayim	גּוֹזֵז צִיפּוֹרְנַיִים (ז)
tweezers	pin'tseta	פִּינְצֶטָה (נ)

cosmetics	tamrukim	תַּמְרוּקִים (ז״ר)
face mask	maseχa	מַסֵּכָה (נ)
manicure	manikur	מָנִיקוּר (ז)
to have a manicure	la'asot manikur	לַעֲשׂוֹת מָנִיקוּר
pedicure	pedikur	פֶּדִיקוּר (ז)

make-up bag	tik ipur	תִּיק אִיפּוּר (ז)
face powder	'pudra	פּוּדְרָה (נ)
powder compact	pudriya	פּוּדְרִיָּה (נ)
blusher	'somek	סוֹמֶק (ז)

perfume (bottled)	'bosem	בּוֹשֶׂם (ז)
toilet water (lotion)	mei 'bosem	מֵי בּוֹשֶׂם (ז״ר)
lotion	mei panim	מֵי פָּנִים (ז״ר)
cologne	mei 'bosem	מֵי בּוֹשֶׂם (ז״ר)

eyeshadow	tslalit	צְלָלִית (נ)
eyeliner	ai 'lainer	אַי לַיינֶר (ז)
mascara	'maskara	מַסְקָרָה (נ)

lipstick	sfaton	שְׂפָתוֹן (ז)
nail polish, enamel	'laka letsipor'nayim	לַכָּה לְצִיפּוֹרְנַיִים (נ)
hair spray	tarsis lese'ar	תַּרְסִיס לְשֵׂיעָר (ז)
deodorant	de'odo'rant	דֶּאוֹדוֹרַנְט (ז)

cream	krem	קְרֶם (ז)
face cream	krem panim	קְרֶם פָּנִים (ז)
hand cream	krem ya'dayim	קְרֶם יָדַיִים (ז)
anti-wrinkle cream	krem 'neged kmatim	קְרֶם נֶגֶד קְמָטִים (ז)
day cream	krem yom	קְרֶם יוֹם (ז)
night cream	krem 'laila	קְרֶם לַיְלָה (ז)
day (as adj)	yomi	יוֹמִי
night (as adj)	leili	לֵילִי

tampon	tampon	טַמְפּוֹן (ז)
toilet paper (toilet roll)	neyar tu'alet	נְיָיר טוּאָלֶט (ז)
hair dryer	meyabeʃ se'ar	מְיַיבֵּשׁ שֵׂיעָר (ז)

40. Watches. Clocks

watch (wristwatch)	ʃe'on yad	שְׁעוֹן יָד (ז)
dial	'luaχ ʃa'on	לוּחַ שָׁעוֹן (ז)
hand (of clock, watch)	maχog	מָחוֹג (ז)
metal watch band	tsamid	צָמִיד (ז)
watch strap	retsu'a leʃa'on	רְצוּעָה לְשָׁעוֹן (נ)

battery	solela	סוֹלְלָה (נ)
to be dead (battery)	lehitroken	לְהִתְרוֹקֵן
to change a battery	lehaχlif	לְהַחֲלִיף
to run fast	lemaher	לְמַהֵר

to run slow	lefager	לְפַגֵּר
wall clock	ʃe'on kir	שְׁעוֹן קִיר (ז)
hourglass	ʃe'on χol	שְׁעוֹן חוֹל (ז)
sundial	ʃe'on 'ʃemeʃ	שְׁעוֹן שֶׁמֶשׁ (ז)
alarm clock	ʃa'on me'orer	שָׁעוֹן מְעוֹרֵר (ז)
watchmaker	ʃa'an	שָׁעָן (ז)
to repair (vt)	letaken	לְתַקֵּן

EVERYDAY EXPERIENCE

T&P Books Publishing

money	'kesef	כֶּסֶף (ז)
currency exchange	hamara	הֲמָרָה (נ)
exchange rate	ʃa'ar χalifin	שַׁעַר חֲלִיפִין (ז)
ATM	kaspomat	כַּספּוֹמָט (ז)
coin	mat'be'a	מַטבֵּעַ (ז)
dollar	'dolar	דוֹלָר (ז)
euro	'eiro	אֵירוֹ (ז)
lira	'lira	לִירָה (נ)
Deutschmark	mark germani	מַרק גֶּרמָנִי (ז)
franc	frank	פרַנק (ז)
pound sterling	'lira 'sterling	לִירָה שׁטֶרלִינג (נ)
yen	yen	יֶן (ז)
debt	χov	חוֹב (ז)
debtor	'ba'al χov	בַּעַל חוֹב (ז)
to lend (money)	lehalvot	לְהַלווֹת
to borrow (vi, vt)	lilvot	לִלווֹת
bank	bank	בַּנק (ז)
account	χeʃbon	חֶשׁבּוֹן (ז)
to deposit (vt)	lehafkid	לְהַפקִיד
to deposit into the account	lehafkid leχeʃbon	לְהַפקִיד לְחֶשׁבּוֹן
to withdraw (vt)	limʃoχ meχeʃbon	לִמשׁוֹך מֵחֶשׁבּוֹן
credit card	kartis aʃrai	כַּרטִיס אַשׁרַאי (ז)
cash	mezuman	מְזוּמָן
check	tʃek	צֶ'ק (ז)
to write a check	liχtov tʃek	לִכתוֹב צֶ'ק
checkbook	pinkas 'tʃekim	פִּנקַס צֶ'קִים (ז)
wallet	arnak	אַרנָק (ז)
change purse	arnak lematbe''ot	אַרנָק לְמַטבְּעוֹת (ז)
safe	ka'sefet	כַּסֶפֶת (נ)
heir	yoreʃ	יוֹרֵשׁ (ז)
inheritance	yeruʃa	יְרוּשָׁה (נ)
fortune (wealth)	'oʃer	עוֹשֶׁר (ז)
lease	χoze sχirut	חוֹזֶה שׂכִירוּת (ז)
rent (money)	sχar dira	שׂכַר דִּירָה (ז)
to rent (sth from sb)	liskor	לִשׂכּוֹר
price	meχir	מְחִיר (ז)

cost	alut	עָלוּת (נ)
sum	sχum	סְכוּם (ז)
to spend (vt)	lehotsi	לְהוֹצִיא
expenses	hotsa'ot	הוֹצָאוֹת (נ־ר)
to economize (vi, vt)	laχasoχ	לַחֲסוֹךְ
economical	χesχoni	חֶסְכוֹנִי
to pay (vi, vt)	leʃalem	לְשַׁלֵם
payment	taʃlum	תַשְׁלוּם (ז)
change (give the ~)	'odef	עוֹדֶף (ז)
tax	mas	מַס (ז)
fine	knas	קְנָס (ז)
to fine (vt)	liknos	לִקְנוֹס

42. Post. Postal service

post office	'do'ar	דוֹאַר (ז)
mail (letters, etc.)	'do'ar	דוֹאַר (ז)
mailman	davar	דַוָור (ז)
opening hours	ʃa'ot avoda	שְׁעוֹת עֲבוֹדָה (נ־ר)
letter	miχtav	מִכְתָב (ז)
registered letter	miχtav raʃum	מִכְתָב רָשׁוּם (ז)
postcard	gluya	גְלוּיָה (נ)
telegram	mivrak	מִבְרָק (ז)
package (parcel)	χavila	חֲבִילָה (נ)
money transfer	ha'avarat ksafim	הַעֲבָרַת כְּסָפִים (נ)
to receive (vt)	lekabel	לְקַבֵּל
to send (vt)	liʃ'loaχ	לִשְׁלוֹחַ
sending	ʃliχa	שְׁלִיחָה (נ)
address	'ktovet	כְּתוֹבֶת (נ)
ZIP code	mikud	מִיקוּד (ז)
sender	ʃo'leaχ	שׁוֹלֵחַ (ז)
receiver	nim'an	נִמְעָן (ז)
name (first name)	ʃem prati	שֵׁם פְּרָטִי (ז)
surname (last name)	ʃem miʃpaχa	שֵׁם מִשְׁפָּחָה (ז)
postage rate	ta'arif	תַעֲרִיף (ז)
standard (adj)	ragil	רָגִיל
economical (adj)	χesχoni	חֶסְכוֹנִי
weight	miʃkal	מִשְׁקָל (ז)
to weigh (~ letters)	liʃkol	לִשְׁקוֹל
envelope	ma'atafa	מַעֲטָפָה (נ)
postage stamp	bul 'do'ar	בּוּל דוֹאַר (ז)
to stamp an envelope	lehadbik bul	לְהַדְבִּיק בּוּל

43. Banking

bank	bank	בַּנק (ז)
branch (of bank, etc.)	snif	סנִיף (ז)
bank clerk, consultant	yo'ets	יוֹעֵץ (ז)
manager (director)	menahel	מְנַהֵל (ז)
bank account	xeʃbon	חֶשבּוֹן (ז)
account number	mispar xeʃbon	מִספַּר חֶשבּוֹן (ז)
checking account	xeʃbon over vaʃav	חֶשבּוֹן עוֹבֵר וָשָב (ז)
savings account	xeʃbon xisaxon	חֶשבּוֹן חִסָכוֹן (ז)
to open an account	liftoax xeʃbon	לִפתוֹחַ חֶשבּוֹן
to close the account	lisgor xeʃbon	לִסגוֹר חֶשבּוֹן
to deposit into the account	lehafkid lexeʃbon	לְהַפקִיד לְחֶשבּוֹן
to withdraw (vt)	limʃox mexeʃbon	לִמשוֹך מֵחֶשבּוֹן
deposit	pikadon	פִּיקָדוֹן (ז)
to make a deposit	lehafkid	לְהַפקִיד
wire transfer	ha'avara banka'it	הַעֲבָרָה בַּנקָאִית (נ)
to wire, to transfer	leha'avir 'kesef	לְהַעֲבִיר כֶּסֶף
sum	sxum	סכוּם (ז)
How much?	'kama?	כַּמָה?
signature	xatima	חֲתִימָה (נ)
to sign (vt)	laxtom	לַחתוֹם
credit card	kartis aʃrai	כַּרטִיס אַשרַאי (ז)
code (PIN code)	kod	קוֹד (ז)
credit card number	mispar kartis aʃrai	מִספַּר כַּרטִיס אַשרַאי (ז)
ATM	kaspomat	כַּספּוֹמָט (ז)
check	tʃek	צֶ׳ק (ז)
to write a check	lixtov tʃek	לִכתוֹב צֶ׳ק
checkbook	pinkas 'tʃekim	פִּנקָס צֶ׳קִים (ז)
loan (bank ~)	halva'a	הַלוָואָה (נ)
to apply for a loan	levakeʃ halva'a	לְבַקֵש הַלוָואָה
to get a loan	lekabel halva'a	לְקַבֵּל הַלוָואָה
to give a loan	lehalvot	לְהַלווֹת
guarantee	arvut	עַרבוּת (נ)

44. Telephone. Phone conversation

telephone	'telefon	טֶלֶפוֹן (ז)
cell phone	'telefon nayad	טֶלֶפוֹן נַייָד (ז)
answering machine	meʃivon	מְשִיבוֹן (ז)

to call (by phone)	letsaltsel	לְצַלְצֵל
phone call	siχat 'telefon	שִׂיחַת טֶלֶפוֹן (נ)
to dial a number	leχayeg mispar	לְחַיֵּג מִסְפָּר
Hello!	'halo!	הָלוֹ!
to ask (vt)	lif'ol	לִשְׁאוֹל
to answer (vi, vt)	la'anot	לַעֲנוֹת
to hear (vt)	lif'mo'a	לִשְׁמוֹעַ
well (adv)	tov	טוֹב
not well (adv)	lo tov	לֹא טוֹב
noises (interference)	hafra'ot	הַפְרָעוֹת (נ-ר)
receiver	ffo'feret	שְׁפוֹפֶרֶת (נ)
to pick up (~ the phone)	leharim ffo'feret	לְהָרִים שְׁפוֹפֶרֶת
to hang up (~ the phone)	leha'niaχ ffo'feret	לְהָנִיחַ שְׁפוֹפֶרֶת
busy (engaged)	tafus	תָּפוּס
to ring (ab. phone)	letsaltsel	לְצַלְצֵל
telephone book	'sefer tele'fonim	סֵפֶר טֶלֶפוֹנִים (ז)
local (adj)	mekomi	מְקוֹמִי
local call	siχa mekomit	שִׂיחָה מְקוֹמִית (נ)
long distance (~ call)	bein ironi	בֵּין עִירוֹנִי
long-distance call	siχa bein ironit	שִׂיחָה בֵּין עִירוֹנִית (נ)
international (adj)	benle'umi	בֵּינְלְאוּמִי
international call	siχa benle'umit	שִׂיחָה בֵּינְלְאוּמִית (נ)

45. Cell phone

cell phone	'telefon nayad	טֶלֶפוֹן נַיָּד (ז)
display	masaχ	מָסָךְ (ז)
button	kaftor	כַּפְתּוֹר (ז)
SIM card	kartis sim	כַּרְטִיס סִים (ז)
battery	solela	סוֹלְלָה (נ)
to be dead (battery)	lehitroken	לְהִתְרוֹקֵן
charger	mit'an	מַטְעָן (ז)
menu	tafrit	תַּפְרִיט (ז)
settings	hagdarot	הַגְדָּרוֹת (נ-ר)
tune (melody)	mangina	מַנְגִּינָה (נ)
to select (vt)	livχor	לִבְחוֹר
calculator	maχfevon	מַחְשְׁבוֹן (ז)
voice mail	ta koli	תָּא קוֹלִי (ז)
alarm clock	fa'on me'orer	שָׁעוֹן מְעוֹרֵר (ז)
contacts	anfei 'kefer	אַנְשֵׁי קֶשֶׁר (ז-ר)
SMS (text message)	misron	מִסְרוֹן (ז)
subscriber	manui	מָנוּי (ז)

46. Stationery

ballpoint pen	et kaduri	עֵט כַּדוּרִי (ז)
fountain pen	et no've'a	עֵט נוֹבֵעַ (ז)
pencil	iparon	עִיפָּרוֹן (ז)
highlighter	'marker	מַרקֵר (ז)
felt-tip pen	tuʃ	טוּש (ז)
notepad	pinkas	פִּנקָס (ז)
agenda (diary)	yoman	יוֹמָן (ז)
ruler	sargel	סַרגֵל (ז)
calculator	maxʃevon	מַחשְבוֹן (ז)
eraser	'maxak	מַחַק (ז)
thumbtack	'na'aʦ	נַעַץ (ז)
paper clip	mehadek	מְהַדֵק (ז)
glue	'devek	דֶבֶק (ז)
stapler	ʃadxan	שַדכָן (ז)
hole punch	menakev	מְנַקֵב (ז)
pencil sharpener	maxded	מַחדֵד (ז)

47. Foreign languages

language	safa	שָׂפָה (נ)
foreign (adj)	zar	זָר
foreign language	safa zara	שָׂפָה זָרָה (נ)
to study (vt)	lilmod	לִלמוֹד
to learn (language, etc.)	lilmod	לִלמוֹד
to read (vi, vt)	likro	לִקרוֹא
to speak (vi, vt)	ledaber	לְדַבֵּר
to understand (vt)	lehavin	לְהָבִין
to write (vt)	lixtov	לִכתוֹב
fast (adv)	maher	מַהֵר
slowly (adv)	le'at	לְאַט
fluently (adv)	xofʃi	חוֹפשִי
rules	klalim	כּלָלִים (ז-ר)
grammar	dikduk	דִקדוּק (ז)
vocabulary	oʦar milim	אוֹצַר מִילִים (ז)
phonetics	torat ha'hege	תוֹרַת הַהֶגֶה (נ)
textbook	'sefer limud	סֵפֶר לִימוּד (ז)
dictionary	milon	מִילוֹן (ז)
teach-yourself book	'sefer lelimud aʦmi	סֵפֶר לְלִימוּד עַצמִי (ז)
phrasebook	sixon	שִׂיחוֹן (ז)

cassette, tape	ka'letet	קַלֶטֶת (נ)
videotape	ka'letet 'vide'o	קַלֶטֶת וִידֵיאוֹ (נ)
CD, compact disc	taklitor	תַקְלִיטוֹר (ז)
DVD	di vi di	דִי. וִי. דִי. (ז)

alphabet	alefbeit	אָלֶפְבֵּית (ז)
to spell (vt)	le'ayet	לְאַיֵּת
pronunciation	hagiya	הֲגִיָּה (נ)

accent	mivta	מִבְטָא (ז)
with an accent	im mivta	עִם מִבְטָא
without an accent	bli mivta	בְּלִי מִבְטָא

| word | mila | מִילָה (נ) |
| meaning | maʃma'ut | מַשְׁמָעוּת (נ) |

course (e.g., a French ~)	kurs	קוּרְס (ז)
to sign up	leheraʃem lekurs	לְהֵירָשֵׁם לְקוּרְס
teacher	more	מוֹרֶה (ז)

translation (process)	tirgum	תִּרְגוּם (ז)
translation (text, etc.)	tirgum	תִּרְגוּם (ז)
translator	metargem	מְתַרְגֵם (ז)
interpreter	meturgeman	מְתוּרְגְמָן (ז)

| polyglot | poliglot | פּוֹלִיגְלוֹט (ז) |
| memory | zikaron | זִיכָּרוֹן (ז) |

MEALS. RESTAURANT

T&P Books Publishing

48. Table setting

spoon	kaf	כַּף (ז)
knife	sakin	סַכִּין (ז. נ)
fork	mazleg	מַזְלֵג (ז)
cup (e.g., coffee ~)	'sefel	סֵפֶל (ז)
plate (dinner ~)	tsa'laxat	צַלַּחַת (נ)
saucer	taxtit	תַּחְתִּית (נ)
napkin (on table)	mapit	מַפִּית (נ)
toothpick	keisam ʃi'nayim	קֵיסָם שִׁינַיִים (ז)

49. Restaurant

restaurant	mis'ada	מִסְעָדָה (נ)
coffee house	beit kafe	בֵּית קָפֶה (ז)
pub, bar	bar, pab	בָּר, פָּאב (ז)
tearoom	beit te	בֵּית תֵּה (ז)
waiter	meltsar	מֶלְצָר (ז)
waitress	meltsarit	מֶלְצָרִית (נ)
bartender	'barmen	בַּרְמֶן (ז)
menu	tafrit	תַּפְרִיט (ז)
wine list	reʃimat yeynot	רְשִׁימַת יֵינוֹת (נ)
to book a table	lehazmin ʃulxan	לְהַזְמִין שׁוּלְחָן
course, dish	mana	מָנָה (נ)
to order (meal)	lehazmin	לְהַזְמִין
to make an order	lehazmin	לְהַזְמִין
aperitif	maʃke meta'aven	מַשְׁקֶה מְתַאֲבֵן (ז)
appetizer	meta'aven	מְתָאֲבֵן (ז)
dessert	ki'nuax	קִינּוּחַ (ז)
check	xeʃbon	חֶשְׁבּוֹן (ז)
to pay the check	leʃalem	לְשַׁלֵּם
to give change	latet 'odef	לָתֵת עוֹדֶף
tip	tip	טִיפ (ז)

50. Meals

food	'oxel	אוֹכֶל (ז)
to eat (vi, vt)	le'exol	לֶאֱכוֹל

breakfast	aruχat 'boker	אֲרוּחַת בּוֹקֶר (ז)
to have breakfast	le'eχol aruχat 'boker	לֶאֱכוֹל אֲרוּחַת בּוֹקֶר
lunch	aruχat tsaha'rayim	אֲרוּחַת צָהֳרַיִם (ז)
to have lunch	le'eχol aruχat tsaha'rayim	לֶאֱכוֹל אֲרוּחַת צָהֳרַיִם
dinner	aruχat 'erev	אֲרוּחַת עֶרֶב (ז)
to have dinner	le'eχol aruχat 'erev	לֶאֱכוֹל אֲרוּחַת עֶרֶב
appetite	te'avon	תֵּיאָבוֹן (ז)
Enjoy your meal!	betei'avon!	בְּתֵיאָבוֹן!
to open (~ a bottle)	lif'toaχ	לִפְתּוֹחַ
to spill (liquid)	liʃpoχ	לִשְׁפּוֹךְ
to spill out (vi)	lehiʃapeχ	לְהִישָׁפֵךְ
to boil (vi)	lir'toaχ	לִרְתּוֹחַ
to boil (vt)	lehar'tiaχ	לְהַרְתִּיחַ
boiled (~ water)	ra'tuaχ	רָתוּחַ
to chill, cool down (vt)	lekarer	לְקָרֵר
to chill (vi)	lehitkarer	לְהִתְקָרֵר
taste, flavor	'ta'am	טַעַם (ז)
aftertaste	'ta'am levai	טַעַם לְוַואי (ז)
to slim down (lose weight)	lirzot	לִרְזוֹת
diet	di''eta	דִּיאָטָה (נ)
vitamin	vitamin	וִיטָמִין (ז)
calorie	ka'lorya	קָלוֹרְיָה (נ)
vegetarian (n)	tsimχoni	צִמְחוֹנִי (ז)
vegetarian (adj)	tsimχoni	צִמְחוֹנִי
fats (nutrient)	ʃumanim	שׁוּמָנִים (ז"ר)
proteins	χelbonim	חֶלְבּוֹנִים (ז"ר)
carbohydrates	paχmema	פַּחְמֵימָה (נ)
slice (of lemon, ham)	prusa	פְּרוּסָה (נ)
piece (of cake, pie)	χatiχa	חֲתִיכָה (נ)
crumb	perur	פֵּירוּר (ז)
(of bread, cake, etc.)		

51. Cooked dishes

course, dish	mana	מָנָה (נ)
cuisine	mitbaχ	מִטְבָּח (ז)
recipe	matkon	מַתְכּוֹן (ז)
portion	mana	מָנָה (נ)
salad	salat	סָלָט (ז)
soup	marak	מָרָק (ז)
clear soup (broth)	marak tsaχ, tsir	מָרָק צַח, צִיר (ז)
sandwich (bread)	kariχ	כָּרִיךְ (ז)

fried eggs	beitsat ain	בֵּיצַת עַיִן (נ)
hamburger (beefburger)	'hamburger	הַמְבּוּרְגֶּר (ז)
beefsteak	umtsa, steik	אוּמְצָה (נ), סְטֵייק (ז)

side dish	to'sefet	תּוֹסֶפֶת (נ)
spaghetti	spa'geti	סְפָּגֶטִי (ז)
mashed potatoes	mexit tapuxei adama	מְחִית תַּפּוּחֵי אֲדָמָה (נ)
pizza	'pitsa	פִּיצָה (נ)
porridge (oatmeal, etc.)	daysa	דַּייסָה (נ)
omelet	xavita	חֲבִיתָה (נ)

boiled (e.g., ~ beef)	mevuʃal	מְבוּשָׁל
smoked (adj)	me'uʃan	מְעוּשָׁן
fried (adj)	metugan	מְטוּגָּן
dried (adj)	meyubaʃ	מְיוּבָּשׁ
frozen (adj)	kafu	קָפוּא
pickled (adj)	kavuʃ	כָּבוּשׁ

sweet (sugary)	matok	מָתוֹק
salty (adj)	ma'luax	מָלוּחַ
cold (adj)	kar	קַר
hot (adj)	xam	חַם
bitter (adj)	marir	מָרִיר
tasty (adj)	ta'im	טָעִים

to cook in boiling water	levaʃel be'mayim rotxim	לְבַשֵּׁל בְּמַיִם רוֹתְחִים
to cook (dinner)	levaʃel	לְבַשֵּׁל
to fry (vt)	letagen	לְטַגֵּן
to heat up (food)	lexamem	לְחַמֵּם

to salt (vt)	leham'liax	לְהַמְלִיחַ
to pepper (vt)	lefalpel	לְפַלְפֵּל
to grate (vt)	lerasek	לְרַסֵּק
peel (n)	klipa	קְלִיפָה (נ)
to peel (vt)	lekalef	לְקַלֵּף

52. Food

meat	basar	בָּשָׂר (ז)
chicken	of	עוֹף (ז)
Rock Cornish hen (poussin)	pargit	פַּרְגִּית (נ)
duck	barvaz	בַּרְווָז (ז)
goose	avaz	אַווָז (ז)
game	'tsayid	צַיִד (ז)
turkey	'hodu	הוֹדוּ (ז)
pork	basar xazir	בָּשָׂר חֲזִיר (ז)
veal	basar 'egel	בָּשָׂר עֵגֶל (ז)
lamb	basar 'keves	בָּשָׂר כֶּבֶשׂ (ז)

beef	bakar	בָּקָר (ז)
rabbit	arnav	אַרְנָב (ז)
sausage (bologna, pepperoni, etc.)	naknik	נַקְנִיק (ז)
vienna sausage (frankfurter)	naknikiya	נַקְנִיקִייָה (נ)
bacon	'kotel χazir	קוֹתֶל חֲזִיר (ז)
ham	basar χazir me'uʃan	בָּשָׂר חֲזִיר מְעוּשָׁן (ז)
gammon	'kotel χazir me'uʃan	קוֹתֶל חֲזִיר מְעוּשָׁן (ז)
pâté	pate	פָּטֶה (ז)
liver	kaved	כָּבֵד (ז)
hamburger (ground beef)	basar taχun	בָּשָׂר טָחוּן (ז)
tongue	laʃon	לָשׁוֹן (נ)
egg	beitsa	בֵּיצָה (נ)
eggs	beitsim	בֵּיצִים (נ-ר)
egg white	χelbon	חֶלְבּוֹן (ז)
egg yolk	χelmon	חֶלְמוֹן (ז)
fish	dag	דָּג (ז)
seafood	perot yam	פֵּירוֹת יָם (ז-ר)
crustaceans	sartana'im	סַרְטָנָאִים (ז-ר)
caviar	kavyar	קָווִיאָר (ז)
crab	sartan yam	סַרְטָן יָם (ז)
shrimp	ʃrimps	שְׁרִימְפְּס (ז-ר)
oyster	tsidpat ma'aχal	צִדְפַּת מַאֲכָל (נ)
spiny lobster	'lobster kotsani	לוֹבְּסְטֶר קוֹצָנִי (ז)
octopus	tamnun	תַּמְנוּן (ז)
squid	kala'mari	קָלָמָארִי (ז)
sturgeon	basar haχidkan	בָּשָׂר הַחִדְקָן (ז)
salmon	'salmon	סַלְמוֹן (ז)
halibut	putit	פּוּטִית (נ)
cod	ʃibut	שִׁיבּוּט (ז)
mackerel	kolyas	קוֹלְיָס (ז)
tuna	'tuna	טוּנָה (נ)
eel	tslofaχ	צְלוֹפָח (ז)
trout	forel	פּוֹרֶל (ז)
sardine	sardin	סַרְדִין (ז)
pike	ze'ev 'mayim	זְאֵב מַיִם (ז)
herring	ma'liaχ	מָלִיחַ (ז)
bread	'leχem	לֶחֶם (ז)
cheese	gvina	גבִינָה (נ)
sugar	sukar	סוּכָּר (ז)
salt	'melaχ	מֶלַח (ז)
rice	'orez	אוֹרֶז (ז)

pasta (macaroni)	'pasta	פַּסְטָה (נ)
noodles	irtiyot	אִטְרִיּוֹת (נ־ר)
butter	xem'a	חֶמְאָה (נ)
vegetable oil	ʃemen tsimxi	שֶׁמֶן צִמְחִי (ז)
sunflower oil	ʃemen xamaniyot	שֶׁמֶן חַמָּנִיּוֹת (ז)
margarine	marga'rina	מַרְגָּרִינָה (נ)
olives	zeitim	זֵיתִים (ז־ר)
olive oil	ʃemen 'zayit	שֶׁמֶן זַיִת (ז)
milk	xalav	חָלָב (ז)
condensed milk	xalav merukaz	חָלָב מְרוּכָּז (ז)
yogurt	'yogurt	יוֹגוּרט (ז)
sour cream	ʃa'menet	שַׁמֶּנֶת (נ)
cream (of milk)	ʃa'menet	שַׁמֶּנֶת (נ)
mayonnaise	mayonez	מָיוֹנֶז (ז)
buttercream	ka'tsefet xem'a	קַצֶּפֶת חֶמְאָה (נ)
cereal grains (wheat, etc.)	grisim	גְּרִיסִים (ז־ר)
flour	'kemax	קֶמַח (ז)
canned food	ʃimurim	שִׁימּוּרִים (ז־ר)
cornflakes	ptitei 'tiras	פְּתִיתֵי תִּירָס (ז־ר)
honey	dvaʃ	דְּבַשׁ (ז)
jam	riba	רִיבָּה (נ)
chewing gum	'mastik	מַסְטִיק (ז)

53. Drinks

water	'mayim	מַיִם (ז־ר)
drinking water	mei ʃtiya	מֵי שְׁתִיָּה (ז־ר)
mineral water	'mayim mine'raliyim	מַיִם מִינֵרָלִיִּים (ז־ר)
still (adj)	lo mugaz	לֹא מוּגָז
carbonated (adj)	mugaz	מוּגָז
sparkling (adj)	mugaz	מוּגָז
ice	'kerax	קֶרַח (ז)
with ice	im 'kerax	עִם קֶרַח
non-alcoholic (adj)	natul alkohol	נְטוּל אֲלְכּוֹהוֹל
soft drink	maʃke kal	מַשְׁקֶה קַל (ז)
refreshing drink	maʃke mera'anen	מַשְׁקֶה מְרַעֲנֵן (ז)
lemonade	limo'nada	לִימוֹנָדָה (נ)
liquors	maʃka'ot xarifim	מַשְׁקָאוֹת חֲרִיפִים (ז־ר)
wine	'yayin	יַיִן (ז)
white wine	'yayin lavan	יַיִן לָבָן (ז)
red wine	'yayin adom	יַיִן אָדוֹם (ז)

liqueur	liker	ליקר (ז)
champagne	ʃam'panya	שמפניה (נ)
vermouth	'vermut	ורמוט (ז)

whiskey	'viski	ויסקי (ז)
vodka	'vodka	וודקה (נ)
gin	dʒin	ג׳ין (ז)
cognac	'konyak	קוניאק (ז)
rum	rom	רום (ז)

coffee	kafe	קפה (ז)
black coffee	kafe ʃaxor	קפה שחור (ז)
coffee with milk	kafe hafux	קפה הפוך (ז)
cappuccino	kapu'tʃino	קפוצ׳ינו (ז)
instant coffee	kafe names	קפה נמס (ז)

milk	xalav	חלב (ז)
cocktail	kokteil	קוקטייל (ז)
milkshake	'milkʃeik	מילקשייק (ז)

juice	mits	מיץ (ז)
tomato juice	mits agvaniyot	מיץ עגבניות (ז)
orange juice	mits tapuzim	מיץ תפוזים (ז)
freshly squeezed juice	mits saxut	מיץ סחוט (ז)

beer	'bira	בירה (נ)
light beer	'bira bahira	בירה בהירה (נ)
dark beer	'bira keha	בירה כהה (נ)

tea	te	תה (ז)
black tea	te ʃaxor	תה שחור (ז)
green tea	te yarok	תה ירוק (ז)

54. Vegetables

| vegetables | yerakot | ירקות (ז״ר) |
| greens | 'yerek | ירק (ז) |

tomato	agvaniya	עגבנייה (נ)
cucumber	melafefon	מלפפון (ז)
carrot	'gezer	גזר (ז)
potato	ta'puax adama	תפוח אדמה (ז)
onion	batsal	בצל (ז)
garlic	ʃum	שום (ז)

cabbage	kruv	כרוב (ז)
cauliflower	kruvit	כרובית (נ)
Brussels sprouts	kruv nitsanim	כרוב ניצנים (ז)
broccoli	'brokoli	ברוקולי (ז)
beetroot	'selek	סלק (ז)

eggplant	χatsil	(ז) חָצִיל
zucchini	kiʃu	(ז) קִישׁוּא
pumpkin	'dla'at	(נ) דְּלַעַת
turnip	'lefet	(נ) לֶפֶת

parsley	petro'zilya	(נ) פֶּטְרוֹזִילְיָה
dill	ʃamir	(ז) שָׁמִיר
lettuce	'χasa	(נ) חַסָּה
celery	'seleri	(ז) סֶלֶרִי
asparagus	aspa'ragos	(ז) אַסְפָּרָגוֹס
spinach	'tered	(ז) תֶּרֶד

pea	afuna	(נ) אֲפוּנָה
beans	pol	(ז) פּוֹל
corn (maize)	'tiras	(ז) תִּירָס
kidney bean	ʃu'it	(נ) שְׁעוּעִית

bell pepper	'pilpel	(ז) פִּלְפֵּל
radish	tsnonit	(נ) צְנוֹנִית
artichoke	artiʃok	(ז) אַרְטִישׁוֹק

55. Fruits. Nuts

fruit	pri	(ז) פְּרִי
apple	ta'puaχ	(ז) תַּפּוּחַ
pear	agas	(ז) אַגָּס
lemon	limon	(ז) לִימוֹן
orange	tapuz	(ז) תַּפּוּז
strawberry (garden ~)	tut sade	(ז) תּוּת שָׂדֶה

mandarin	klemen'tina	(נ) קְלֶמֶנְטִינָה
plum	ʃezif	(ז) שְׁזִיף
peach	afarsek	(ז) אֲפַרְסֵק
apricot	'miʃmeʃ	(ז) מִשְׁמֵשׁ
raspberry	'petel	(ז) פֶּטֶל
pineapple	'ananas	(ז) אַנָּנָס

banana	ba'nana	(נ) בַּנָּנָה
watermelon	ava'tiaχ	(ז) אֲבַטִּיחַ
grape	anavim	(ז-ר) עֲנָבִים
sour cherry	duvdevan	(ז) דּוּבְדְּבָן
sweet cherry	gudgedan	(ז) גּוּדְגְּדָן
melon	melon	(ז) מֶלוֹן

grapefruit	eʃkolit	(נ) אֶשְׁכּוֹלִית
avocado	avo'kado	(ז) אֲבוֹקָדוֹ
papaya	pa'paya	(נ) פַּפָּאיָה
mango	'mango	(ז) מַנְגּוֹ
pomegranate	rimon	(ז) רִימוֹן
redcurrant	dumdemanit aduma	(נ) דּוּמְדְּמָנִית אֲדוּמָה

blackcurrant	dumdemanit ʃxora	דומדמנית שחורה (נ)
gooseberry	xazarzar	חֲזַרְזַר (ז)
bilberry	uxmanit	אוכְמָנִית (נ)
blackberry	'petel ʃaxor	פֶּטֶל שָׁחוֹר (ז)
raisin	tsimukim	צִימוּקִים (ז״ר)
fig	te'ena	תְּאֵנָה (נ)
date	tamar	תָּמָר (ז)
peanut	botnim	בּוֹטְנִים (ז״ר)
almond	ʃaked	שָׁקֵד (ז)
walnut	egoz 'melex	אֱגוֹז מֶלֶךְ (ז)
hazelnut	egoz ilsar	אֱגוֹז אִלְסָר (ז)
coconut	'kokus	קוֹקוּס (ז)
pistachios	'fistuk	פִּיסְטוּק (ז)

56. Bread. Candy

bakers' confectionery (pastry)	mutsrei kondi'torya	מוּצְרֵי קוֹנְדִיטוֹרְיָה (ז״ר)
bread	'lexem	לֶחֶם (ז)
cookies	ugiya	עוּגִיָּה (נ)
chocolate (n)	'ʃokolad	שׁוֹקוֹלָד (ז)
chocolate (as adj)	mi'ʃokolad	מְשׁוֹקוֹלָד
candy (wrapped)	sukariya	סוּכָּרִיָּה (נ)
cake (e.g., cupcake)	uga	עוּגָה (נ)
cake (e.g., birthday ~)	uga	עוּגָה (נ)
pie (e.g., apple ~)	pai	פַּאי (ז)
filling (for cake, pie)	milui	מִילּוּי (ז)
jam (whole fruit jam)	riba	רִיבָּה (נ)
marmalade	marme'lada	מַרְמֶלָדָה (נ)
waffles	'vaflim	וָפְלִים (ז״ר)
ice-cream	'glida	גְּלִידָה (נ)
pudding	'puding	פּוּדִינְג (ז)

57. Spices

salt	'melax	מֶלַח (ז)
salty (adj)	ma'luax	מָלוּחַ
to salt (vt)	leham'liax	לְהַמְלִיחַ
black pepper	'pilpel ʃaxor	פִּלְפֵּל שָׁחוֹר (ז)
red pepper (milled ~)	'pilpel adom	פִּלְפֵּל אָדוֹם (ז)
mustard	xardal	חַרְדָּל (ז)
horseradish	xa'zeret	חֲזֶרֶת (נ)

condiment	'rotev	רוֹטֶב (ז)
spice	tavlin	תַבלין (ז)
sauce	'rotev	רוֹטֶב (ז)
vinegar	'χomets	חוֹמֶץ (ז)
anise	kamnon	כַּמנוֹן (ז)
basil	reχan	רֵיחָן (ז)
cloves	tsi'poren	צִיפּוֹרֶן (ז)
ginger	'dʒindʒer	ג׳ינג׳ר (ז)
coriander	'kusbara	כּוּסבָּרָה (נ)
cinnamon	kinamon	קינָמוֹן (ז)
sesame	'ʃumʃum	שומשום (ז)
bay leaf	ale dafna	עָלֶה דַפנָה (ז)
paprika	'paprika	פַּפּרִיקה (נ)
caraway	'kimel	קימֶל (ז)
saffron	ze'afran	זַעֲפרָן (ז)

PERSONAL
INFORMATION. FAMILY

T&P Books Publishing

58. Personal information. Forms

name (first name)	ʃem	שֵׁם (ז)
surname (last name)	ʃem miʃpaχa	שֵׁם מִשְׁפָּחָה (ז)
date of birth	ta'ariχ leda	תַּאֲרִיךְ לֵידָה (ז)
place of birth	mekom leda	מְקוֹם לֵידָה (ז)
nationality	le'om	לְאוֹם (ז)
place of residence	mekom megurim	מְקוֹם מְגוּרִים (ז)
country	medina	מְדִינָה (נ)
profession (occupation)	mik'tso'a	מִקְצוֹעַ (ז)
gender, sex	min	מִין (ז)
height	'gova	גּוֹבַה (ז)
weight	miʃkal	מִשְׁקָל (ז)

59. Family members. Relatives

mother	em	אֵם (נ)
father	av	אָב (ז)
son	ben	בֵּן (ז)
daughter	bat	בַּת (נ)
younger daughter	habat haktana	הַבַּת הַקְּטַנָה (נ)
younger son	haben hakatan	הַבֵּן הַקָּטָן (ז)
eldest daughter	habat habχora	הַבַּת הַבְּכוֹרָה (נ)
eldest son	haben habχor	הַבֵּן הַבְּכוֹר (ז)
brother	aχ	אָח (ז)
elder brother	aχ gadol	אָח גָּדוֹל (ז)
younger brother	aχ katan	אָח קָטָן (ז)
sister	aχot	אָחוֹת (נ)
elder sister	aχot gdola	אָחוֹת גְּדוֹלָה (נ)
younger sister	aχot ktana	אָחוֹת קְטַנָה (נ)
cousin (masc.)	ben dod	בֶּן דּוֹד (ז)
cousin (fem.)	bat 'doda	בַּת דּוֹדָה (נ)
mom, mommy	'ima	אִמָּא (נ)
dad, daddy	'aba	אַבָּא (ז)
parents	horim	הוֹרִים (ז״ר)
child	'yeled	יֶלֶד (ז)
children	yeladim	יְלָדִים (ז״ר)
grandmother	'savta	סָבְתָא (נ)
grandfather	'saba	סָבָא (ז)

156

grandson	'neχed	נֶכֶד (ז)
granddaughter	neχda	נֶבְדָּה (נ)
grandchildren	neχadim	נְכָדִים (ז״ר)
uncle	dod	דּוֹד (ז)
aunt	'doda	דּוֹדָה (נ)
nephew	aχyan	אַחְיָן (ז)
niece	aχyanit	אַחְיָנִית (נ)
mother-in-law (wife's mother)	χamot	חָמוֹת (נ)
father-in-law (husband's father)	χam	חָם (ז)
son-in-law (daughter's husband)	χatan	חָתָן (ז)
stepmother	em χoreget	אֵם חוֹרֶגֶת (נ)
stepfather	av χoreg	אָב חוֹרֵג (ז)
infant	tinok	תִּינוֹק (ז)
baby (infant)	tinok	תִּינוֹק (ז)
little boy, kid	pa'ot	פָּעוֹט (ז)
wife	iʃa	אִשָּׁה (נ)
husband	'ba‘al	בַּעַל (ז)
spouse (husband)	ben zug	בֶּן זוּג (ז)
spouse (wife)	bat zug	בַּת זוּג (נ)
married (masc.)	nasui	נָשׂוּי
married (fem.)	nesu'a	נְשׂוּאָה
single (unmarried)	ravak	רַוָּק
bachelor	ravak	רַוָּק (ז)
divorced (masc.)	garuʃ	גָּרוּשׁ
widow	almana	אַלְמָנָה (נ)
widower	alman	אַלְמָן (ז)
relative	karov miʃpaχa	קָרוֹב מִשְׁפָּחָה (ז)
close relative	karov miʃpaχa	קָרוֹב מִשְׁפָּחָה (ז)
distant relative	karov raχok	קָרוֹב רָחוֹק (ז)
relatives	krovei miʃpaχa	קְרוֹבֵי מִשְׁפָּחָה (ז״ר)
orphan (boy)	yatom	יָתוֹם (ז)
orphan (girl)	yetoma	יְתוֹמָה (נ)
guardian (of a minor)	apo'tropos	אַפּוֹטְרוֹפּוֹס (ז)
to adopt (a boy)	le'amets	לְאַמֵּץ
to adopt (a girl)	le'amets	לְאַמֵּץ

60. Friends. Coworkers

| friend (masc.) | χaver | חָבֵר (ז) |
| friend (fem.) | χavera | חֲבֵרָה (נ) |

friendship	yedidut	יְדִידוּת (נ)
to be friends	lihyot yadidim	לִהְיוֹת יָדִידִים
buddy (masc.)	xaver	חָבֵר (ז)
buddy (fem.)	xavera	חֲבֵרָה (נ)
partner	ʃutaf	שׁוֹתָף (ז)
chief (boss)	menahel, roʃ	מְנַהֵל (ז), רֹאשׁ (ז)
superior (n)	memune	מְמוּנֶה (ז)
owner, proprietor	be'alim	בְּעָלִים (ז)
subordinate (n)	kafuf le	כָּפוּף ל (ז)
colleague	amit	עָמִית (ז)
acquaintance (person)	makar	מַכָּר (ז)
fellow traveler	ben levaya	בֶּן לְוָיָה (ז)
classmate	xaver lekita	חָבֵר לְכִּיתָה (ז)
neighbor (masc.)	ʃaxen	שָׁכֵן (ז)
neighbor (fem.)	ʃxena	שׁכֵנָה (נ)
neighbors	ʃxenim	שׁכֵנִים (ז-ר)

HUMAN BODY.
MEDICINE

T&P Books Publishing

61. Head

head	roʃ	רֹאשׁ (ז)
face	panim	פָּנִים (ז״ר)
nose	af	אַף (ז)
mouth	pe	פֶּה (ז)
eye	'ayin	עַיִן (נ)
eyes	ei'nayim	עֵינַיִים (נ״ר)
pupil	iʃon	אִישׁוֹן (ז)
eyebrow	gaba	גַּבָּה (נ)
eyelash	ris	רִיס (ז)
eyelid	af'af	עַפְעַף (ז)
tongue	laʃon	לָשׁוֹן (נ)
tooth	ʃen	שֵׁן (נ)
lips	sfa'tayim	שְׂפָתַיִים (נ״ר)
cheekbones	atsamot leχa'yayim	עַצְמוֹת לְחָיַים (נ״ר)
gum	χani'χayim	חֲנִיכַיִים (ז״ר)
palate	χeχ	חֵךְ (ז)
nostrils	neχi'rayim	נְחִירַיִים (ז״ר)
chin	santer	סַנְטֵר (ז)
jaw	'leset	לֶסֶת (נ)
cheek	'leχi	לֶחִי (נ)
forehead	'metsaχ	מֵצַח (ז)
temple	raka	רַקָּה (נ)
ear	'ozen	אֹוֹזֶן (נ)
back of the head	'oref	עֹרֶף (ז)
neck	tsavar	צַוָּאר (ז)
throat	garon	גָּרוֹן (ז)
hair	se'ar	שֵׂיעָר (ז)
hairstyle	tis'roket	תִּסְרוֹקֶת (נ)
haircut	tis'poret	תִּסְפֹּרֶת (נ)
wig	pe'a	פֵּאָה (נ)
mustache	safam	שָׂפָם (ז)
beard	zakan	זָקָן (ז)
to have (a beard, etc.)	legadel	לְגַדֵּל
braid	tsama	צַמָּה (נ)
sideburns	pe'ot leχa'yayim	פֵּאוֹת לְחָיַים (נ״ר)
red-haired (adj)	'dʒindʒi	גִּ'ינגִ'י
gray (hair)	kasuf	כָּסוּף

bald (adj)	ke'reaχ	קֵירֵחַ
bald patch	ka'raχat	קָרַחַת (נ)
ponytail	'kuku	קוּקוּ (ז)
bangs	'poni	פּוֹנִי (ז)

62. Human body

hand	kaf yad	כַּף יָד (נ)
arm	yad	יָד (נ)
finger	'etsba	אֶצְבַּע (נ)
toe	'bohen	בּוֹהֶן (נ)
thumb	agudal	אֲגוּדָל (ז)
little finger	'zeret	זֶרֶת (נ)
nail	tsi'poren	צִיפּוֹרֶן (נ)
fist	egrof	אֶגְרוֹף (ז)
palm	kaf yad	כַּף יָד (נ)
wrist	'ʃoreʃ kaf hayad	שׁוֹרֶשׁ כַּף הַיָד (ז)
forearm	ama	אַמָה (נ)
elbow	marpek	מַרְפֵּק (ז)
shoulder	katef	כָּתֵף (נ)
leg	'regel	רֶגֶל (נ)
foot	kaf 'regel	כַּף רֶגֶל (נ)
knee	'bereχ	בֶּרֶךְ (נ)
calf (part of leg)	ʃok	שׁוֹק (נ)
hip	yareχ	יָרֵךְ (ז)
heel	akev	עָקֵב (ז)
body	guf	גוּף (ז)
stomach	'beten	בֶּטֶן (נ)
chest	χaze	חָזֶה (ז)
breast	ʃad	שַׁד (ז)
flank	tsad	צַד (ז)
back	gav	גַב (ז)
lower back	mot'nayim	מוֹתְנַיִים (ז״ר)
waist	'talya	טַלְיָה (נ)
navel (belly button)	tabur	טַבּוּר (ז)
buttocks	aχo'rayim	אֲחוֹרַיִים (ז״ר)
bottom	yaʃvan	יַשְׁבָן (ז)
beauty mark	nekudat χen	נְקוּדַת חֵן (נ)
birthmark (café au lait spot)	'ketem leida	כֶּתֶם לֵידָה (ז)
tattoo	ka'a'ku'a	קַעֲקוּעַ (ז)
scar	tsa'leket	צַלֶקֶת (נ)

63. Diseases

sickness	maχala	מַחֲלָה (נ)
to be sick	lihyot χole	לִהְיוֹת חוֹלֶה
health	bri'ut	בְּרִיאוּת (נ)
runny nose (coryza)	na'zelet	נַזֶּלֶת (נ)
tonsillitis	da'leket ʃkedim	דַּלֶּקֶת שְׁקֵדִים (נ)
cold (illness)	hitstanenut	הִצְטַנְּנוּת (נ)
to catch a cold	lehitstanen	לְהִצְטַנֵּן
bronchitis	bron'χitis	בְּרוֹנְכִיטִיס (ז)
pneumonia	da'leket re'ot	דַּלֶּקֶת רֵיאוֹת (נ)
flu, influenza	ʃa'pa'at	שַׁפַּעַת (נ)
nearsighted (adj)	ktsar re'iya	קְצַר רְאִיָּה
farsighted (adj)	reχok re'iya	רְחוֹק־רְאִיָּה
strabismus (crossed eyes)	pzila	פְּזִילָה (נ)
cross-eyed (adj)	pozel	פּוֹזֵל
cataract	katarakt	קָטָרַקְט (ז)
glaucoma	gla'u'koma	גְּלָאוּקוֹמָה (נ)
stroke	ʃavats moχi	שָׁבָץ מוֹחִי (ז)
heart attack	hetkef lev	הֶתְקֵף לֵב (ז)
myocardial infarction	'otem ʃrir halev	אוֹטֶם שְׁרִיר הַלֵּב (ז)
paralysis	ʃituk	שִׁיתּוּק (ז)
to paralyze (vt)	leʃatek	לְשַׁתֵּק
allergy	a'lergya	אֲלֶרְגְּיָה (נ)
asthma	'astma, ka'tseret	אַסְתְמָה, קַצֶּרֶת (נ)
diabetes	su'keret	סוּכֶּרֶת (נ)
toothache	ke'ev ʃi'nayim	כְּאֵב שִׁינַיִים (ז)
caries	a'ʃeʃet	עֲשֶׁשֶׁת (נ)
diarrhea	ʃilʃul	שִׁלְשׁוּל (ז)
constipation	atsirut	עֲצִירוּת (נ)
stomach upset	kilkul keiva	קִלְקוּל קֵיבָה (ז)
food poisoning	har'alat mazon	הַרְעָלַת מָזוֹן (נ)
to get food poisoning	laχatof har'alat mazon	לַחֲטוֹף הַרְעָלַת מָזוֹן
arthritis	da'leket mifrakim	דַּלֶּקֶת מִפְרָקִים (נ)
rickets	ra'keχet	רַכֶּכֶת (נ)
rheumatism	ʃigaron	שִׁיגָּרוֹן (ז)
atherosclerosis	ar'teryo skle'rosis	אַרְטֶרְיוֹ־סְקְלֶרוֹסִיס (ז)
gastritis	da'leket keiva	דַּלֶּקֶת קֵיבָה (נ)
appendicitis	da'leket toseftan	דַּלֶּקֶת תּוֹסֶפְתָּן (נ)
cholecystitis	da'leket kis hamara	דַּלֶּקֶת כִּיס הַמָּרָה (נ)
ulcer	'ulkus, kiv	אוּלְקוּס, כִּיב (ז)
measles	χa'tsevet	חַצֶּבֶת (נ)

rubella (German measles)	a'demet	אַדֶּמֶת (נ)
jaundice	tsa'hevet	צַהֶבֶת (נ)
hepatitis	da'leket kaved	דַּלֶּקֶת כָּבֵד (נ)
schizophrenia	sχizo'frenya	סכִיזוֹפרֶניָה (נ)
rabies (hydrophobia)	ka'levet	כַּלֶּבֶת (נ)
neurosis	noi'roza	נוֹירוֹזָה (נ)
concussion	za'a'zu'a 'moaχ	זַעֲזוּעַ מוֹחַ (ז)
cancer	sartan	סַרטָן (ז)
sclerosis	ta'refet	טָרֶשֶׁת (נ)
multiple sclerosis	ta'refet nefotsa	טָרֶשֶׁת נְפוֹצָה (נ)
alcoholism	alkoholizm	אַלכּוֹהוֹלִיזם (ז)
alcoholic (n)	alkoholist	אַלכּוֹהוֹלִיסט (ז)
syphilis	a'gevet	עַגֶּבֶת (נ)
AIDS	eids	אֵיידס (ז)
tumor	gidul	גִּידוּל (ז)
malignant (adj)	mam'ir	מַמאִיר
benign (adj)	ʃapir	שַׁפִּיר
fever	ka'daχat	קַדַּחַת (נ)
malaria	ma'larya	מָלַריָה (נ)
gangrene	gan'grena	גַּנגרֶנָה (נ)
seasickness	maχalat yam	מַחֲלַת יָם (נ)
epilepsy	maχalat hanefila	מַחֲלַת הַנְּפִילָה (נ)
epidemic	magefa	מַגֵּיפָה (נ)
typhus	'tifus	טִיפוּס (ז)
tuberculosis	ʃa'χefet	שַׁחֶפֶת (נ)
cholera	ko'lera	כּוֹלֵרָה (נ)
plague (bubonic ~)	davar	דֶּבֶר (ז)

64. Symptoms. Treatments. Part 1

symptom	simptom	סִימפּטוֹם (ז)
temperature	χom	חוֹם (ז)
high temperature (fever)	χom ga'voha	חוֹם גָּבוֹהַּ (ז)
pulse	'dofek	דּוֹפֶק (ז)
dizziness (vertigo)	sχar'χoret	סחַרחוֹרֶת (נ)
hot (adj)	χam	חַם
shivering	tsmar'moret	צְמַרמוֹרֶת (נ)
pale (e.g., ~ face)	χiver	חִיוֵּר
cough	ʃi'ul	שִׁיעוּל (ז)
to cough (vi)	lehiʃta'el	לְהִשׁתַּעֵל
to sneeze (vi)	lehit'ateʃ	לְהִתעַטֵּשׁ
faint	ilafon	עִילָפוֹן (ז)

to faint (vi)	lehit'alef	לְהִתעַלֵף
bruise (hématome)	χabura	חַבּוּרָה (נ)
bump (lump)	blita	בּלִיטָה (נ)
to bang (bump)	lekabel maka	לְקַבֵּל מַכָּה
contusion (bruise)	maka	מַכָּה (נ)
to get a bruise	lekabel maka	לְקַבֵּל מַכָּה

to limp (vi)	lits'lo'a	לְצלוֹעַ
dislocation	'neka	נֶקַע (ז)
to dislocate (vt)	lin'ko'a	לִנקוֹעַ
fracture	'ʃever	שֶבֶר (ז)
to have a fracture	liʃbor	לִשבּוֹר

cut (e.g., paper ~)	χataχ	חָתָך (ז)
to cut oneself	lehiχateχ	לְהִיחָתֵך
bleeding	dimum	דִימוּם (ז)

| burn (injury) | kviya | כּוֹוִיָיה (נ) |
| to get burned | laχatof kviya | לַחֲטוֹף כּוֹוִיָיה |

to prick (vt)	lidkor	לִדקוֹר
to prick oneself	lehidaker	לְהִידָקֵר
to injure (vt)	lif'tso'a	לִפצוֹעַ
injury	ptsi'a	פּצִיעָה (נ)
wound	'petsa	פֶּצַע (ז)
trauma	'tra'uma	טרָאוּמָה (נ)

to be delirious	lahazot	לַהֲזוֹת
to stutter (vi)	legamgem	לְגַמגֵם
sunstroke	makat 'ʃemeʃ	מַכַּת שֶמֶש (נ)

65. Symptoms. Treatments. Part 2

| pain, ache | ke'ev | כּאֵב (ז) |
| splinter (in foot, etc.) | kots | קוֹץ (ז) |

sweat (perspiration)	ze'a	זֵיעָה (נ)
to sweat (perspire)	leha'zi'a	לְהַזִיעַ
vomiting	haka'a	הֲקָאָה (נ)
convulsions	pirkusim	פִּירכּוּסִים (ז-ר)

pregnant (adj)	hara	הָרָה
to be born	lehivaled	לְהִיוָולֵד
delivery, labor	leda	לֵידָה (נ)
to deliver (~ a baby)	la'ledet	לָלֶדֶת
abortion	hapala	הַפָּלָה (נ)

breathing, respiration	neʃima	נְשִימָה (נ)
in-breath (inhalation)	ʃe'ifa	שְאִיפָה (נ)
out-breath (exhalation)	neʃifa	נְשִיפָה (נ)

to exhale (breathe out)	linʃof	לִנְשׁוֹף
to inhale (vi)	liʃof	לִשְׁאוֹף
disabled person	naχe	נָכֶה (ז)
cripple	naχe	נָכֶה (ז)
drug addict	narkoman	נַרְקוֹמָן (ז)
deaf (adj)	χereʃ	חֵירֵשׁ
mute (adj)	ilem	אִילֵם
deaf mute (adj)	χereʃ-ilem	חֵירֵשׁ־אִילֵם
mad, insane (adj)	meʃuga	מְשׁוּגָע
madman (demented person)	meʃuga	מְשׁוּגָע (ז)
madwoman	meʃu'ga'at	מְשׁוּגַעַת (נ)
to go insane	lehiʃta'ge'a	לְהִשְׁתַּגֵּעַ
gene	gen	גֵּן (ז)
immunity	χasinut	חֲסִינוּת (נ)
hereditary (adj)	toraʃti	תּוֹרַשְׁתִּי
congenital (adj)	mulad	מוּלָד
virus	'virus	וִירוּס (ז)
microbe	χaidak	חַיְידַק (ז)
bacterium	bak'terya	בַּקְטֶרְיָה (נ)
infection	zihum	זִיהוּם (ז)

66. Symptoms. Treatments. Part 3

hospital	beit χolim	בֵּית חוֹלִים (ז)
patient	metupal	מְטוּפָּל (ז)
diagnosis	avχana	אַבְחָנָה (נ)
cure	ripui	רִיפּוּי (ז)
medical treatment	tipul refu'i	טִיפּוּל רְפוּאִי (ז)
to get treatment	lekabel tipul	לְקַבֵּל טִיפּוּל
to treat (~ a patient)	letapel be…	לְטַפֵּל בְּ…
to nurse (look after)	letapel be…	לְטַפֵּל בְּ…
care (nursing ~)	tipul	טִיפּוּל (ז)
operation, surgery	ni'tuaχ	נִיתוּחַ (ז)
to bandage (head, limb)	laχboʃ	לַחְבּוֹשׁ
bandaging	χaviʃa	חֲבִישָׁה (נ)
vaccination	χisun	חִיסוּן (ז)
to vaccinate (vt)	leχasen	לְחַסֵּן
injection, shot	zrika	זְרִיקָה (נ)
to give an injection	lehazrik	לְהַזְרִיק
attack	hetkef	הֶתְקֵף (ז)
amputation	kti'a	קְטִיעָה (נ)

to amputate (vt)	lik'to'a	לִקְטוֹעַ
coma	tar'demet	תַּרְדֶּמֶת (נ)
to be in a coma	lihyot betar'demet	לִהְיוֹת בְּתַרְדֶּמֶת
intensive care	tipul nimrats	טִיפּוּל נִמְרָץ (ז)

to recover (~ from flu)	lehaχlim	לְהַחְלִים
condition (patient's ~)	matsav	מַצָּב (ז)
consciousness	hakara	הַכָּרָה (נ)
memory (faculty)	zikaron	זִיכָּרוֹן (ז)

to pull out (tooth)	la'akor	לַעֲקוֹר
filling	stima	סְתִימָה (נ)
to fill (a tooth)	la'asot stima	לַעֲשׂוֹת סְתִימָה

| hypnosis | hip'noza | הִיפְּנוֹזָה (נ) |
| to hypnotize (vt) | lehapnet | לְהַפְנֵט |

67. Medicine. Drugs. Accessories

medicine, drug	trufa	תְּרוּפָה (נ)
remedy	trufa	תְּרוּפָה (נ)
to prescribe (vt)	lirʃom	לִרְשׁוֹם
prescription	mirʃam	מִרְשָׁם (ז)

tablet, pill	kadur	כַּדּוּר (ז)
ointment	miʃχa	מִשְׁחָה (נ)
ampule	'ampula	אַמְפּוּלָה (נ)
mixture	ta'a'rovet	תַּעֲרוֹבֶת (נ)
syrup	sirop	סִירוֹפּ (ז)
pill	gluya	גְּלוּיָה (נ)
powder	avka	אַבְקָה (נ)

gauze bandage	taχ'boʃet 'gaza	תַּחְבּוֹשֶׁת גָּאזָה (נ)
cotton wool	'tsemer 'gefen	צֶמֶר גֶּפֶן (ז)
iodine	yod	יוֹד (ז)

| Band-Aid | 'plaster | פְּלַסְטֶר (ז) |
| eyedropper | taf'tefet | טַפְטֶפֶת (נ) |

| thermometer | madχom | מַדְחוֹם (ז) |
| syringe | mazrek | מַזְרֵק (ז) |

| wheelchair | kise galgalim | כִּיסֵא גַּלְגַּלִים (ז) |
| crutches | ka'bayim | קַבַּיִים (ז"ר) |

painkiller	meʃakeχ ke'evim	מְשַׁכֵּךְ כְּאֵבִים (ז)
laxative	trufa meʃal'ʃelet	תְּרוּפָה מְשַׁלְשֶׁלֶת (נ)
spirits (ethanol)	'kohal	כּוֹהַל (ז)
medicinal herbs	isvei marpe	עִשְׂבֵי מַרְפֵּא (ז"ר)
herbal (~ tea)	ʃel asavim	שֶׁל עֲשָׂבִים

APARTMENT

T&P Books Publishing

68. Apartment

apartment	dira	דִּירָה (נ)
room	'xeder	חֶדֶר (ז)
bedroom	xadar ʃena	חֲדַר שֵׁינָה (ז)
dining room	pinat 'oxel	פִּינַת אוֹכֶל (נ)
living room	salon	סָלוֹן (ז)
study (home office)	xadar avoda	חֲדַר עֲבוֹדָה (ז)
entry room	prozdor	פְּרוֹזְדוֹר (ז)
bathroom (room with a bath or shower)	xadar am'batya	חֲדַר אַמְבַּטְיָה (ז)
half bath	ʃerutim	שֵׁירוּתִים (ז״ר)
ceiling	tikra	תִּקְרָה (נ)
floor	ritspa	רִצְפָּה (נ)
corner	pina	פִּינָה (נ)

69. Furniture. Interior

furniture	rehitim	רָהִיטִים (ז״ר)
table	ʃulxan	שׁוּלְחָן (ז)
chair	kise	כִּסֵא (ז)
bed	mita	מִיטָה (נ)
couch, sofa	sapa	סַפָּה (נ)
armchair	kursa	כּוּרְסָה (נ)
bookcase	aron sfarim	אֲרוֹן סְפָרִים (ז)
shelf	madaf	מַדָּף (ז)
wardrobe	aron bgadim	אֲרוֹן בְּגָדִים (ז)
coat rack (wall-mounted ~)	mitle	מִתְלֶה (ז)
coat stand	mitle	מִתְלֶה (ז)
bureau, dresser	ʃida	שִׁידָה (נ)
coffee table	ʃulxan itonim	שׁוּלְחָן עִיתּוֹנִים (ז)
mirror	mar'a	מַרְאָה (נ)
carpet	ʃa'tiax	שָׁטִיחַ (ז)
rug, small carpet	ʃa'tiax	שָׁטִיחַ (ז)
fireplace	ax	אָח (נ)
candle	ner	נֵר (ז)
candlestick	pamot	פָּמוֹט (ז)

drapes	vilonot	וִילוֹנוֹת (ז״ר)
wallpaper	tapet	טַפֶּט (ז)
blinds (jalousie)	trisim	תְּרִיסִים (ז״ר)
table lamp	menorat ʃulχan	מְנוֹרַת שׁוּלחָן (נ)
wall lamp (sconce)	menorat kir	מְנוֹרַת קִיר (נ)
floor lamp	menora o'medet	מְנוֹרָה עוֹמֶדֶת (נ)
chandelier	niv'reʃet	נִבְרֶשֶׁת (נ)
leg (of chair, table)	'regel	רֶגֶל (נ)
armrest	miʃ'enet yad	מִשׁעֶנֶת יָד (נ)
back (backrest)	miʃ'enet	מִשׁעֶנֶת (נ)
drawer	megera	מְגֵירָה (נ)

70. Bedding

bedclothes	matsa'im	מַצָּעִים (ז״ר)
pillow	karit	כָּרִית (נ)
pillowcase	tsipit	צִיפִּית (נ)
duvet, comforter	smiχa	שׂמִיכָה (נ)
sheet	sadin	סָדִין (ז)
bedspread	kisui mita	כִּיסוּי מִיטָה (ז)

71. Kitchen

kitchen	mitbaχ	מִטבָּח (ז)
gas	gaz	גָּז (ז)
gas stove (range)	tanur gaz	תַּנוּר גָּז (ז)
electric stove	tanur χaʃmali	תַּנוּר חַשׁמַלִי (ז)
oven	tanur afiya	תַּנוּר אֲפִייָה (ז)
microwave oven	mikrogal	מִיקרוֹגַל (ז)
refrigerator	mekarer	מְקָרֵר (ז)
freezer	makpi	מַקפִּיא (ז)
dishwasher	me'diaχ kelim	מֵדִיחַ כֵּלִים (ז)
meat grinder	matχenat basar	מַטחֵנַת בָּשָׂר (נ)
juicer	masχeta	מַסחֵטָה (נ)
toaster	'toster	טוֹסטֶר (ז)
mixer	'mikser	מִיקסֶר (ז)
coffee machine	meχonat kafe	מְכוֹנַת קָפֶה (נ)
coffee pot	findʒan	פִינגָ׳אן (ז)
coffee grinder	matχenat kafe	מַטחֵנַת קָפֶה (נ)
kettle	kumkum	קוּמקוּם (ז)
teapot	kumkum	קוּמקוּם (ז)
lid	miχse	מִכסֶה (ז)

tea strainer	mis'nenet te	מְסַנֶּנֶת תֵּה (נ)
spoon	kaf	כַּף (נ)
teaspoon	kapit	כַּפִּית (נ)
soup spoon	kaf	כַּף (נ)
fork	mazleg	מַזְלֵג (ז)
knife	sakin	סַכִּין (ז, נ)
tableware (dishes)	kelim	כֵּלִים (ז"ר)
plate (dinner ~)	tsa'laxat	צַלַּחַת (נ)
saucer	taxtit	תַּחְתִּית (נ)
shot glass	kosit	כּוֹסִית (נ)
glass (tumbler)	kos	כּוֹס (נ)
cup	'sefel	סֵפֶל (ז)
sugar bowl	mis'keret	מִסְכֶּרֶת (נ)
salt shaker	milxiya	מִלְחִיָּה (נ)
pepper shaker	pilpeliya	פִּלְפְּלִיָּיה (נ)
butter dish	maxame'a	מַחֲמָאָה (נ)
stock pot (soup pot)	sir	סִיר (ז)
frying pan (skillet)	maxvat	מַחֲבַת (נ)
ladle	tarvad	תַּרְוָד (ז)
colander	mis'nenet	מְסַנֶּנֶת (נ)
tray (serving ~)	magaʃ	מַגָּשׁ (ז)
bottle	bakbuk	בַּקְבּוּק (ז)
jar (glass)	tsin'tsenet	צִנְצֶנֶת (נ)
can	paxit	פַּחִית (נ)
bottle opener	potxan bakbukim	פּוֹתְחָן בַּקְבּוּקִים (ז)
can opener	potxan kufsa'ot	פּוֹתְחָן קוּפְסָאוֹת (ז)
corkscrew	maxlets	מַחְלֵץ (ז)
filter	'filter	פִילְטֶר (ז)
to filter (vt)	lesanen	לְסַנֵּן
trash, garbage (food waste, etc.)	'zevel	זֶבֶל (ז)
trash can (kitchen ~)	pax 'zevel	פַּח זֶבֶל (ז)

72. Bathroom

bathroom	xadar am'batya	חֲדַר אַמְבַּטְיָה (ז)
water	'mayim	מַיִם (ז"ר)
faucet	'berez	בֶּרֶז (ז)
hot water	'mayim xamim	מַיִם חַמִּים (ז"ר)
cold water	'mayim karim	מַיִם קָרִים (ז"ר)
toothpaste	miʃxat ʃi'nayim	מִשְׁחַת שִׁינַיִים (נ)
to brush one's teeth	letsax'tseax ʃi'nayim	לְצַחְצֵחַ שִׁינַיִים

toothbrush	miv'refet ʃi'nayim	מִבְרֶשֶׁת שִׁנַּיִים (נ)
to shave (vi)	lehitga'leaχ	לְהִתְגַּלֵּחַ
shaving foam	'ketsef gi'luaχ	קֶצֶף גִּילּוּחַ (ז)
razor	'ta'ar	תַּעַר (ז)

to wash (one's hands, etc.)	liʃtof	לִשְׁטוֹף
to take a bath	lehitraχets	לְהִתְרַחֵץ
shower	mik'laχat	מִקְלַחַת (נ)
to take a shower	lehitka'leaχ	לְהִתְקַלֵּחַ

bathtub	am'batya	אַמְבַּטְיָה (נ)
toilet (toilet bowl)	asla	אַסְלָה (נ)
sink (washbasin)	kiyor	כִּיּוֹר (ז)

| soap | sabon | סַבּוֹן (ז) |
| soap dish | saboniya | סַבּוֹנִיָּה (נ) |

sponge	sfog 'lifa	סְפוֹג לִיפָה (ז)
shampoo	ʃampu	שַׁמְפּוּ (ז)
towel	ma'gevet	מַגֶּבֶת (נ)
bathrobe	χaluk raχatsa	חָלוּק רַחְצָה (ז)

laundry (process)	kvisa	כְּבִיסָה (נ)
washing machine	meχonat kvisa	מְכוֹנַת כְּבִיסָה (נ)
to do the laundry	leχabes	לְכַבֵּס
laundry detergent	avkat kvisa	אַבְקַת כְּבִיסָה (נ)

73. Household appliances

TV set	tele'vizya	טֶלֶווִיזְיָה (נ)
tape recorder	teip	טֵייפּ (ז)
VCR (video recorder)	maχʃir 'vide'o	מַכְשִׁיר וִידֵאוֹ (ז)
radio	'radyo	רַדְיוֹ (ז)
player (CD, MP3, etc.)	nagan	נַגָּן (ז)

video projector	makren	מַקְרֵן (ז)
home movie theater	kol'no'a beiti	קוֹלְנוֹעַ בֵּיתִי (ז)
DVD player	nagan dividi	נַגָּן DVD (ז)
amplifier	magber	מַגְבֵּר (ז)
video game console	maχʃir plei'steiʃen	מַכְשִׁיר פְּלֵייסְטֵיישֶׁן (ז)

video camera	matslemat 'vide'o	מַצְלֵמַת וִידֵאוֹ (נ)
camera (photo)	matslema	מַצְלֵמָה (נ)
digital camera	matslema digi'talit	מַצְלֵמָה דִּיגִיטָלִית (נ)

vacuum cleaner	ʃo'ev avak	שׁוֹאֵב אָבָק (ז)
iron (e.g., steam ~)	maghets	מַגְהֵץ (ז)
ironing board	'kereʃ gihuts	קֶרֶשׁ גִּיהוּץ (ז)
telephone	'telefon	טֶלֶפוֹן (ז)
cell phone	'telefon nayad	טֶלֶפוֹן נַיָּיד (ז)

typewriter	meχonat ktiva	מְכוֹנַת כּתִיבָה (נ)
sewing machine	meχonat tfira	מְכוֹנַת תפִירָה (נ)
microphone	mikrofon	מִיקרוֹפוֹן (ז)
headphones	ozniyot	אוֹזנִיוֹת (נ-ר)
remote control (TV)	'ʃelet	שֶלֶט (ז)
CD, compact disc	taklitor	תַקלִיטוֹר (ז)
cassette, tape	ka'letet	קַלֶטֶת (נ)
vinyl record	taklit	תַקלִיט (ז)

THE EARTH. WEATHER

T&P Books Publishing

space	χalal	חָלָל (ז)
space (as adj)	ʃel χalal	שֶׁל חָלָל
outer space	χalal χitson	חָלָל חִיצוֹן (ז)
world	olam	עוֹלָם (ז)
universe	yekum	יְקוּם (ז)
galaxy	ga'laksya	גָלַקְסְיָה (נ)
star	koχav	כּוֹכָב (ז)
constellation	tsvir koχavim	צְבִיר כּוֹכָבִים (ז)
planet	koχav 'leχet	כּוֹכָב לֶכֶת (ז)
satellite	lavyan	לַוְיָן (ז)
meteorite	mete'orit	מֶטֶאוֹרִיט (ז)
comet	koχav ʃavit	כּוֹכָב שָׁבִיט (ז)
asteroid	aste'ro'id	אַסְטְרוֹאִיד (ז)
orbit	maslul	מַסְלוּל (ז)
to revolve (~ around the Earth)	lesovev	לְסוֹבֵב
atmosphere	atmos'fera	אַטְמוֹסְפֶרָה (נ)
the Sun	'ʃemeʃ	שֶׁמֶשׁ (נ)
solar system	ma'a'reχet ha'ʃemeʃ	מַעֲרֶכֶת הַשֶּׁמֶשׁ (נ)
solar eclipse	likui χama	לִיקוּי חַמָה (ז)
the Earth	kadur ha''arets	כַּדוּר הָאָרֶץ (ז)
the Moon	ya'reaχ	יָרֵחַ (ז)
Mars	ma'adim	מַאְדִים (ז)
Venus	'noga	נוֹגָה (ז)
Jupiter	'tsedek	צֶדֶק (ז)
Saturn	ʃabtai	שַׁבְתַּאי (ז)
Mercury	koχav χama	כּוֹכָב חַמָה (ז)
Uranus	u'ranus	אוּרָנוּס (ז)
Neptune	neptun	נֶפְטוּן (ז)
Pluto	'pluto	פלוטו (ז)
Milky Way	ʃvil haχalav	שְׁבִיל הֶחָלָב (ז)
Great Bear (Ursa Major)	duba gdola	דוּבָּה גדוֹלָה (נ)
North Star	koχav hatsafon	כּוֹכָב הַצָפוֹן (ז)
Martian	toʃav ma'adim	תוֹשָׁב מַאְדִים (ז)
extraterrestrial (n)	χutsan	חוּצָן (ז)

alien	χaizar	חַייָזָר (ז)
flying saucer	tsa'laχat me'o'fefet	צַלַחַת מְעוֹפֶפֶת (נ)
spaceship	χalalit	חַלָלִית (נ)
space station	taχanat χalal	תַחֲנַת חָלָל (נ)
blast-off	hamra'a	הַמרָאָה (נ)
engine	ma'no'a	מָנוֹעַ (ז)
nozzle	neχir	נְחִיר (ז)
fuel	'delek	דֶלֶק (ז)
cockpit, flight deck	'kokpit	קוֹקפִּיט (ז)
antenna	an'tena	אַנטֶנָה (נ)
porthole	eʃnav	אֶשׁנָב (ז)
solar panel	'luaχ so'lari	לוּחַ סוֹלָרִי (ז)
spacesuit	χalifat χalal	חֲלִיפַת חָלָל (נ)
weightlessness	'χoser miʃkal	חוֹסֶר מִשׁקָל (ז)
oxygen	χamtsan	חַמצָן (ז)
docking (in space)	agina	עֲגִינָה (נ)
to dock (vi, vt)	la'agon	לַעֲגוֹן
observatory	mitspe koχavim	מִצפֵּה כּוֹכָבִים (ז)
telescope	teleskop	טֶלֶסקוֹפ (ז)
to observe (vt)	liʃpot, lehaʃkif	לִצפּוֹת, לְהַשׁקִיף
to explore (vt)	laχkor	לַחקוֹר

75. The Earth

the Earth	kadur ha''arets	כַּדוּר הָאָרֶץ (ז)
the globe (the Earth)	kadur ha''arets	כַּדוּר הָאָרֶץ (ז)
planet	koχav 'leχet	כּוֹכַב לֶכֶת (ז)
atmosphere	atmos'fera	אַטמוֹספֵרָה (נ)
geography	ge'o'grafya	גִיאוֹגרַפיָה (נ)
nature	'teva	טֶבַע (ז)
globe (table ~)	'globus	גלוֹבּוּס (ז)
map	mapa	מַפָּה (נ)
atlas	'atlas	אַטלָס (ז)
Europe	ei'ropa	אֵירוֹפָּה (נ)
Asia	'asya	אַסיָה (נ)
Africa	'afrika	אַפרִיקָה (נ)
Australia	ost'ralya	אוֹסטרַליָה (נ)
America	a'merika	אָמֶרִיקָה (נ)
North America	a'merika hatsfonit	אָמֶרִיקָה הַצפוֹנִית (נ)
South America	a'merika hadromit	אָמֶרִיקָה הַדרוֹמִית (נ)

| Antarctica | ya'beʃet an'tarktika | יַבֶּשֶׁת אַנְטַארקְטִיקָה (נ) |
| the Arctic | 'arktika | אַרקְטִיקָה (נ) |

76. Cardinal directions

north	tsafon	צָפוֹן (ז)
to the north	tsa'fona	צָפוֹנָה
in the north	batsafon	בַּצָפוֹן
northern (adj)	tsfoni	צפוֹנִי

south	darom	דָרוֹם (ז)
to the south	da'roma	דָרוֹמָה
in the south	badarom	בַּדָרוֹם
southern (adj)	dromi	דרוֹמִי

west	ma'arav	מַעֲרָב (ז)
to the west	ma'a'rava	מַעֲרָבָה
in the west	bama'arav	בַּמַעֲרָב
western (adj)	ma'aravi	מַעֲרָבִי

east	mizraχ	מִזְרָח (ז)
to the east	miz'raχa	מִזְרָחָה
in the east	bamizraχ	בַּמִזְרָח
eastern (adj)	mizraχi	מִזְרָחִי

77. Sea. Ocean

sea	yam	יָם (ז)
ocean	ok'yanos	אוֹקְיָאנוֹס (ז)
gulf (bay)	mifrats	מִפְרָץ (ז)
straits	meitsar	מֵיצַר (ז)

land (solid ground)	yabaʃa	יַבָּשָׁה (נ)
continent (mainland)	ya'beʃet	יַבֶּשֶׁת (נ)
island	i	אִי (ז)
peninsula	χatsi i	חֲצִי אִי (ז)
archipelago	arχipelag	אַרכִיפֶּלָג (ז)

bay, cove	mifrats	מִפְרָץ (ז)
harbor	namal	נָמָל (ז)
lagoon	la'guna	לָגוּנָה (נ)
cape	kef	כֵּף (ז)

atoll	atol	אָטוֹל (ז)
reef	ʃunit	שׁוֹנִית (נ)
coral	almog	אַלמוֹג (ז)
coral reef	ʃunit almogim	שׁוֹנִית אַלמוֹגִים (נ)
deep (adj)	amok	עָמוֹק

depth (deep water)	'omek	עוֹמֶק (ז)
abyss	tehom	תְּהוֹם (נ)
trench (e.g., Mariana ~)	maxteʃ	מַכתֵּש (ז)
current (Ocean ~)	'zerem	זֶרֶם (ז)
to surround (bathe)	lehakif	לְהַקִיף
shore	χof	חוֹף (ז)
coast	χof yam	חוֹף יָם (ז)
flow (flood tide)	ge'ut	גְאוּת (נ)
ebb (ebb tide)	'ʃefel	שֶׁפֶל (ז)
shoal	sirton	שִׂרטוֹן (ז)
bottom (~ of the sea)	karka'it	קַרקָעִית (נ)
wave	gal	גַל (ז)
crest (~ of a wave)	pisgat hagal	פִּסגַת הַגַל (נ)
spume (sea foam)	'keʦef	קֶצֶף (ז)
storm (sea storm)	sufa	סוּפָה (נ)
hurricane	hurikan	הוּרִיקָן (ז)
tsunami	ʦu'nami	צוּנָאמִי (ז)
calm (dead ~)	'roga	רוֹגַע (ז)
quiet, calm (adj)	ʃalev	שָׁלֵו
pole	'kotev	קוֹטֶב (ז)
polar (adj)	kotbi	קוֹטבִּי
latitude	kav 'roχav	קַו רוֹחַב (ז)
longitude	kav 'oreχ	קַו אוֹרֶך (ז)
parallel	kav 'roχav	קַו רוֹחַב (ז)
equator	kav hamaʃve	קַו הַמַשׁוֶוה (ז)
sky	ʃa'mayim	שָׁמַיִם (ז-ר)
horizon	'ofek	אוֹפֶק (ז)
air	avir	אֲווִיר (ז)
lighthouse	migdalor	מִגדָלוֹר (ז)
to dive (vi)	liʦlol	לִצלוֹל
to sink (ab. boat)	lit'bo'a	לִטבּוֹעַ
treasures	oʦarot	אוֹצָרוֹת (ז-ר)

78. Seas' and Oceans' names

Atlantic Ocean	ha'ok'yanus ha'at'lanti	הָאוֹקיָינוֹס הָאַטלַנטִי (ז)
Indian Ocean	ha'ok'yanus ha'hodi	הָאוֹקיָינוֹס הַהוֹדִי (ז)
Pacific Ocean	ha'ok'yanus haʃaket	הָאוֹקיָינוֹס הַשָׁקֵט (ז)
Arctic Ocean	ok'yanos ha'keraχ haʦfoni	אוֹקיָינוֹס הַקֶרַח הַצפוֹנִי (ז)
Black Sea	hayam haʃaχor	הַיָם הַשָׁחוֹר (ז)
Red Sea	yam suf	יַם סוּף (ז)

177

Yellow Sea	hayam hatsahov	הַיָּם הַצָּהוֹב (ז)
White Sea	hayam halavan	הַיָּם הַלָּבָן (ז)
Caspian Sea	hayam ha'kaspi	הַיָּם הַכַּסְפִּי (ז)
Dead Sea	yam ha'melax	יַם הַמֶּלַח (ז)
Mediterranean Sea	hayam hatixon	הַיָּם הַתִּיכוֹן (ז)
Aegean Sea	hayam ha'e'ge'i	הַיָּם הָאֶגֵאִי (ז)
Adriatic Sea	hayam ha'adri'yati	הַיָּם הָאַדְרִיָאתִי (ז)
Arabian Sea	hayam ha'aravi	הַיָּם הָעֲרָבִי (ז)
Sea of Japan	hayam haya'pani	הַיָּם הַיַפָּנִי (ז)
Bering Sea	yam 'bering	יַם בֶּרִינג (ז)
South China Sea	yam sin hadromi	יַם סִין הַדְרוֹמִי (ז)
Coral Sea	yam ha'almogim	יַם הָאַלְמוֹגִים (ז)
Tasman Sea	yam tasman	יַם טַסְמַן (ז)
Caribbean Sea	hayam haka'ribi	הַיָּם הַקָרִיבִּי (ז)
Barents Sea	yam 'barents	ים בָּרֶנץ (ז)
Kara Sea	yam 'kara	יַם קָאְרָה (ז)
North Sea	hayam hatsfoni	הַיָּם הַצְפוֹנִי (ז)
Baltic Sea	hayam ha'balti	הַיָּם הַבָּלְטִי (ז)
Norwegian Sea	hayam hanor'vegi	הַיָּם הַנוֹרְבֶּגִי (ז)

79. Mountains

mountain	har	הַר (ז)
mountain range	'rexes harim	רֶכֶס הָרִים (ז)
mountain ridge	'rexes har	רֶכֶס הַר (ז)
summit, top	pisga	פִּסְגָּה (נ)
peak	pisga	פִּסְגָּה (נ)
foot (~ of the mountain)	margelot	מַרְגְלוֹת (נ־ר)
slope (mountainside)	midron	מִדְרוֹן (ז)
volcano	har ga'aʃ	הַר גַעַש (ז)
active volcano	har 'ga'aʃ pa'il	הַר גַעַש פָּעִיל (ז)
dormant volcano	har 'ga'aʃ radum	הַר גַעַש רָדוּם (ז)
eruption	hitpartsut	הִתְפָּרְצוּת (נ)
crater	lo'a	לוֹעַ (ז)
magma	megama	מֶגְמָה (נ)
lava	'lava	לָאבָה (נ)
molten (~ lava)	lohet	לוֹהֵט
canyon	kanyon	קָנִיוֹן (ז)
gorge	gai	גַיְא (ז)
crevice	'beka	בֶּקַע (ז)

abyss (chasm)	tehom	תְּהוֹם (ז)
pass, col	ma'avar harim	מַעֲבַר הָרִים (ז)
plateau	rama	רָמָה (נ)
cliff	tsuk	צוּק (ז)
hill	giv'a	גִבְעָה (נ)

glacier	karχon	קַרְחוֹן (ז)
waterfall	mapal 'mayim	מַפַּל מַיִם (ז)
geyser	'geizer	גֵייזֶר (ז)
lake	agam	אֲגַם (ז)

plain	miʃor	מִישׁוֹר (ז)
landscape	nof	נוֹף (ז)
echo	hed	הֵד (ז)

alpinist	metapes harim	מְטַפֵּס הָרִים (ז)
rock climber	metapes sla'im	מְטַפֵּס סְלָעִים (ז)
to conquer (in climbing)	liχboʃ	לִכְבּוֹשׁ
climb (an easy ~)	tipus	טִיפּוּס (ז)

80. Mountains names

The Alps	harei ha''alpim	הָרֵי הָאַלְפִּים (ז"ר)
Mont Blanc	mon blan	מוֹן בְּלָאן (ז)
The Pyrenees	pire'ne'im	פִּירֶנֶאִים (ז"ר)

The Carpathians	kar'patim	קַרְפָּטִים (ז"ר)
The Ural Mountains	harei ural	הָרֵי אוּרָל (ז"ר)
The Caucasus Mountains	harei hakavkaz	הָרֵי הַקַוְוקָז (ז"ר)
Mount Elbrus	elbrus	אֶלְבְּרוּס (ז)

The Altai Mountains	harei altai	הָרֵי אַלְטַאי (ז"ר)
The Tian Shan	tyan ʃan	טִיאָן שָׁאן (ז)
The Pamir Mountains	harei pamir	הָרֵי פָּאמִיר (ז"ר)
The Himalayas	harei hehima'laya	הָרֵי הֶהִימָלָאיָה (ז"ר)
Mount Everest	everest	אֶוֶורֶסְט (ז)

| The Andes | harei ha''andim | הָרֵי הָאָנְדִים (ז"ר) |
| Mount Kilimanjaro | kiliman'dʒaro | קִילִימַנְגֹ'רוֹ (ז) |

81. Rivers

river	nahar	נָהָר (ז)
spring (natural source)	ma'ayan	מַעְיָין (ז)
riverbed (river channel)	afik	אָפִיק (ז)
basin (river valley)	agan nahar	אֲגַן נָהָר (ז)
to flow into …	lehiʃapeχ	לְהִישָׁפֵּךְ
tributary	yuval	יוּבַל (ז)

bank (of river)	χof	חוֹף (ז)
current (stream)	'zerem	זֶרֶם (ז)
downstream (adv)	bemorad hanahar	בְּמוֹרַד הַנָּהָר
upstream (adv)	bema'ale hanahar	בְּמַעֲלֵה הַזֶּרֶם
inundation	hatsafa	הֲצָפָה (נ)
flooding	ʃitafon	שִׁיטָפוֹן (ז)
to overflow (vi)	la'alot al gdotav	לַעֲלוֹת עַל גְדוֹתָיו
to flood (vt)	lehatsif	לְהָצִיף
shallow (shoal)	sirton	שִׂרְטוֹן (ז)
rapids	'eʃed	אֶשֶׁד (ז)
dam	'seχer	סֶכֶר (ז)
canal	te'ala	תְּעָלָה (נ)
reservoir (artificial lake)	ma'agar 'mayim	מַאֲגַר מַיִם (ז)
sluice, lock	ta 'ʃayit	תָּא שַׁיִט (ז)
water body (pond, etc.)	ma'agar 'mayim	מַאֲגַר מַיִם (ז)
swamp (marshland)	bitsa	בִּיצָה (נ)
bog, marsh	bitsa	בִּיצָה (נ)
whirlpool	me'ar'bolet	מְעַרבּוֹלֶת (נ)
stream (brook)	'naχal	נַחַל (ז)
drinking (ab. water)	ʃel ʃtiya	שֶׁל שתִיָּה
fresh (~ water)	metukim	מְתוּקִים
ice	'keraχ	קֶרַח (ז)
to freeze over (ab. river, etc.)	likpo	לִקְפּוֹא

82. Rivers' names

Seine	hasen	הַסֶן (ז)
Loire	lu'ar	לוֹאָר (ז)
Thames	'temza	תֶמזָה (ז)
Rhine	hrain	הרַיין (ז)
Danube	da'nuba	דָנוּבָּה (ז)
Volga	'volga	וֹולגָה (ז)
Don	nahar don	נָהָר דוֹן (ז)
Lena	'lena	לֶנָה (ז)
Yellow River	hvang ho	הוֹוַנג הוֹ (ז)
Yangtze	yangtse	יַאנגצֶה (ז)
Mekong	mekong	מֶקוֹנג (ז)
Ganges	'ganges	גַנגֶס (ז)
Nile River	'nilus	נִילוּס (ז)
Congo River	'kongo	קוֹנגוֹ (ז)

Okavango River	ok'vango	אוֹקְבַנְגּוֹ (ז)
Zambezi River	zam'bezi	זַמְבֶּזִי (ז)
Limpopo River	limpopo	לִימְפּוֹפּוֹ (ז)
Mississippi River	misi'sipi	מִיסִיסִיפִּי (ז)

83. Forest

forest, wood	'ya'ar	יַעַר (ז)
forest (as adj)	ʃel 'ya'ar	שֶׁל יַעַר
thick forest	avi ha'ya'ar	עֲבִי הַיַעַר (ז)
grove	χurʃa	חוּרְשָׁה (נ)
forest clearing	ka'raχat 'ya'ar	קָרַחַת יַעַר (נ)
thicket	svaχ	סְבַךְ (ז)
scrubland	'siaχ	שִׂיחַ (ז)
footpath (troddenpath)	ʃvil	שְׁבִיל (ז)
gully	'emek tsar	עֶמֶק צַר (ז)
tree	ets	עֵץ (ז)
leaf	ale	עָלֶה (ז)
leaves (foliage)	alva	עַלְוָה (נ)
fall of leaves	ʃa'leχet	שַׁלֶכֶת (נ)
to fall (ab. leaves)	linʃor	לִנְשׁוֹר
top (of the tree)	tsa'meret	צַמֶרֶת (נ)
branch	anaf	עָנָף (ז)
bough	anaf ave	עָנָף עָבֶה (ז)
bud (on shrub, tree)	nitsan	נִיצָן (ז)
needle (of pine tree)	'maχat	מַחַט (נ)
pine cone	itstrubal	אִצְטְרוּבָּל (ז)
hollow (in a tree)	χor ba'ets	חוֹר בָּעֵץ (ז)
nest	ken	קֵן (ז)
burrow (animal hole)	meχila	מְחִילָה (נ)
trunk	'geza	גֶּזַע (ז)
root	'ʃoreʃ	שׁוֹרֶשׁ (ז)
bark	klipa	קְלִיפָּה (נ)
moss	taχav	טַחַב (ז)
to uproot (remove trees or tree stumps)	la'akor	לַעֲקוֹר
to chop down	liχrot	לִכְרוֹת
to deforest (vt)	levare	לְבָרֵא
tree stump	'gedem	גֶּדֶם (ז)
campfire	medura	מְדוּרָה (נ)
forest fire	srefa	שְׂרֵיפָה (נ)

to extinguish (vt)	leχabot	לְכַבּוֹת
forest ranger	ʃomer 'ya'ar	שׁוֹמֵר יַעַר (ז)
protection	ʃmira	שְׁמִירָה (נ)
to protect (~ nature)	liʃmor	לִשְׁמוֹר
poacher	tsayad lelo reʃut	צַיָּיד לְלא רְשׁוּת (ז)
steel trap	mal'kodet	מַלכּוֹדֶת (נ)

| to gather, to pick (vt) | lelaket | לְלַקֵּט |
| to lose one's way | lit'ot | לִתעוֹת |

84. Natural resources

natural resources	otsarot 'teva	אוֹצָרוֹת טֶבַע (ז״ר)
minerals	mine'ralim	מִינֶרָלִים (ז״ר)
deposits	mirbats	מִרבָּץ (ז)
field (e.g., oilfield)	mirbats	מִרבָּץ (ז)

to mine (extract)	liχrot	לִכרוֹת
mining (extraction)	kriya	כְּרִיָה (נ)
ore	afra	עַפרָה (נ)
mine (e.g., for coal)	miχre	מִכרֶה (ז)
shaft (mine ~)	pir	פִּיר (ז)
miner	kore	כּוֹרֶה (ז)

| gas (natural ~) | gaz | גָז (ז) |
| gas pipeline | tsinor gaz | צִינוֹר גָז (ז) |

oil (petroleum)	neft	נֵפט (ז)
oil pipeline	tsinor neft	צִינוֹר נֵפט (ז)
oil well	be'er neft	בְּאֵר נֵפט (נ)
derrick (tower)	migdal ki'duaχ	מִגדַל קִידוּחַ (ז)
tanker	meχalit	מֵיכָלִית (נ)

sand	χol	חוֹל (ז)
limestone	'even gir	אֶבֶן גִיר (נ)
gravel	χatsats	חָצָץ (ז)
peat	kavul	כָּבוּל (ז)
clay	tit	טִיט (ז)
coal	peχam	פֶּחָם (ז)

iron (ore)	barzel	בַּרזֶל (ז)
gold	zahav	זָהָב (ז)
silver	'kesef	כֶּסֶף (ז)
nickel	'nikel	נִיקֶל (ז)
copper	ne'χoʃet	נְחוֹשֶׁת (נ)

zinc	avats	אָבָץ (ז)
manganese	mangan	מַנגָן (ז)
mercury	kaspit	כַּספִּית (נ)
lead	o'feret	עוֹפֶרֶת (נ)

mineral	mineral	מִינֶרָל (ז)
crystal	gaviʃ	גָבִיש (ז)
marble	ʃayiʃ	שַיִש (ז)
uranium	u'ranyum	אוּרָניוּם (ז)

85. Weather

weather	'mezeg avir	מֶזֶג אֲוִויר (ז)
weather forecast	taχazit 'mezeg ha'avir	תַחֲזִית מֶזֶג הָאֲוִויר (נ)
temperature	tempera'tura	טֶמפֶּרָטוּרָה (נ)
thermometer	madχom	מַדחוֹם (ז)
barometer	ba'rometer	בָּרוֹמֶטֶר (ז)

humid (adj)	laχ	לַח
humidity	laχut	לַחוּת (נ)
heat (extreme ~)	χom	חוֹם (ז)
hot (torrid)	χam	חַם
it's hot	χam	חַם

| it's warm | χamim | חָמִים |
| warm (moderately hot) | χamim | חָמִים |

it's cold	kar	קַר
cold (adj)	kar	קַר
sun	'ʃemeʃ	שֶמֶש (נ)
to shine (vi)	lizhor	לִזהוֹר
sunny (day)	ʃimʃi	שמשי
to come up (vi)	liz'roaχ	לִזרוֹחַ
to set (vi)	liʃ'ko'a	לִשקוֹעַ

cloud	anan	עָנָן (ז)
cloudy (adj)	me'unan	מְעוּנָן
rain cloud	av	עָב (ז)
somber (gloomy)	sagriri	סַגרִירִי

rain	'geʃem	גֶשֶם (ז)
it's raining	yored 'geʃem	יוֹרֵד גֶשֶם
rainy (~ day, weather)	gaʃum	גָשוּם
to drizzle (vi)	letaftef	לְטַפטֵף

pouring rain	matar	מָטָר (ז)
downpour	mabul	מַבּוּל (ז)
heavy (e.g., ~ rain)	χazak	חָזָק
puddle	ʃlulit	שלוּלִית (נ)
to get wet (in rain)	lehitratev	לְהִתרַטֵב

fog (mist)	arapel	עֲרָפֶל (ז)
foggy	me'urpal	מְעוּרפָּל
snow	'ʃeleg	שֶלֶג (ז)
it's snowing	yored 'ʃeleg	יוֹרֵד שֶלֶג

86. Severe weather. Natural disasters

thunderstorm	sufat re'amim	סוּפַת רְעָמִים (נ)
lightning (~ strike)	barak	בָּרָק (ז)
to flash (vi)	livhok	לבהוק
thunder	'ra'am	רַעַם (ז)
to thunder (vi)	lir'om	לרעוֹם
it's thundering	lir'om	לרעוֹם
hail	barad	בָּרָד (ז)
it's hailing	yored barad	יוֹרֵד בָּרָד
to flood (vt)	lehatsif	לְהָצִיף
flood, inundation	ʃitafon	שִׁיטָפוֹן (ז)
earthquake	re'idat adama	רְעִידַת אֲדָמָה (נ)
tremor, quake	re'ida	רְעִידָה (נ)
epicenter	moked	מוֹקֵד (ז)
eruption	hitpartsut	הִתְפָּרְצוּת (נ)
lava	'lava	לָאבָה (נ)
twister	hurikan	הוֹרִיקָן (ז)
tornado	tor'nado	טוֹרְנָדוֹ (ז)
typhoon	taifun	טַייפוּן (ז)
hurricane	hurikan	הוֹרִיקָן (ז)
storm	sufa	סוּפָה (נ)
tsunami	tsu'nami	צוּנָאמִי (ז)
cyclone	tsiklon	צִיקלוֹן (ז)
bad weather	sagrir	סַגרִיר (ז)
fire (accident)	srefa	שׂרֵיפָה (נ)
disaster	ason	אָסוֹן (ז)
meteorite	mete'orit	מֶטְאוֹרִיט (ז)
avalanche	ma'polet ʃlagim	מַפּוֹלֶת שׁלָגִים (נ)
snowslide	ma'polet ʃlagim	מַפּוֹלֶת שׁלָגִים (נ)
blizzard	sufat ʃlagim	סוּפַת שׁלָגִים (נ)
snowstorm	sufat ʃlagim	סוּפַת שׁלָגִים (נ)

FAUNA

T&P Books Publishing

predator	χayat 'teref	חַיַּת טֶרֶף (נ)
tiger	'tigris	טִיגְרִיס (ז)
lion	arye	אַרְיֵה (ז)
wolf	ze'ev	זְאֵב (ז)
fox	ʃu'al	שׁוּעָל (ז)
jaguar	yagu'ar	יָגוּאָר (ז)
leopard	namer	נָמֵר (ז)
cheetah	bardelas	בַּרְדְּלָס (ז)
black panther	panter	פַּנְתֵּר (ז)
puma	'puma	פּוּמָה (נ)
snow leopard	namer 'ʃeleg	נָמֵר שֶׁלֶג (ז)
lynx	ʃunar	שׁוּנָר (ז)
coyote	ze'ev ha'aravot	זְאֵב הָעֲרָבוֹת (ז)
jackal	tan	תַּן (ז)
hyena	tsa'vo'a	צָבוֹעַ (ז)

animal	'ba'al χayim	בַּעַל חַיִּים (ז)
beast (animal)	χaya	חַיָּה (נ)
squirrel	sna'i	סְנָאִי (ז)
hedgehog	kipod	קִיפּוֹד (ז)
hare	arnav	אַרְנָב (ז)
rabbit	ʃafan	שָׁפָן (ז)
badger	girit	גִּירִית (נ)
raccoon	dvivon	דְּבִיבוֹן (ז)
hamster	oger	אוֹגֵר (ז)
marmot	mar'mita	מַרְמִיטָה (נ)
mole	χafar'peret	חֲפַרְפֶּרֶת (נ)
mouse	aχbar	עַכְבָּר (ז)
rat	χulda	חוּלְדָּה (נ)
bat	atalef	עֲטַלֵּף (ז)
ermine	hermin	הֶרְמִין (ז)
sable	tsobel	צוֹבֶּל (ז)
marten	dalak	דָּלָק (ז)

weasel	χamus	חָמוּס (ז)
mink	χorfan	חוֹרְפָן (ז)
beaver	bone	בּוֹנֶה (ז)
otter	lutra	לוּטְרָה (נ)
horse	sus	סוּס (ז)
moose	ayal hakore	אַיָּיל הַקּוֹרֵא (ז)
deer	ayal	אַיָּיל (ז)
camel	gamal	גָּמָל (ז)
bison	bizon	בִּיזוֹן (ז)
wisent	bizon ei'ropi	בִּיזוֹן אֵירוֹפִי (ז)
buffalo	te'o	תְּאוֹ (ז)
zebra	'zebra	זֶבְּרָה (נ)
antelope	anti'lopa	אַנְטִילוֹפָּה (נ)
roe deer	ayal hakarmel	אַיָּיל הַכַּרְמֶל (ז)
fallow deer	yaχmur	יַחְמוּר (ז)
chamois	ya'el	יָעֵל (ז)
wild boar	χazir bar	חֲזִיר בָּר (ז)
whale	livyatan	לִוְויָתָן (ז)
seal	'kelev yam	כֶּלֶב יָם (ז)
walrus	sus yam	סוּס יָם (ז)
fur seal	dov yam	דּוֹב יָם (ז)
dolphin	dolfin	דּוֹלְפִין (ז)
bear	dov	דּוֹב (ז)
polar bear	dov 'kotev	דּוֹב קוֹטֶב (ז)
panda	'panda	פַּנְדָּה (נ)
monkey	kof	קוֹף (ז)
chimpanzee	ʃimpanze	שִׁימְפַּנְזֶה (נ)
orangutan	orang utan	אוֹרַנְג-אוּטָן (ז)
gorilla	go'rila	גּוֹרִילָה (נ)
macaque	makak	מָקָק (ז)
gibbon	gibon	גִּיבּוֹן (ז)
elephant	pil	פִּיל (ז)
rhinoceros	karnaf	קַרְנַף (ז)
giraffe	dʒi'rafa	גִ'ירָפָה (נ)
hippopotamus	hipopotam	הִיפוֹפּוֹטָם (ז)
kangaroo	'kenguru	קֶנְגּוּרוּ (ז)
koala (bear)	ko''ala	קוֹאָלָה (ז)
mongoose	nemiya	נְמִייָה (נ)
chinchilla	tʃin'tʃila	צִ'ינְצִ'ילָה (נ)
skunk	bo'eʃ	בּוֹאֵשׁ (ז)
porcupine	darban	דַּרְבָּן (ז)

89. Domestic animals

cat	χatula	חֲתוּלָה (נ)
tomcat	χatul	חָתוּל (ז)
dog	'kelev	כֶּלֶב (ז)
horse	sus	סוּס (ז)
stallion (male horse)	sus harba'a	סוּס הַרְבָּעָה (ז)
mare	susa	סוּסָה (נ)
cow	para	פָּרָה (נ)
bull	ʃor	שׁוֹר (ז)
ox	ʃor	שׁוֹר (ז)
sheep (ewe)	kivsa	כִּבְשָׂה (נ)
ram	'ayil	אַיִל (ז)
goat	ez	עֵז (נ)
billy goat, he-goat	'tayiʃ	תַּיִשׁ (ז)
donkey	χamor	חֲמוֹר (ז)
mule	'pered	פֶּרֶד (ז)
pig, hog	χazir	חֲזִיר (ז)
piglet	χazarzir	חֲזַרְזִיר (ז)
rabbit	arnav	אַרְנָב (ז)
hen (chicken)	tarne'golet	תַּרְנְגוֹלֶת (נ)
rooster	tarnegol	תַּרְנְגוֹל (ז)
duck	barvaz	בַּרְוָז (ז)
drake	barvaz	בַּרְוָז (ז)
goose	avaz	אֲוָז (ז)
tom turkey, gobbler	tarnegol 'hodu	תַּרְנְגוֹל הוֹדוּ (ז)
turkey (hen)	tarne'golet 'hodu	תַּרְנְגוֹלֶת הוֹדוּ (נ)
domestic animals	χayot 'bayit	חַיוֹת בַּיִת (נ"ר)
tame (e.g., ~ hamster)	mevuyat	מְבוּיָת
to tame (vt)	levayet	לְבַיֵּת
to breed (vt)	lehar'bi'a	לְהַרְבִּיעַ
farm	χava	חַוָּה (נ)
poultry	ofot 'bayit	עוֹפוֹת בַּיִת (נ"ר)
cattle	bakar	בָּקָר (ז)
herd (cattle)	'eder	עֵדֶר (ז)
stable	urva	אוּרְוָה (נ)
pigpen	dir χazirim	דִּיר חֲזִירִים (ז)
cowshed	'refet	רֶפֶת (נ)
rabbit hutch	arnaviya	אַרְנְבִיָּה (נ)
hen house	lul	לוּל (ז)

90. Birds

bird	tsipor	צִיפּוֹר (נ)
pigeon	yona	יוֹנָה (נ)
sparrow	dror	דְּרוֹר (ז)
tit (great tit)	yargazi	יַרְגָזִי (ז)
magpie	orev neχalim	עוֹרֵב נְחָלִים (ז)

raven	orev ʃaχor	עוֹרֵב שָׁחוֹר (ז)
crow	orev afor	עוֹרֵב אָפוֹר (ז)
jackdaw	ka'ak	קָאָק (ז)
rook	orev hamizra	עוֹרֵב הַמִזְרָע (ז)

duck	barvaz	בַּרְוָז (ז)
goose	avaz	אָוָז (ז)
pheasant	pasyon	פַּסיוֹן (ז)

eagle	'ayit	עַיִט (ז)
hawk	nets	נֵץ (ז)
falcon	baz	בַּז (ז)
vulture	ozniya	עוֹזְנִיָּה (נ)
condor (Andean ~)	kondor	קוֹנְדוֹר (ז)

swan	barbur	בַּרְבּוּר (ז)
crane	agur	עָגוּר (ז)
stork	χasida	חֲסִידָה (נ)

parrot	'tuki	תוּכִּי (ז)
hummingbird	ko'libri	קוֹלִיבְּרִי (ז)
peacock	tavas	טָוָוס (ז)

ostrich	bat ya'ana	בַּת יַעֲנָה (נ)
heron	anafa	אֲנָפָה (נ)
flamingo	fla'mingo	פְלָמִינגוֹ (ז)
pelican	saknai	שַׂקְנַאי (ז)

| nightingale | zamir | זָמִיר (ז) |
| swallow | snunit | סְנוּנִית (נ) |

thrush	kiχli	קִיכְלִי (ז)
song thrush	kiχli mezamer	קִיכְלִי מְזַמֵר (ז)
blackbird	kiχli ʃaχor	קִיכְלִי שָׁחוֹר (ז)

swift	sis	סִיס (ז)
lark	efroni	עֶפְרוֹנִי (ז)
quail	slav	שְׂלָיו (ז)

woodpecker	'neker	נֶקֶר (ז)
cuckoo	kukiya	קוּקִיָּה (נ)
owl	yanʃuf	יַנְשׁוּף (ז)
eagle owl	'oaχ	אוֹחַ (ז)

wood grouse	seχvi 'ya'ar	שְׂכְוִוי יַעַר (ז)
black grouse	seχvi	שְׂכְוִוי (ז)
partridge	χogla	חוֹגְלָה (נ)

starling	zarzir	זַרְזִיר (ז)
canary	ka'narit	קָנָרִית (נ)
hazel grouse	seχvi haya'arot	שְׂכְוִוי הַיְּעָרוֹת (ז)
chaffinch	paroʃ	פָּרוֹשׁ (ז)
bullfinch	admonit	אַדְמוֹנִית (נ)

seagull	ʃaχaf	שַׁחַף (ז)
albatross	albatros	אַלְבַּטְרוֹס (ז)
penguin	pingvin	פִּינְגְּוִוין (ז)

91. Fish. Marine animals

bream	avroma	אַבְרוֹמָה (נ)
carp	karpiyon	קַרְפִּיוֹן (ז)
perch	'okunus	אוֹקוּנוּס (ז)
catfish	sfamnun	שְׂפַמְנוּן (ז)
pike	ze'ev 'mayim	זְאֵב מַיִם (ז)

| salmon | 'salmon | סַלְמוֹן (ז) |
| sturgeon | χidkan | חִדְקָן (ז) |

herring	ma'liaχ	מָלִיחַ (ז)
Atlantic salmon	iltit	אִילְתִּית (נ)
mackerel	makarel	מָקָרֶל (ז)
flatfish	dag moʃe ra'benu	דָּג מֹשֶׁה רַבֵּנוּ (ז)

zander, pike perch	amnun	אַמְנוּן (ז)
cod	ʃibut	שִׁיבּוּט (ז)
tuna	'tuna	טוּנָה (נ)
trout	forel	פּוֹרֶל (ז)

eel	tslofaχ	צְלוֹפַח (ז)
electric ray	trisanit	תְּרִיסָנִית (נ)
moray eel	mo'rena	מוֹרֶנָה (נ)
piranha	pi'ranya	פִּירַנְיָה (נ)

shark	kariʃ	כָּרִישׁ (ז)
dolphin	dolfin	דּוֹלְפִין (ז)
whale	livyatan	לִוְוְיָתָן (ז)

crab	sartan	סַרְטָן (ז)
jellyfish	me'duza	מֶדוּזָה (נ)
octopus	tamnun	תַּמְנוּן (ז)

| starfish | koχav yam | כּוֹכָב יָם (ז) |
| sea urchin | kipod yam | קִיפוֹד יָם (ז) |

seahorse	suson yam	סוסוֹן יָם (ז)
oyster	tsidpa	צִדְפָּה (נ)
shrimp	χasilon	חֲסִילוֹן (ז)
lobster	'lobster	לוֹבְּסְטֶר (ז)
spiny lobster	'lobster kotsani	לוֹבְּסְטֶר קוֹצָנִי (ז)

92. Amphibians. Reptiles

snake	naχaʃ	נָחָשׁ (ז)
venomous (snake)	arsi	אַרְסִי
viper	'tsefa	צֶפַע (ז)
cobra	'peten	פֶּתֶן (ז)
python	piton	פִּיתוֹן (ז)
boa	χanak	חֶנֶק (ז)
grass snake	naχaʃ 'mayim	נָחָשׁ מַיִם (ז)
rattle snake	ʃfifon	שְׁפִיפוֹן (ז)
anaconda	ana'konda	אֲנָקוֹנְדָה (נ)
lizard	leta'a	לְטָאָה (נ)
iguana	igu''ana	אִיגוּאָנָה (נ)
monitor lizard	'koaχ	כּוֹחַ (ז)
salamander	sala'mandra	סָלָמַנְדְּרָה (נ)
chameleon	zikit	זִיקִית (נ)
scorpion	akrav	עַקְרָב (ז)
turtle	tsav	צָב (ז)
frog	tsfar'de'a	צְפַרְדֵעַ (נ)
toad	karpada	קַרְפָּדָה (נ)
crocodile	tanin	תַנִּין (ז)

93. Insects

insect, bug	χarak	חָרָק (ז)
butterfly	parpar	פַּרְפַּר (ז)
ant	nemala	נְמָלָה (נ)
fly	zvuv	זְבוּב (ז)
mosquito	yatuʃ	יַתּוּשׁ (ז)
beetle	χipuʃit	חִיפּוּשִׁית (נ)
wasp	tsir'a	צִרְעָה (נ)
bee	dvora	דְּבוֹרָה (נ)
bumblebee	dabur	דַּבּוּר (ז)
gadfly (botfly)	zvuv hasus	זְבוּב הַסּוּס (ז)
spider	akaviʃ	עַכָּבִישׁ (ז)
spiderweb	kurei akaviʃ	קוּרֵי עַכָּבִישׁ (ז״ר)

dragonfly	ʃapirit	שְׁפִירִית (נ)
grasshopper	χagav	חָגָב (ז)
moth (night butterfly)	aʃ	עָשׁ (ז)
cockroach	makak	מַקָק (ז)
tick	kartsiya	קַרְצִיָּה (נ)
flea	parʻoʃ	פַּרְעוֹשׁ (ז)
midge	yavχuʃ	יַבְחוּשׁ (ז)
locust	arbe	אַרְבֶּה (ז)
snail	χilazon	חִילָזוֹן (ז)
cricket	tsartsar	צְרָצַר (ז)
lightning bug	gaχlilit	גַחְלִילִית (נ)
ladybug	parat moʃe raʻbenu	פָּרַת מֹשֶׁה רַבֵּנוּ (נ)
cockchafer	χipuʃit aviv	חִיפוּשִׁית אָבִיב (נ)
leech	aluka	עֲלוּקָה (נ)
caterpillar	zaχal	זַחַל (ז)
earthworm	toʻlaʿat	תּוֹלַעַת (נ)
larva	ʻderen	דֶּרֶן (ז)

FLORA

T&P Books Publishing

tree	eʦ	עֵץ (ז)
deciduous (adj)	naʃir	נָשִׁיר
coniferous (adj)	maxtani	מַחְטָנִי
evergreen (adj)	yarok ad	יָרוֹק עַד
apple tree	ta'puax	תַּפּוּחַ (ז)
pear tree	agas	אַגָּס (ז)
sweet cherry tree	gudgedan	גּוּדְגְּדָן (ז)
sour cherry tree	duvdevan	דּוּבְדְּבָן (ז)
plum tree	ʃezif	שְׁזִיף (ז)
birch	ʃadar	שַׁדָּר (ז)
oak	alon	אַלוֹן (ז)
linden tree	'tilya	טִילְיָה (נ)
aspen	aspa	אַסְפָּה (נ)
maple	'eder	אֶדֶר (ז)
spruce	a'ʃuax	אַשּׁוּחַ (ז)
pine	'oren	אוֹרֶן (ז)
larch	arzit	אַרְזִית (נ)
fir tree	a'ʃuax	אַשּׁוּחַ (ז)
cedar	'erez	אֶרֶז (ז)
poplar	ʦaftsefa	צַפְצָפָה (נ)
rowan	ben xuzrar	בֶּן־חוּזְרָר (ז)
willow	arava	עֲרָבָה (נ)
alder	alnus	אַלְנוּס (ז)
beech	aʃur	אָשׁוּר (ז)
elm	bu'kiʦa	בּוּקִיצָה (נ)
ash (tree)	mela	מֵילָה (נ)
chestnut	armon	עַרְמוֹן (ז)
magnolia	mag'nolya	מַגְנוֹלְיָה (נ)
palm tree	'dekel	דֶּקֶל (ז)
cypress	broʃ	בְּרוֹשׁ (ז)
mangrove	mangrov	מַנְגְּרוֹב (ז)
baobab	ba'obab	בָּאוֹבָּב (ז)
eucalyptus	eika'liptus	אֵיקָלִיפְּטוּס (ז)
sequoia	sek'voya	סֶקְווֹיָה (נ)

95. Shrubs

bush	'siaχ	שִׂיחַ (ז)
shrub	'siaχ	שִׂיחַ (ז)
grapevine	'gefen	גֶּפֶן (ז)
vineyard	'kerem	כֶּרֶם (ז)
raspberry bush	'petel	פֶּטֶל (ז)
blackcurrant bush	'siaχ dumdemaniyot ʃχorot	שִׂיחַ דּוּמְדְּמָנִיּוֹת שְׁחוֹרוֹת (ז)
redcurrant bush	'siaχ dumdemaniyot adumot	שִׂיחַ דּוּמְדְּמָנִיּוֹת אֲדוּמּוֹת (ז)
gooseberry bush	χazarzar	חֲזַרְזַר (ז)
acacia	ʃita	שִׁיטָה (נ)
barberry	berberis	בֶּרְבֶּרִיס (ז)
jasmine	yasmin	יַסְמִין (ז)
juniper	ar'ar	עַרְעָר (ז)
rosebush	'siaχ vradim	שִׂיחַ וְרָדִים (ז)
dog rose	'vered bar	וֶרֶד בָּר (ז)

96. Fruits. Berries

fruit	pri	פְּרִי (ז)
fruits	perot	פֵּירוֹת (ז"ר)
apple	ta'puaχ	תַּפּוּחַ (ז)
pear	agas	אַגָּס (ז)
plum	ʃezif	שְׁזִיף (ז)
strawberry (garden ~)	tut sade	תּוּת שָׂדֶה (ז)
sour cherry	duvdevan	דּוּבְדְּבָן (ז)
sweet cherry	gudgedan	גּוּדְגְּדָן (ז)
grape	anavim	עֲנָבִים (ז"ר)
raspberry	'petel	פֶּטֶל (ז)
blackcurrant	dumdemanit ʃχora	דּוּמְדְּמָנִית שְׁחוֹרָה (נ)
redcurrant	dumdemanit aduma	דּוּמְדְּמָנִית אֲדוּמָּה (נ)
gooseberry	χazarzar	חֲזַרְזַר (ז)
cranberry	χamutsit	חֲמוּצִית (נ)
orange	tapuz	תַּפּוּז (ז)
mandarin	klemen'tina	קְלֶמֶנְטִינָה (נ)
pineapple	'ananas	אֲנָנָס (ז)
banana	ba'nana	בַּנָנָה (נ)
date	tamar	תָּמָר (ז)
lemon	limon	לִימוֹן (ז)
apricot	'miʃmeʃ	מִשְׁמֵשׁ (ז)

peach	afarsek	אֲפַרְסֵק (ז)
kiwi	'kivi	קִיוִוי (ז)
grapefruit	eʃkolit	אֶשְׁכּוֹלִית (נ)
berry	garger	גַּרְגֵּר (ז)
berries	gargerim	גַּרְגְּרִים (ז״ר)
cowberry	uχmanit aduma	אוּכְמָנִית אֲדוּמָה (נ)
wild strawberry	tut 'ya'ar	תּוּת יַעַר (ז)
bilberry	uχmanit	אוּכְמָנִית (נ)

97. Flowers. Plants

flower	'peraχ	פֶּרַח (ז)
bouquet (of flowers)	zer	זֵר (ז)
rose (flower)	'vered	וֶרֶד (ז)
tulip	tsiv'oni	צִבְעוֹנִי (ז)
carnation	tsi'poren	צִיפּוֹרֶן (ז)
gladiolus	glad'yola	גְּלַדִיוֹלָה (נ)
cornflower	dganit	דְּגָנִית (נ)
harebell	pa'amonit	פַּעֲמוֹנִית (נ)
dandelion	ʃinan	שִׁינָן (ז)
camomile	kamomil	קָמוֹמִיל (ז)
aloe	alvai	אַלְוַוי (ז)
cactus	'kaktus	קַקְטוּס (ז)
rubber plant, ficus	'fikus	פִיקוּס (ז)
lily	ʃoʃana	שׁוֹשַׁנָּה (נ)
geranium	ge'ranyum	גֶּרַנְיוּם (ז)
hyacinth	yakinton	יָקִינְטוֹן (ז)
mimosa	mi'moza	מִימוֹזָה (נ)
narcissus	narkis	נַרְקִיס (ז)
nasturtium	'kova hanazir	כּוֹבַע הַנָּזִיר (ז)
orchid	saχlav	סַחְלָב (ז)
peony	admonit	אַדְמוֹנִית (נ)
violet	sigalit	סִיגָּלִית (נ)
pansy	amnon vetamar	אַמְנוֹן וְתָמָר (ז)
forget-me-not	ziχ'rini	זִכְרִינִי (ז)
daisy	marganit	מַרְגָּנִית (נ)
poppy	'pereg	פֶּרֶג (ז)
hemp	ka'nabis	קָנָאבִּיס (ז)
mint	'menta	מֶנְתָה (נ)
lily of the valley	zivanit	זִיווָנִית (נ)
snowdrop	ga'lantus	גָּלַנְטוּס (ז)

nettle	sirpad	סִרְפָּד (ז)
sorrel	χum'a	חוּמְעָה (נ)
water lily	nufar	נוּפָר (ז)
fern	ʃaraχ	שָׁרָךְ (ז)
lichen	χazazit	חֲזָזִית (נ)

greenhouse (tropical ~)	χamama	חֲמָמָה (נ)
lawn	midʃa'a	מִדְשָׁאָה (נ)
flowerbed	arugat praχim	עֲרוּגַת פְּרָחִים (נ)

plant	'tsemaχ	צֶמַח (ז)
grass	'deʃe	דֶּשֶׁא (ז)
blade of grass	giv'ol 'esev	גִּבְעוֹל עֵשֶׂב (ז)

leaf	ale	עָלֶה (ז)
petal	ale ko'teret	עָלֵה כּוֹתֶרֶת (ז)
stem	giv'ol	גִּבְעוֹל (ז)
tuber	'pka'at	פְּקַעַת (נ)

young plant (shoot)	'nevet	נֶבֶט (ז)
thorn	kots	קוֹץ (ז)

to blossom (vi)	lifʼroaχ	לִפְרוֹחַ
to fade, to wither	linbol	לִנְבּוֹל
smell (odor)	'reaχ	רֵיחַ (ז)
to cut (flowers)	ligzom	לִגְזוֹם
to pick (a flower)	liktof	לִקְטוֹף

98. Cereals, grains

grain	tvu'a	תְּבוּאָה (נ)
cereal crops	dganim	דְּגָנִים (ז״ר)
ear (of barley, etc.)	ʃi'bolet	שִׁיבּוֹלֶת (נ)

wheat	χita	חִיטָה (נ)
rye	ʃifon	שִׁיפוֹן (ז)
oats	ʃi'bolet ʃu'al	שִׁיבּוֹלֶת שׁוּעָל (נ)

millet	'doχan	דּוֹחַן (ז)
barley	se'ora	שְׂעוֹרָה (נ)

corn	'tiras	תִּירָס (ז)
rice	'orez	אוֹרֶז (ז)
buckwheat	ku'semet	כּוּסֶמֶת (נ)

pea plant	afuna	אֲפוּנָה (נ)
kidney bean	ʃu'it	שְׁעוּעִית (נ)
soy	'soya	סוֹיָה (נ)
lentil	adaʃim	עֲדָשִׁים (ז״ר)
beans (pulse crops)	pol	פּוֹל (ז)

COUNTRIES OF
THE WORLD

T&P Books Publishing

Afghanistan	afganistan	אַפְגָּנִיסְטָן (ז)
Albania	al'banya	אַלְבַּנְיָה (נ)
Argentina	argen'tina	אַרְגֶּנְטִינָה (נ)
Armenia	ar'menya	אַרְמֶנְיָה (נ)
Australia	ost'ralya	אוֹסְטְרַלְיָה (נ)
Austria	'ostriya	אוֹסְטְרִיָה (נ)
Azerbaijan	azerbaidʒan	אָזֶרְבַּיְגָ'ן (ז)
The Bahamas	iyey ba'hama	אִיֵּי בָּהָאמָה (ז-ר)
Bangladesh	bangladeʃ	בַּנְגְלָדֶשׁ (נ)
Belarus	'belarus	בֶּלָרוּס (ז)
Belgium	'belgya	בֶּלְגְיָה (נ)
Bolivia	bo'livya	בּוֹלִיבִיָה (נ)
Bosnia and Herzegovina	'bosniya	בּוֹסְנְיָה (נ)
Brazil	brazil	בְּרָזִיל (ז)
Bulgaria	bul'garya	בּוּלְגָּרִיָה (נ)
Cambodia	kam'bodya	קַמְבּוֹדִיָה (נ)
Canada	'kanada	קָנָדָה (נ)
Chile	'tʃile	צִ'ילֶה (נ)
China	sin	סִין (נ)
Colombia	ko'lombya	קוֹלוֹמְבִּיָה (נ)
Croatia	kro''atya	קְרוֹאָטְיָה (נ)
Cuba	'kuba	קוּבָּה (נ)
Cyprus	kafrisin	קַפְרִיסִין (ז)
Czech Republic	'tʃeχya	צֶ'כְיָה (נ)
Denmark	'denemark	דֶנְמַרְק (נ)
Dominican Republic	hare'publika hadomeni'kanit	הָרֶפּוּבְּלִיקָה הַדוֹמִינִיקָנִית (נ)
Ecuador	ekvador	אֶקְוָודוֹר (ז)
Egypt	mits'rayim	מִצְרַיִם (נ)
England	'angliya	אַנְגְלִיָה (נ)
Estonia	es'tonya	אֶסְטוֹנְיָה (נ)
Finland	'finland	פִינְלַנד (נ)
France	tsarfat	צָרְפַת (נ)
French Polynesia	poli'nezya hatsarfatit	פּוֹלִינֶזְיָה הַצָרְפָתִית (נ)
Georgia	'gruzya	גרוזיָה (נ)
Germany	ger'manya	גֶרְמַנְיָה (נ)
Ghana	'gana	גָאנָה (נ)
Great Britain	bri'tanya hagdola	בְּרִיטַנְיָה הַגדוֹלָה (נ)
Greece	yavan	יָוָון (נ)
Haiti	ha'iti	הָאִיטִי (נ)
Hungary	hun'garya	הוּנְגַרִיָה (נ)

100. Countries. Part 2

Iceland	'island	אִיסלֶנד (נ)
India	'hodu	הוֹדוּ (נ)
Indonesia	indo'nezya	אִינדוֹנֶזיָה (נ)
Iran	iran	אִירָן (נ)
Iraq	irak	עִירָאק (נ)
Ireland	'irland	אִירלַנד (נ)
Israel	yisra'el	יִשׂרָאֵל (נ)
Italy	i'talya	אִיטַליָה (נ)

Jamaica	dʒa'maika	גָ'מַייקָה (נ)
Japan	yapan	יָפָן (נ)
Jordan	yarden	יַרדֵן (נ)
Kazakhstan	kazaχstan	קָזחסטָן (נ)
Kenya	'kenya	קֶניָה (נ)
Kirghizia	kirgizstan	קִירגִיזסטָן (נ)
Kuwait	kuveit	כּוּוֵית (נ)
Laos	la'os	לָאוֹס (נ)
Latvia	'latviya	לַטבִיָה (נ)
Lebanon	levanon	לְבָנוֹן (נ)
Libya	luv	לוּב (נ)
Liechtenstein	liχtenʃtain	לִיכטֶנשטַיין (נ)
Lithuania	'lita	לִיטָא (נ)
Luxembourg	luksemburg	לוּקסֶמבּוּרג (נ)

Macedonia (Republic of ~)	make'donya	מָקֶדוֹניָה (נ)
Madagascar	madagaskar	מָדָגַסקָר (ז)
Malaysia	ma'lezya	מָלֶזיָה (נ)
Malta	'malta	מַלטָה (נ)
Mexico	'meksiko	מֶקסִיקוֹ (נ)
Moldova, Moldavia	mol'davya	מוֹלדָבִיָה (נ)

Monaco	mo'nako	מוֹנָקוֹ (נ)
Mongolia	mon'golya	מוֹנגוֹליָה (נ)
Montenegro	monte'negro	מוֹנטֶנֶגרוֹ (נ)
Morocco	ma'roko	מָרוֹקוֹ (נ)
Myanmar	miyanmar	מִיַאנמָר (נ)
Namibia	na'mibya	נָמִיבִיָה (נ)
Nepal	nepal	נֶפָּאל (נ)
Netherlands	'holand	הוֹלַנד (נ)
New Zealand	nyu 'ziland	ניו זִילַנד (נ)
North Korea	ko'rei'a hatsfonit	קוֹרֵיאָה הַצפוֹנִית (נ)
Norway	nor'vegya	נוֹרבֶגיָה (נ)

101. Countries. Part 3

Pakistan	pakistan	פָּקִיסטָן (נ)
Palestine	falastin	פָּלֶסטִין (נ)

Panama	pa'nama	פָּנָמָה (נ)
Paraguay	paragvai	פָּרַגוּוַאי (נ)
Peru	peru	פֶּרוּ (נ)
Poland	polin	פּוֹלִין (נ)
Portugal	portugal	פּוֹרטוּגָל (נ)
Romania	ro'manya	רוֹמַניָה (נ)
Russia	'rusya	רוּסיָה (נ)
Saudi Arabia	arav hasa'udit	עֲרָב הַסָעוּדִית (נ)
Scotland	'skotland	סקוֹטלַנד (נ)
Senegal	senegal	סֶנֶגָל (נ)
Serbia	'serbya	סֶרבִּיָה (נ)
Slovakia	slo'vakya	סלוֹבַקיָה (נ)
Slovenia	slo'venya	סלוֹבֶנִיָה (נ)
South Africa	drom 'afrika	דרוֹם אַפרִיקָה (נ)
South Korea	ko'rei'a hadromit	קוֹרֵיאָה הַדרוֹמִית (נ)
Spain	sfarad	סְפָרַד (נ)
Suriname	surinam	סוּרִינָאם (נ)
Sweden	'ʃvedya	שבֶדִיָה (נ)
Switzerland	'ʃvaits	שוֵויץ (נ)
Syria	'surya	סוּרִיָה (נ)
Taiwan	taivan	טַייוָון (נ)
Tajikistan	tadʒikistan	טָגִ'יקִיסטָן (נ)
Tanzania	tan'zanya	טַנזַנִיָה (נ)
Tasmania	tas'manya	טַסמַניָה (נ)
Thailand	'tailand	תָאִילַנד (נ)
Tunisia	tu'nisya	טוּנִיסיָה (נ)
Turkey	'turkiya	טוּרקִיָה (נ)
Turkmenistan	turkmenistan	טוּרקמֶנִיסטָן (נ)
Ukraine	uk'rayna	אוּקרַאִינָה (נ)
United Arab Emirates	iχud ha'emi'royot ha'araviyot	אִיחוּד הָאֱמִירוּיוֹת הָעַרָבִיוֹת (ז)
United States of America	artsot habrit	אַרצוֹת הַברִית (נ-ר)
Uruguay	urugvai	אוּרוּגוַוואי (נ)
Uzbekistan	uzbekistan	אוּזבֶּקִיסטָן (נ)
Vatican	vatikan	וָתִיקָן (ז)
Venezuela	venetsu''ela	וֶנֶצוּאֶלָה (נ)
Vietnam	vyetnam	וִייֶטנָאם (נ)
Zanzibar	zanzibar	זָנזִיבָּר (נ)

GASTRONOMIC GLOSSARY

This section contains a lot of
words and terms associated
with food. This dictionary will
make it easier for you to
understand the menu at a
restaurant and choose
the right dish

T&P Books Publishing

aftertaste	'ta'am levai	טַעַם לְוַואי (ז)
almond	ʃaked	שָׁקֵד (ז)
anise	kamnon	כַּמְנוֹן (ז)
aperitif	maʃke meta'aven	מַשְׁקֵה מְתַאֲבֵן (ז)
appetite	te'avon	תֵּיאָבוֹן (ז)
appetizer	meta'aven	מְתַאֲבֵן (ז)
apple	ta'puaχ	תַּפּוּחַ (ז)
apricot	'miʃmeʃ	מִשְׁמֵשׁ (ז)
artichoke	artiʃok	אַרְטִישׁוֹק (ז)
asparagus	aspa'ragos	אַסְפָּרָגוֹס (ז)
Atlantic salmon	iltit	אִילְתִּית (נ)
avocado	avo'kado	אָבוֹקָדוֹ (ז)
bacon	'kotel χazir	קוֹתֶל חֲזִיר (ז)
banana	ba'nana	בַּנָּנָה (נ)
barley	se'ora	שְׂעוֹרָה (נ)
bartender	'barmen	בַּרְמֶן (ז)
basil	reχan	רֵיחָן (ז)
bay leaf	ale dafna	עָלֶה דַּפְנָה (ז)
beans	pol	פּוֹל (ז)
beef	bakar	בָּקָר (ז)
beer	'bira	בִּירָה (נ)
beetroot	'selek	סֶלֶק (ז)
bell pepper	'pilpel	פִּלְפֵּל (ז)
berries	gargerim	גַּרְגְּרִים (ז-ר)
berry	garger	גַּרְגֵּר (ז)
bilberry	uχmanit	אוּכְמָנִית (נ)
birch bolete	pitriyat 'ya'ar	פִּטְרִיַּת יַעַר (נ)
bitter	marir	מָרִיר
black coffee	kafe ʃaχor	קָפֶה שָׁחוֹר (ז)
black pepper	'pilpel ʃaχor	פִּלְפֵּל שָׁחוֹר (ז)
black tea	te ʃaχor	תֵּה שָׁחוֹר (ז)
blackberry	'petel ʃaχor	פֶּטֶל שָׁחוֹר (ז)
blackcurrant	dumdemanit ʃχora	דּוּמְדְּמָנִית שְׁחוֹרָה (נ)
boiled	mevuʃal	מְבוּשָׁל
bottle opener	potχan bakbukim	פּוֹתְחָן בַּקְבּוּקִים (ז)
bread	'leχem	לֶחֶם (ז)
breakfast	aruχat 'boker	אֲרוּחַת בּוֹקֶר (נ)
bream	avroma	אַבְרוֹמָה (נ)
broccoli	'brokoli	בְּרוֹקוֹלִי (ז)
Brussels sprouts	kruv nitsanim	כְּרוּב נִצָּנִים (ז)
buckwheat	ku'semet	כּוּסֶּמֶת (נ)
butter	χem'a	חֶמְאָה (נ)
buttercream	ka'tsefet χem'a	קַצֶּפֶת חֶמְאָה (נ)
cabbage	kruv	כְּרוּב (ז)

cake	uga	עוּגָה (נ)
cake	uga	עוּגָה (נ)
calorie	ka'lorya	קָלוֹרְיָה (נ)
can opener	potχan kufsa'ot	פּוֹתְחַן קוּפְסָאוֹת (ז)
candy	sukariya	סוּכָּרִיָּה (נ)
canned food	ʃimurim	שִׁמּוּרִים (ז״ר)
cappuccino	kapu'tʃino	קָפּוּצִ׳ינוֹ (ז)
caraway	'kimel	קִימֶל (ז)
carbohydrates	paχmema	פַּחְמֵימָה (נ)
carbonated	mugaz	מוּגָז
carp	karpiyon	קַרְפִּיוֹן (ז)
carrot	'gezer	גֶּזֶר (ז)
catfish	sfamnun	שְׂפַמְנוּן (ז)
cauliflower	kruvit	כְּרוּבִית (נ)
caviar	kavyar	קָוְויָאר (ז)
celery	'seleri	סֶלֶרִי (ז)
cep	por'tʃini	פּוֹרְצִ׳יני (ז)
cereal crops	dganim	דְּגָנִים (ז״ר)
cereal grains	grisim	גְּרִיסִים (ז״ר)
champagne	ʃam'panya	שַׁמְפַּנְיָה (נ)
chanterelle	gvi'onit ne'e'χelet	גְּבִיעוֹנִית נֶאֱכֶלֶת (נ)
check	χeʃbon	חֶשְׁבּוֹן (ז)
cheese	gvina	גְּבִינָה (נ)
chewing gum	'mastik	מַסְטִיק (ז)
chicken	of	עוֹף (ז)
chocolate	'ʃokolad	שׁוֹקוֹלָד (ז)
chocolate	mi'ʃokolad	מִשׁוֹקוֹלָד
cinnamon	kinamon	קִינָמוֹן (ז)
clear soup	marak tsaχ, tsir	מָרָק צַח, צִיר (ז)
cloves	tsi'poren	צִיפּוֹרֶן (ז)
cocktail	kokteil	קוֹקְטֵיל (ז)
coconut	'kokus	קוֹקוּס (ז)
cod	ʃibut	שִׁיבּוּט (ז)
coffee	kafe	קָפֶה (ז)
coffee with milk	kafe hafuχ	קָפֶה הָפוּךְ (ז)
cognac	'konyak	קוֹנְיָאק (ז)
cold	kar	קָר
condensed milk	χalav merukaz	חָלָב מְרוּכָּז (ז)
condiment	'rotev	רוֹטֶב (ז)
confectionery	mutsrei kondi'torya	מוּצְרֵי קוֹנְדִיטוֹרְיָה (ז״ר)
cookies	ugiya	עוּגִיָה (נ)
coriander	'kusbara	כּוּסְבָּרָה (נ)
corkscrew	maχlets	מַחְלֵץ (ז)
corn	'tiras	תִּירָס (ז)
corn	'tiras	תִּירָס (ז)
cornflakes	ptitei 'tiras	פְּתִיתֵי תִּירָס (ז״ר)
course, dish	mana	מָנָה (נ)
cowberry	uχmanit aduma	אוּכְמָנִית אֲדוּמָה (נ)
crab	sartan yam	סַרְטָן יָם (ז)
cranberry	χamutsit	חֲמוּצִית (נ)
cream	ʃa'menet	שְׁמֶנֶת (נ)
crumb	perur	פֵּירוּר (ז)

crustaceans	sartana'im	סַרְטָנָאִים (ז״ר)
cucumber	melafefon	מְלָפְפוֹן (ז)
cuisine	mitbaχ	מִטְבָּח (ז)
cup	'sefel	סֵפֶל (ז)
dark beer	'bira keha	בִּירָה כֵּהָה (נ)
date	tamar	תָּמָר (ז)
death cap	pitriya ra'ila	פְּטרִייָה רָעִילָה (נ)
dessert	ki'nuaχ	קִינּוּחַ (ז)
diet	di''eta	דִּיאֶטָה (נ)
dill	ʃamir	שָׁמִיר (ז)
dinner	aruχat 'erev	אֲרוּחַת עֶרֶב (נ)
dried	meyubaʃ	מְיוּבָּש
drinking water	mei ʃtiya	מֵי שתִייָה (ז״ר)
duck	barvaz	בַּרוָז (ז)
ear	ʃi'bolet	שִׁיבּוֹלֶת (נ)
edible mushroom	pitriya ra'uya lema'aχal	פְּטרִייָה רְאוּיָה לְמַאֲכָל (נ)
eel	tslofaχ	צְלוֹפָח (ז)
egg	beitsa	בֵּיצָה (נ)
egg white	χelbon	חֶלבּוֹן (ז)
egg yolk	χelmon	חֶלמוֹן (ז)
eggplant	χatsil	חָצִיל (ז)
eggs	beitsim	בֵּיצִים (נ־ר)
Enjoy your meal!	betei'avon!	בְּתֵיאָבוֹן!
fats	ʃumanim	שׁוּמָנִים (ז״ר)
fig	te'ena	תְּאֵנָה (נ)
filling	milui	מִילּוּי (ז)
fish	dag	דָג (ז)
flatfish	dag moʃe ra'benu	דָג מֹשֶׁה רַבֵּנוּ (ז)
flour	'kemaχ	קֶמַח (ז)
fly agaric	zvuvanit	זבוּבָנִית (נ)
food	'oχel	אוֹכֶל (ז)
fork	mazleg	מַזלֵג (ז)
freshly squeezed juice	mits saχut	מִיץ סָחוּט (ז)
fried	metugan	מְטוּגָּן
fried eggs	beitsat ain	בֵּיצַת עַיִן (נ)
frozen	kafu	קָפוּא
fruit	pri	פְּרִי (ז)
fruits	perot	פֵּירוֹת (ז־ר)
game	'tsayid	צַיִד (ז)
gammon	'kotel χazir me'uʃan	קוֹתֶל חֲזִיר מְעוּשָׁן (ז)
garlic	ʃum	שׁוּם (ז)
gin	dʒin	ג׳ין (ז)
ginger	'dʒindʒer	גִ׳ינגֶ׳ר (ז)
glass	kos	כּוֹס (נ)
glass	ga'vi'a	גָּבִיעַ (ז)
goose	avaz	אֲווָז (ז)
gooseberry	χazarzar	חֲזַרזַר (ז)
grain	tvu'a	תבוּאָה (נ)
grape	anavim	עֲנָבִים (ז־ר)
grapefruit	eʃkolit	אֶשׁכּוֹלִית (נ)
green tea	te yarok	תֵּה יָרוֹק (ז)
greens	'yerek	יֶרֶק (ז)

halibut	putit	פּוטִית (נ)
ham	basar χazir me'uʃan	בָּשָׂר חֲזִיר מְעוּשָׁן (ז)
hamburger	basar taχun	בָּשָׂר טָחוּן (ז)
hamburger	'hamburger	הַמְבּוּרְגֶר (ז)
hazelnut	egoz ilsar	אֱגוֹז אִלְסָר (ז)
herring	ma'liaχ	מָלִיחַ (ז)
honey	dvaʃ	דבַשׁ (ז)
horseradish	χa'zeret	חֲזֶרֶת (נ)
hot	χam	חַם
ice	'keraχ	קֶרַח (ז)
ice-cream	'glida	גלִידָה (נ)
instant coffee	kafe names	קָפֶּה נָמֵס (ז)
jam	riba	רִיבָּה (נ)
jam	riba	רִיבָּה (נ)
juice	mits	מִיץ (ז)
kidney bean	ʃu'it	שְׁעוּעִית (נ)
kiwi	'kivi	קִיוִוי (ז)
knife	sakin	סַכִּין (ז, נ)
lamb	basar 'keves	בָּשָׂר כֶּבֶשׂ (ז)
lemon	limon	לִימוֹן (ז)
lemonade	limo'nada	לִימוֹנָדָה (נ)
lentil	adaʃim	עֲדָשִׁים (נ-ר)
lettuce	'χasa	חַסָּה (נ)
light beer	'bira bahira	בִּירָה בָּהִירָה (נ)
liqueur	liker	לִיקֶר (ז)
liquors	maʃka'ot χarifim	מַשְׁקָאוֹת חָרִיפִים (ז-ר)
liver	kaved	כָּבֵד (ז)
lunch	aruχat tsaha'rayim	אֲרוּחַת צָהֳרַיִם (נ)
mackerel	kolyas	קוֹלְיָס (ז)
mandarin	klemen'tina	קלֶמֶנְטִינָה (נ)
mango	'mango	מַנגוֹ (ז)
margarine	marga'rina	מַרְגָרִינָה (נ)
marmalade	marme'lada	מַרְמֶלָדָה (נ)
mashed potatoes	meχit tapuχei adama	מְחִית תַּפּוּחֵי אֲדָמָה (נ)
mayonnaise	mayonez	מָיוֹנֵז (ז)
meat	basar	בָּשָׂר (ז)
melon	melon	מֶלוֹן (ז)
menu	tafrit	תַּפרִיט (ז)
milk	χalav	חָלָב (ז)
milkshake	'milkʃeik	מִילקְשֵׁייק (ז)
millet	'doχan	דוֹחַן (ז)
mineral water	'mayim mine'raliyim	מַיִם מִינֵרָלְיִים (ז-ר)
morel	gamtsuts	גַמצוּץ (ז)
mushroom	pitriya	פִּטְרִייָה (נ)
mustard	χardal	חַרְדָל (ז)
non-alcoholic	natul alkohol	נָטוּל אַלכּוֹהוֹל
noodles	irtiyot	אָטרִיוֹת (נ-ר)
oats	ʃi'bolet ʃu'al	שִׁיבּוֹלֶת שׁוּעָל (נ)
olive oil	'ʃemen 'zayit	שֶׁמֶן זַיִת (ז)
olives	zeitim	זֵיתִים (ז-ר)
omelet	χavita	חֲבִיתָה (נ)
onion	batsal	בָּצָל (ז)

207

orange	tapuz	תַּפּוּז (ז)
orange juice	mits tapuzim	מִיץ תַּפּוּזִים (ז)
orange-cap boletus	pitriyat 'kova aduma	פִּטְרִיַּת כּוֹבַע אֲדוּמָה (נ)
oyster	tsidpat ma'axal	צִדְפַּת מַאֲכָל (נ)
pâté	pate	פָּטֶה (ז)
papaya	pa'paya	פַּפָּאיָה (נ)
paprika	'paprika	פַּפְרִיקָה (נ)
parsley	petro'zilya	פֶּטְרוֹזִילְיָה (נ)
pasta	'pasta	פַּסְטָה (נ)
pea	afuna	אֲפוּנָה (נ)
peach	afarsek	אֲפַרְסֵק (ז)
peanut	botnim	בּוֹטְנִים (ז״ר)
pear	agas	אַגָּס (ז)
peel	klipa	קְלִיפָּה (נ)
perch	'okunus	אוֹקוּנוּס (ז)
pickled	kavuʃ	כָּבוּשׁ
pie	pai	פָּאי (ז)
piece	xatixa	חֲתִיכָה (נ)
pike	ze'ev 'mayim	זְאֵב מַיִם (ז)
pike perch	amnun	אַמְנוּן (ז)
pineapple	'ananas	אֲנָנָס (ז)
pistachios	'fistuk	פִּיסְטוּק (ז)
pizza	'pitsa	פִּיצָה (נ)
plate	tsa'laxat	צַלַּחַת (נ)
plum	ʃezif	שְׁזִיף (ז)
poisonous mushroom	pitriya ra'ila	פִּטְרִיָּה רְעִילָה (נ)
pomegranate	rimon	רִימוֹן (ז)
pork	basar xazir	בָּשָׂר חֲזִיר (ז)
porridge	daysa	דַּייסָה (נ)
portion	mana	מָנָה (נ)
potato	ta'puax adama	תַּפּוּחַ אֲדָמָה (ז)
proteins	xelbonim	חֶלְבּוֹנִים (ז״ר)
pub, bar	bar, pab	בָּר, פָּאב (ז)
pudding	'puding	פּוּדִינג (ז)
pumpkin	'dla'at	דְּלַעַת (נ)
rabbit	arnav	אַרְנָב (ז)
radish	tsnonit	צְנוֹנִית (נ)
raisin	tsimukim	צִימוּקִים (ז״ר)
raspberry	'petel	פֶּטֶל (ז)
recipe	matkon	מַתְכּוֹן (ז)
red pepper	'pilpel adom	פִּלְפֵּל אָדוֹם (ז)
red wine	'yayin adom	יַיִן אָדוֹם (ז)
redcurrant	dumdemanit aduma	דּוּמְדְּמָנִית אֲדוּמָה (נ)
refreshing drink	maʃke mera'anen	מַשְׁקֶה מְרַעֲנֵן (ז)
rice	'orez	אוֹרֶז (ז)
rum	rom	רוֹם (ז)
russula	xarifit	חֲרִיפִית (נ)
rye	ʃifon	שִׁיפוֹן (ז)
saffron	ze'afran	זְעַפְרָן (ז)
salad	salat	סָלָט (ז)
salmon	'salmon	סַלְמוֹן (ז)
salt	'melax	מֶלַח (ז)

salty	ma'luax	מָלוּחַ
sandwich	karix	כָּרִיךְ (ז)
sardine	sardin	סַרְדִּין (ז)
sauce	'rotev	רוֹטֶב (ז)
saucer	taxtit	תַּחְתִּית (נ)
sausage	naknik	נַקְנִיק (ז)
seafood	perot yam	פֵּירוֹת יָם (ז״ר)
sesame	'ʃumʃum	שׁוּמְשׁוֹם (ז)
shark	kariʃ	כָּרִישׁ (ז)
shrimp	ʃrimps	שְׁרִימְפְּס (ז״ר)
side dish	to'sefet	תּוֹסֶפֶת (נ)
slice	prusa	פְּרוּסָה (נ)
smoked	me'uʃan	מְעוּשָׁן
soft drink	maʃke kal	מַשְׁקֶה קַל (ז)
soup	marak	מָרָק (ז)
soup spoon	kaf	כַּף (נ)
sour cherry	duvdevan	דּוּבְדְּבָן (ז)
sour cream	ʃa'menet	שַׁמֶּנֶת (נ)
soy	'soya	סוֹיָה (נ)
spaghetti	spa'geti	סְפָּגֶטִי (ז)
sparkling	mugaz	מוּגָז
spice	tavlin	תַּבְלִין (ז)
spinach	'tered	תֶּרֶד (ז)
spiny lobster	'lobster kotsani	לוֹבְּסְטֶר קוֹצָנִי (ז)
spoon	kaf	כַּף (נ)
squid	kala'mari	קָלָמָארִי (ז)
steak	umtsa, steik	אוּמְצָה (נ), סְטֵייק (ז)
still	lo mugaz	לֹא מוּגָז
strawberry	tut sade	תּוּת שָׂדֶה (ז)
sturgeon	basar haxidkan	בָּשָׂר הַחִדְקָן (ז)
sugar	sukar	סוּכָּר (ז)
sunflower oil	'ʃemen xamaniyot	שֶׁמֶן חַמָּנִיוֹת (ז)
sweet	matok	מָתוֹק
sweet cherry	gudgedan	גּוּדְגְּדָן (ז)
taste, flavor	'taʕam	טַעַם (ז)
tasty	ta'ʕim	טָעִים
tea	te	תֵּה (ז)
teaspoon	kapit	כַּפִּית (נ)
tip	tip	טִיפ (ז)
tomato	agvaniya	עַגְבָנִיָּה (נ)
tomato juice	mits agvaniyot	מִיץ עַגְבָנִיוֹת (ז)
tongue	laʃon	לָשׁוֹן (נ)
toothpick	keisam ʃi'nayim	קֵיסָם שִׁינַיִים (ז)
trout	forel	פּוֹרֶל (ז)
tuna	'tuna	טוּנָה (נ)
turkey	'hodu	הוֹדוּ (ז)
turnip	'lefet	לֶפֶת (נ)
veal	basar 'egel	בָּשָׂר עֵגֶל (ז)
vegetable oil	'ʃemen tsimxi	שֶׁמֶן צִמְחִי (ז)
vegetables	yerakot	יְרָקוֹת (ז״ר)
vegetarian	tsimxoni	צִמְחוֹנִי (ז)
vegetarian	tsimxoni	צִמְחוֹנִי

vermouth	'vermut	וֶרְמוּט (ז)
vienna sausage	naknikiya	נַקְנִיקִיָּה (נ)
vinegar	'χomets	חוֹמֶץ (ז)
vitamin	vitamin	וִיטָמִין (ז)
vodka	'vodka	וּוֹדְקָה (נ)
waffles	'vaflim	וָפְלִים (ז"ר)
waiter	meltsar	מֶלְצָר (ז)
waitress	meltsarit	מֶלְצָרִית (נ)
walnut	egoz 'meleχ	אֱגוֹז מֶלֶךְ (ז)
water	'mayim	מַיִם (ז"ר)
watermelon	ava'tiaχ	אֲבַטִּיחַ (ז)
wheat	χita	חִיטָה (נ)
whiskey	'viski	וִיסְקִי (ז)
white wine	'yayin lavan	יַיִן לָבָן (ז)
wild strawberry	tut 'ya'ar	תּוּת יַעַר (ז)
wine	'yayin	יַיִן (ז)
wine list	reʃimat yeynot	רְשִׁימַת יֵינוֹת (נ)
with ice	im 'keraχ	עִם קֶרַח
yogurt	'yogurt	יוֹגוּרט (ז)
zucchini	kiʃu	קִישׁוּא (ז)

תַּחְתִּית (נ)	taχtit	saucer
כּוֹס (נ)	kos	glass
גָּבִיעַ (ז)	ga'vi'a	glass
בָּשָׂר (ז)	basar	meat
עוֹף (ז)	of	chicken
בַּרְוָז (ז)	barvaz	duck
אֲוָז (ז)	avaz	goose
צַיִד (ז)	'tsayid	game
הֹדוּ (ז)	'hodu	turkey
בָּשָׂר חֲזִיר (ז)	basar χazir	pork
בָּשָׂר עֵגֶל (ז)	basar 'egel	veal
בָּשָׂר כֶּבֶשׂ (ז)	basar 'keves	lamb
בָּקָר (ז)	bakar	beef
אַרְנָב (ז)	arnav	rabbit
נַקְנִיק (ז)	naknik	sausage
נַקְנִיקִיָּה (נ)	naknikiya	vienna sausage
קוֹתֶל חֲזִיר (ז)	'kotel χazir	bacon
בָּשָׂר חֲזִיר מְעוּשָּׁן (ז)	basar χazir me'uʃan	ham
קוֹתֶל חֲזִיר מְעוּשָּׁן (ז)	'kotel χazir me'uʃan	gammon
פָּטֶה (ז)	pate	pâté
כָּבֵד (ז)	kaved	liver
בָּשָׂר טָחוּן (ז)	basar taχun	hamburger
לָשׁוֹן (נ)	laʃon	tongue
בֵּיצָה (נ)	beitsa	egg
בֵּיצִים (נ"ר)	beitsim	eggs
חֶלְבּוֹן (ז)	χelbon	egg white
חֶלְמוֹן (ז)	χelmon	egg yolk
דָּג (ז)	dag	fish
פֵּירוֹת יָם (ז"ר)	perot yam	seafood
קַוְויָאר (ז)	kavyar	caviar
סַרְטָן יָם (ז)	sartan yam	crab
שְׁרִימְפְּס (ז"ר)	ʃrimps	shrimp
צִדְפַּת מַאֲכָל (נ)	tsidpat ma'aχal	oyster
לוֹבְּסְטֶר קוֹצָנִי (ז)	'lobster kotsani	spiny lobster
קָלָמָארִי (ז)	kala'mari	squid
בָּשָׂר הַחִדְקָן (ז)	basar haχidkan	sturgeon
סַלְמוֹן (ז)	'salmon	salmon
פּוּטִית (נ)	putit	halibut
שִׁיבּוּט (ז)	ʃibut	cod
קוֹלְיָס (ז)	kolyas	mackerel
טוּנָה (נ)	'tuna	tuna
צְלוֹפָח (ז)	tslofaχ	eel
פּוֹרֶל (ז)	forel	trout
סַרְדִּין (ז)	sardin	sardine

זְאֵב מַיִם (ז)	ze'ev 'mayim	pike
מָלִיחַ (ז)	ma'liaχ	herring
לֶחֶם (ז)	'leχem	bread
גְּבִינָה (נ)	gvina	cheese
סוּכָּר (ז)	sukar	sugar
מֶלַח (ז)	'melaχ	salt
אוֹרֶז (ז)	'orez	rice
פַּסְטָה (נ)	'pasta	pasta
אִטְרִיּוֹת (נ״ר)	irtiyot	noodles
חֶמְאָה (נ)	χem'a	butter
שֶׁמֶן צִמְחִי (ז)	'ʃemen tsimχi	vegetable oil
שֶׁמֶן חַמָנִיּוֹת (ז)	'ʃemen χamaniyot	sunflower oil
מַרְגָּרִינָה (נ)	marga'rina	margarine
זֵיתִים (ז״ר)	zeitim	olives
שֶׁמֶן זַיִת (ז)	'ʃemen 'zayit	olive oil
חָלָב (ז)	χalav	milk
חָלָב מְרוּכָּז (ז)	χalav merukaz	condensed milk
יוֹגוּרְט (ז)	'yogurt	yogurt
שַׁמֶּנֶת (נ)	ʃa'menet	sour cream
שַׁמֶּנֶת (נ)	ʃa'menet	cream
מַיוֹנֵז (ז)	mayonez	mayonnaise
קַצֶּפֶת חֶמְאָה (נ)	ka'tsefet χem'a	buttercream
גְּרִיסִים (ז״ר)	grisim	cereal grains
קֶמַח (ז)	'kemaχ	flour
שִׁימוּרִים (ז״ר)	ʃimurim	canned food
פְּתִיתֵי תִירָס (ז״ר)	ptitei 'tiras	cornflakes
דְּבַשׁ (ז)	dvaʃ	honey
רִיבָּה (נ)	riba	jam
מַסְטִיק (ז)	'mastik	chewing gum
מַיִם (ז״ר)	'mayim	water
מֵי שְׁתִיָּה (ז״ר)	mei ʃtiya	drinking water
מַיִם מִינֶרָלִיִּים (ז״ר)	'mayim mine'raliyim	mineral water
לֹא מוּגָז	lo mugaz	still
מוּגָז	mugaz	carbonated
מוּגָז	mugaz	sparkling
קֶרַח (ז)	'keraχ	ice
עִם קֶרַח	im 'keraχ	with ice
נָטוּל אַלְכּוֹהוֹל	natul alkohol	non-alcoholic
מַשְׁקֶה קַל (ז)	maʃke kal	soft drink
מַשְׁקֶה מְרַעֲנֵן (ז)	maʃke mera'anen	refreshing drink
לִימוֹנָדָה (נ)	limo'nada	lemonade
מַשְׁקָאוֹת חָרִיפִים (ז״ר)	maʃka'ot χarifim	liquors
יַיִן (ז)	'yayin	wine
יַיִן לָבָן (ז)	'yayin lavan	white wine
יַיִן אָדֹם (ז)	'yayin adom	red wine
לִיקֵר (ז)	liker	liqueur
שַׁמְפַּנְיָה (נ)	ʃam'panya	champagne
וֶרְמוּט (ז)	'vermut	vermouth
וִיסְקִי (ז)	'viski	whiskey
ווֹדְקָה (נ)	'vodka	vodka
גְּ׳ין (ז)	dʒin	gin
קוֹנְיָאק (ז)	'konyak	cognac

רוֹם (ז)	rom	rum
קָפֶה (ז)	kafe	coffee
קָפֶה שָׁחוֹר (ז)	kafe ʃaχor	black coffee
קָפֶה הָפוּךְ (ז)	kafe hafuχ	coffee with milk
קְפוּצִ׳ינוֹ (ז)	kapu'tʃino	cappuccino
קָפֶה נָמֵס (ז)	kafe names	instant coffee
קוֹקְטֵיל (ז)	kokteil	cocktail
מִילְקְשֵׁייק (ז)	'milkʃeik	milkshake
מִיץ (ז)	mits	juice
מִיץ עַגְבָנִיוֹת (ז)	mits agvaniyot	tomato juice
מִיץ תַּפּוּזִים (ז)	mits tapuzim	orange juice
מִיץ סָחוּט (ז)	mits saχut	freshly squeezed juice
בִּירָה (נ)	'bira	beer
בִּירָה בָּהִירָה (נ)	'bira bahira	light beer
בִּירָה כֵּהָה (נ)	'bira keha	dark beer
תֵּה (ז)	te	tea
תֵּה שָׁחוֹר (ז)	te ʃaχor	black tea
תֵּה יָרוֹק (ז)	te yarok	green tea
יְרָקוֹת (ז-ר)	yerakot	vegetables
יֶרֶק (ז)	'yerek	greens
עַגְבָנִיָּה (נ)	agvaniya	tomato
מְלָפְפוֹן (ז)	melafefon	cucumber
גֶּזֶר (ז)	'gezer	carrot
תַּפּוּחַ אֲדָמָה (ז)	ta'puaχ adama	potato
בָּצָל (ז)	batsal	onion
שׁוּם (ז)	ʃum	garlic
כְּרוּב (ז)	kruv	cabbage
כְּרוּבִית (נ)	kruvit	cauliflower
כְּרוּב נִצָּנִים (ז)	kruv nitsanim	Brussels sprouts
בְּרוֹקוֹלִי (ז)	'brokoli	broccoli
סֶלֶק (ז)	'selek	beetroot
חָצִיל (ז)	χatsil	eggplant
קִישׁוּא (ז)	kiʃu	zucchini
דְּלַעַת (נ)	'dla'at	pumpkin
לֶפֶת (נ)	'lefet	turnip
פֶּטְרוֹזִילְיָה (נ)	petro'zilya	parsley
שָׁמִיר (ז)	ʃamir	dill
חַסָּה (נ)	'χasa	lettuce
סֶלֶרִי (ז)	'seleri	celery
אַסְפָּרָגוֹס (ז)	aspa'ragos	asparagus
תֶּרֶד (ז)	'tered	spinach
אֲפוּנָה (נ)	afuna	pea
פּוֹל (ז)	pol	beans
תִּירָס (ז)	'tiras	corn
שְׁעוּעִית (נ)	ʃu'it	kidney bean
פִּלְפֵּל (ז)	'pilpel	bell pepper
צְנוֹנִית (נ)	tsnonit	radish
אַרְטִישׁוֹק (ז)	artiʃok	artichoke
פְּרִי (ז)	pri	fruit
תַּפּוּחַ (ז)	ta'puaχ	apple
אַגָּס (ז)	agas	pear
לִימוֹן (ז)	limon	lemon

תַּפוּז (ז)	tapuz	orange
תוּת שָׂדֶה (ז)	tut sade	strawberry
קְלֶמֶנטִינָה (נ)	klemen'tina	mandarin
שְׁזִיף (ז)	ʃezif	plum
אֲפַרסֵק (ז)	afarsek	peach
מִשְׁמֵשׁ (ז)	'miʃmeʃ	apricot
פֶּטֶל (ז)	'petel	raspberry
אָנָנָס (ז)	'ananas	pineapple
בַּנָנָה (נ)	ba'nana	banana
אֲבַטִּיחַ (ז)	ava'tiax	watermelon
עֲנָבִים (ז"ר)	anavim	grape
מֶלוֹן (ז)	melon	melon
אֶשְׁכּוֹלִית (נ)	eʃkolit	grapefruit
אָבוֹקָדוֹ (ז)	avo'kado	avocado
פַּפָּאיָה (נ)	pa'paya	papaya
מַנגוֹ (ז)	'mango	mango
רִימוֹן (ז)	rimon	pomegranate
דומדְמָנִית אֲדוּמָה (נ)	dumdemanit aduma	redcurrant
דומדְמָנִית שׁחוֹרָה (נ)	dumdemanit ʃxora	blackcurrant
חֲזַרזַר (ז)	xazarzar	gooseberry
אוכמָנִית (נ)	uxmanit	bilberry
פֶּטֶל שָׁחוֹר (ז)	'petel ʃaxor	blackberry
צִימוּקִים (ז"ר)	tsimukim	raisin
תְּאֵנָה (נ)	te'ena	fig
תָּמָר (ז)	tamar	date
בּוֹטנִים (ז"ר)	botnim	peanut
שָׁקֵד (ז)	ʃaked	almond
אֱגוֹז מֶלֶךְ (ז)	egoz 'melex	walnut
אֱגוֹז אִלסָר (ז)	egoz ilsar	hazelnut
קוֹקוּס (ז)	'kokus	coconut
פִּיסטוּק (ז)	'fistuk	pistachios
מוֹצרֵי קוֹנדִיטוֹריָה (ז"ר)	mutsrei kondi'torya	confectionery
עוּגִיָה (נ)	ugiya	cookies
שׁוֹקוֹלָד (ז)	'ʃokolad	chocolate
מְשׁוֹקוֹלָד	mi'ʃokolad	chocolate
סוּכָּרִיָה (נ)	sukariya	candy
עוּגָה (נ)	uga	cake
עוּגָה (נ)	uga	cake
פַּאי (ז)	pai	pie
מִילוּי (ז)	milui	filling
רִיבָּה (נ)	riba	jam
מַרמְלָדָה (נ)	marme'lada	marmalade
וַפלִים (ז"ר)	'vaflim	waffles
גלִידָה (נ)	'glida	ice-cream
מָנָה (נ)	mana	course, dish
מִטבָּח (ז)	mitbax	cuisine
מַתכּוֹן (ז)	matkon	recipe
מָנָה (נ)	mana	portion
סָלָט (ז)	salat	salad
מָרָק (ז)	marak	soup
מָרָק צַח, צִיר (ז)	marak tsax, tsir	clear soup
כָּרִיךְ (ז)	karix	sandwich

בֵּיצַת עַיִן (נ)	beitsat ain	fried eggs
הַמְבּוּרְגֶר (ז)	'hamburger	hamburger
אוּמְצָה (נ), סְטֵייק (ז)	umtsa, steik	steak
תּוֹסֶפֶת (נ)	to'sefet	side dish
סְפָּגֶטִי (ז)	spa'geti	spaghetti
מְחִית תַּפּוּחֵי אֲדָמָה (נ)	meχit tapuχei adama	mashed potatoes
פִּיצָה (נ)	'pitsa	pizza
דַּייְסָה (נ)	daysa	porridge
חֲבִיתָה (נ)	χavita	omelet
מְבוּשָׁל	mevuʃal	boiled
מְעוּשָׁן	me'uʃan	smoked
מְטוּגָּן	metugan	fried
מְיוּבָּשׁ	meyubaʃ	dried
קָפוּא	kafu	frozen
כָּבוּשׁ	kavuʃ	pickled
מָתוֹק	matok	sweet
מָלוּחַ	ma'luaχ	salty
קַר	kar	cold
חַם	χam	hot
מָרִיר	marir	bitter
טָעִים	ta'im	tasty
קְלִיפָּה (נ)	klipa	peel
פִּלְפֵּל שָׁחוֹר (ז)	'pilpel ʃaχor	black pepper
פִּלְפֵּל אָדוֹם (ז)	'pilpel adom	red pepper
חַרְדָּל (ז)	χardal	mustard
חֲזֶרֶת (נ)	χa'zeret	horseradish
רוֹטֶב (ז)	'rotev	condiment
תַּבְלִין (ז)	tavlin	spice
רוֹטֶב (ז)	'rotev	sauce
חוֹמֶץ (ז)	'χomets	vinegar
כַּמְנוֹן (ז)	kamnon	anise
רֵיחָן (ז)	reχan	basil
צִיפּוֹרֶן (ז)	tsi'poren	cloves
גִ׳ינְגֶ׳ר (ז)	'dʒindʒer	ginger
כּוּסְבָּרָה (נ)	'kusbara	coriander
קִינָמוֹן (ז)	kinamon	cinnamon
שׁוּמְשׁוּם (ז)	'ʃumʃum	sesame
עָלֶה דַּפְנָה (ז)	ale dafna	bay leaf
פַּפְּרִיקָה (נ)	'paprika	paprika
קִימֶל (ז)	'kimel	caraway
זַעֲפְרָן (ז)	ze'afran	saffron
אוֹכֶל (ז)	'oχel	food
אֲרוּחַת בּוֹקֶר (נ)	aruχat 'boker	breakfast
אֲרוּחַת צָהֳרַיִים (נ)	aruχat tsaha'rayim	lunch
אֲרוּחַת עֶרֶב (נ)	aruχat 'erev	dinner
תֵּיאָבוֹן (ז)	te'avon	appetite
בְּתֵיאָבוֹן!	betei'avon!	Enjoy your meal!
טַעַם (ז)	'ta'am	taste, flavor
טַעַם לְוַואי (ז)	'ta'am levai	aftertaste
דִּיאֶטָה (נ)	di''eta	diet
וִיטָמִין (ז)	vitamin	vitamin
קָלוֹרִיָה (נ)	ka'lorya	calorie

צִמְחוֹנִי (ז)	tsimχoni	vegetarian
צִמְחוֹנִי	tsimχoni	vegetarian
שׁוּמָנִים (ז״ר)	ʃumanim	fats
חֶלְבּוֹנִים (ז״ר)	χelbonim	proteins
פַּחְמֵימָה (נ)	paχmema	carbohydrates
פְּרוּסָה (נ)	prusa	slice
חֲתִיכָה (נ)	χatiχa	piece
פֵּירוּר (ז)	perur	crumb
כַּף (נ)	kaf	spoon
סַכִּין (ז, נ)	sakin	knife
מַזְלֵג (ז)	mazleg	fork
סֵפֶל (ז)	'sefel	cup
צַלַּחַת (נ)	tsa'laχat	plate
קֵיסָם שִׁינַיִים (ז)	keisam ʃi'nayim	toothpick
בָּר, פָּאבּ (ז)	bar, pab	pub, bar
מֶלְצָר (ז)	meltsar	waiter
מֶלְצָרִית (נ)	meltsarit	waitress
בַּרְמֶן (ז)	'barmen	bartender
תַּפְרִיט (ז)	tafrit	menu
רְשִׁימַת יֵינוֹת (נ)	reʃimat yeynot	wine list
מַשְׁקֶה מְתַאֲבֵן (ז)	maʃke meta'aven	aperitif
מְתָאֲבֵן (ז)	meta'aven	appetizer
קִינּוּחַ (ז)	ki'nuaχ	dessert
חֶשְׁבּוֹן (ז)	χeʃbon	check
טִיפּ (ז)	tip	tip
כַּפִּית (נ)	kapit	teaspoon
כַּף (נ)	kaf	soup spoon
פּוֹתְחָן בַּקְבּוּקִים (ז)	potχan bakbukim	bottle opener
פּוֹתְחָן קוּפְסָאוֹת (ז)	potχan kufsa'ot	can opener
מַחְלֵץ (ז)	maχlets	corkscrew
אַבְרוֹמָה (נ)	avroma	bream
קַרְפְּיוֹן (ז)	karpiyon	carp
אוֹקוּנוּס (ז)	'okunus	perch
שְׂפַמְנוּן (ז)	sfamnun	catfish
אִילְתִּית (נ)	iltit	Atlantic salmon
דָּג מֹשֶׁה רַבֵּנוּ (ז)	dag moʃe ra'benu	flatfish
אַמְנוּן (ז)	amnun	pike perch
כָּרִישׁ (ז)	kariʃ	shark
פִּטְרִיָּה (נ)	pitriya	mushroom
פִּטְרִיָּה רְאוּיָה לְמַאֲכָל	pitriya ra'uya lema'aχal	edible mushroom
פִּטְרִיָּה רְעִילָה (נ)	pitriya ra'ila	poisonous mushroom
פּוֹרְצִ׳ינִי (ז)	por'tʃini	cep
פִּטְרִיַּת כּוֹבַע אֲדוּמָה (נ)	pitriyat 'kova aduma	orange-cap boletus
פִּטְרִיַּת יַעַר (נ)	pitriyat 'ya'ar	birch bolete
גְּבִיעוֹנִית נֶאֱכֶלֶת (נ)	gvi'onit ne'e'χelet	chanterelle
חֲרִיפִית (נ)	χarifit	russula
גִּמְצוּץ (ז)	gamtsuts	morel
זְבוּבָנִית (נ)	zvuvanit	fly agaric
פִּטְרִיָּה רְעִילָה (נ)	pitriya ra'ila	death cap
פֵּירוֹת (ז״ר)	perot	fruits
חֲמוּצִית (נ)	χamutsit	cranberry
קִיוִוי (ז)	'kivi	kiwi

גַּרְגֵּר (ז)	garger	berry
גַּרְגְּרִים (ז״ר)	gargerim	berries
אוכְמָנִית אֲדוֹמָה (נ)	uxmanit aduma	cowberry
תּוּת יַעַר (ז)	tut 'ya'ar	wild strawberry
תְּבוּאָה (נ)	tvu'a	grain
דְּגָנִים (ז״ר)	dganim	cereal crops
שִׁיבּוֹלֶת (נ)	ʃi'bolet	ear
חִיטָה (נ)	xita	wheat
שִׁיפוֹן (ז)	ʃifon	rye
שִׁיבּוֹלֶת שׁוּעָל (נ)	ʃi'bolet ʃu'al	oats
דּוֹחַן (ז)	'doxan	millet
שְׂעוֹרָה (נ)	se'ora	barley
תִּירָס (ז)	'tiras	corn
כּוּסֶמֶת (נ)	ku'semet	buckwheat
סוֹיָה (נ)	'soya	soy
עֲדָשִׁים (נ״ר)	adaʃim	lentil
סַרְטָנָאִים (ז״ר)	sartana'im	crustaceans
דּוּבדְּבָן (ז)	duvdevan	sour cherry
גוֹדגְּדָן (ז)	gudgedan	sweet cherry
פּוּדִינג (ז)	'puding	pudding

Made in the USA
Middletown, DE
05 September 2021